Broken Bottles, Broken Dreams
Understanding and Helping the Children of Alcoholics

Broken Bottles
Broken Dreams

Understanding and Helping the Children of Alcoholics

CHARLES DEUTSCH

*Formerly Education Specialist,
Cambridge and Somerville Program of
Alcoholism Rehabilitation (CASPAR)*

Teachers College, Columbia University
New York / London

Published by Teachers College Press
1234 Amsterdam Avenue
New York, NY 10027

ACKNOWLEDGEMENT
Lines from the lyric of the song LIVERPOOL LULLABY (Words and Music by Stan Kelly). © Copyright 1964 Heathside Music Ltd., London, England. TRO—Melody Trails, Inc., New York, controls all publication rights for the U.S.A. and Canada. Used by permission.

Library of Congress Cataloging in Publication Data

Deutsch, Charles, 1947–
  Broken bottles, broken dreams.

  Bibliography: p.
  Includes index.
  1. Children of alcoholic parents.   I. Title.
[DNLM: 1. Alcoholism.   2. Child health services.
3. Parent-child relations.   WM 274 D486]
HV5132.D43   362.8'28   81-5729
                      AACR2
ISBN 0-8077-2664-8
ISBN 0-8077-2663-X (pbk.)

Manufactured in the United States of America

86 85   5 6

To
the memory of my mother

Liverpool Lullaby

Oh you are a mucky kid,
Dirty as a dustbin lid.
When he finds out the things you did
You'll get a belt from your dad!
Oh you have your father's nose,
So crimson in the dark it glows.
If you're not asleep when the boozers close
You'll get a belt from your dad! . . .

Oh you have your father's face,
You're growing up a real hard case,
But there's no one else can take your place.
Go fast asleep, for mummy.©

—*Stan Kelly*

CONTENTS

Part Two   HELPING

PREFACE

In his Introduction to the *Fourth Special Report to the U.S. Congress on Alcohol and Health* (January 1981), John R. DeLuca, Director of the National Institute on Alcohol Abuse and Alcoholism, DHHS, wrote:

[A] study by the Institute of Medicine [found that] heart and vascular disease costs society about the same amount as alcoholism, yet heart and vascular disease research receives 17 times more money than alcoholism research. Cancer costs society considerably less than alcoholism, yet cancer research receives 39 times more money. . . . All are dread diseases; all have a devastating impact on our society. . . .

Broken Bottles, Broken Dreams is concerned with approximately fifteen million school-age children who suffer from the impact of alcoholism in the most damaging, enduring, and ultimately the most preventable way. As DeLuca and most other authorities have noted, great strides have been made in combatting alcoholism over the last decade. But the children of alcoholics have been left behind. Probably not more than 5 percent are getting the help they need. Unless they start getting systematic assistance, they will continue to have serious problems with which we will all have to contend sooner or later.

There is no question that children of alcoholics are more likely than other children to develop alcoholism, for whatever combination of genetic and environmental reasons. And a growing body of research, supporting clinical observation and widespread experience, shows that children of alcoholics are a population of greater than average risk for a variety of physical, psychological, situational, developmental, and interpersonal problems.

It is not difficult to see why children of alcoholics might have severe problems. But it is not generally understood that their problems are often less the result of the alcoholic's behavior than of the children's misunderstanding and misinterpretation of it. The children's problems don't end when the alcoholic stops drinking; and they are by no means insoluble before the alcoholic becomes sober. The children's feelings about themselves and their families, their ways of contending with the situation in the home, their outlets for frustration, anger, and shame can be different and healthier for everyone, if they can get insight and support. The family illness can become a source of strength even if the alcoholic continues to drink. Help for the children need not and cannot be contingent upon treating the parents. Children who understand alcoholism can be potent catalysts of family recovery.

The nature of family alcoholism precludes relying upon parents and other family members to give the children the perspective and the support they need. Similarly, given their shame, guilt, fear, and hopelessness, the children can hardly be expected to identify their problem and seek help on their own. Nor will media messages suffice—many children don't even notice them until they have had an actual conversation about alcoholism with someone they trust.

Systematic help for children of alcoholics depends upon the intervention of the many kinds of youth professionals with whom the children have regular, natural, and relatively trustful contact. These include teachers, guidance counselors, school nurses, administrators, and coaches; social workers, psychologists and other mental health workers; clergy, scout leaders, and recreation workers; nurses and physicians; probation officers, employment counselors, and alcoholism clinicians. Their work toward the healthy emotional, educational, and social development of children is greatly compromised if they do not recognize the barriers to that development. The world's best reading teacher will not get far with a child who is constantly preoccupied with the safety of an alcoholic mother.

Youth professionals are already overworked and underappreciated. This book does not urge new obligations on them or propose that they interfere with family matters. Its thesis is simple: There are a great many children who need assistance in understanding and coping with family alcoholism before they can really use the skills and knowledge that may be the main business of the professional. Professionals who work with young people have to know something about family alcoholism and its effects. With that knowledge they can play an intervention role that is limited but crucial: They can help children acknowledge their problem and find ongoing help with it.

The organization of this book reflects six years of experience in training youth professionals. I have tried most of all to be concrete, pragmatic, and motivating in the book's approach. The first part describes the children: the way they feel, the way they react, and the hazardous consequences of their upbringing. To see the children clearly we first have to examine certain assumptions and myths about alcoholism. The second part is about the youth professional's role in the helping process. Helpers need to be clear about their own biases and reservations, expectations and goals; they need concrete strategies to try; and they need information and insight into existing referral resources, as well as encouragement to help create inexpensive and effective new resources. Finally, they need some guidelines for recognizing children of alcoholics, and the names of books, pamphlets, films, and other resources for their own and for children's use.

The timing of this book is propitious. Because of cutbacks, staff reductions, a focus on basic services in many programs, it is not a good time to call for something new. But if we still hope to reduce the incidence or mitigate the severity of the problems of a host of today's adolescents (tomorrow's adults)—problems ranging from alcoholism to suicide to interpersonal aggression—we can no longer afford to overlook family alcoholism as a preventable predisposing factor. We don't need a phalanx of new specialists and costly programs. We need to train, motivate, and support the people who are already doing so much with our children and adolescents; and we need to promote realistic models that can provide ongoing support.

Not all children of alcoholics need even the short-term peer-based help that this book espouses. But a great many do; and they rely upon the intervention of youth professionals.

C.G.D.

ACKNOWLEDGMENTS

Of the many people who contributed to this book, those who relived their childhood experiences in families with alcoholism are surely the first to be thanked. Some had never before discussed the subject at such length and with such painful candor. Many of the young people and adults whose words and stories fill the book asked not to be acknowledged by name. For them, as for those cited below, gratification rests in the hope that their insights may make it easier for other children of alcoholics.

The heart of the book, and the inspiration for writing it, has always been the CASPAR peer leaders. All 35 teenagers who served as alcohol educators in Somerville (Mass.) between 1975 and 1979 added to the book. For extraordinary patience, openness, perceptiveness, and encouragement I want especially to thank Ann Kisich, Harold Mason, Maryetta O'Brien, Michele Reidy and Cathy Santos. Ann and Cathy also helped with eleventh-hour research. Marie Kearns, one of the first peer leaders, deserves special recognition: The entire CASPAR program for children of alcoholics owes a great deal to Marie's courage, vision, and persistence.

Their combination of personal experience and clinical training made Noel Jette and Bob Ziegler exceptionally valuable. Louise Dussault, Larry Heaton, and Paul Montgomery are three contributors who can be mentioned for their dual perspective, as children of alcoholics and as human service workers.

My mentors and colleagues at CASPAR—Lena DiCicco, Dixie Mills, and Hilma Unterberger—got me into this field, taught and learned with me, promoted the book from the beginning, and read much of the draft. Gail Levine-Reid, Beth Aronson, Ruth Davis, and Laura Derman also lent assistance and encouragement.

Karen Schaeffer and Suzanne Pratt of the Pre-School Unit, Cambridge-Somerville Mental Health and Retardation Center, recounted cases that appear in Chapter 8. Norma McGann of the same center's Alcoholism Program provided much of the information about Al-Anon's structure in Chapter 10.

Really good teachers are an embattled, some say an endangered species. They have to do a good deal more than satisfy the educational needs of 30 to 150 youngsters. They have to contend with administrators, parents, school boards, and bureaucracies that don't always make their jobs easier. They have to weather political cross-currents and financial crises. Never have the school-based professions, including counselors, school nurses, coaches, and administrators been so beleaguered. Through the work that preceded this book, and the interviews with Somerville school personnel for its compilation, I felt an infusion of optimism regarding the state of public education. These are the people most responsible for that optimism: Alan Ballek, John Campagna, Bob Colozzo, Diane Depczenski, Donna Dupee, Pat Johnston, Ken Lonergan, Linda McGillicuddy, Barbara Melley, Christine Morris, Mary Mullally, Kevin O'Malley, Doris O'Meara, Emilie Rose, Florence Sotiros, Nora Stackpole, Mary Sullivan, Paul Tighe, Steve Tucelli, and Peggy Turko.

Arthur Evans was most helpful when I was preparing the book proposal. The Women's Mental Health Collective provided my typewriter with a temporary home. Elisabeth Bouche did a superb job typing the manuscript, and Juliana Wu and Laura Whitehall were fine editors.

Most of all I want to thank my wife, Emily Schatzow, for everything she gives to me and asks of me; and my daughter Rachel for her ceaseless bright-eyed wonder.

Part One

THE CHILDREN

Chapter 1

INTRODUCTION

I never admitted that there was a problem. I just hated my mother for drinking; I hated seeing her drunk. I don't remember ever having a laugh with my mother. I felt shame and hate, that's all. I don't ever recall a time when I liked my mother. I had three older sisters and we never talked about it, never ever once said a word about Ma drinking, my whole life. I just hated her. And boy, did I hate myself!

Once I had a problem and I was terrified to tell him. But he was okay about it. The next time I had the same feelings he got up and started screaming, "You never do anything right!" The unpredictability drove me crazy. Even when you get what you want, you feel shitty. You just feel worse about all the times you didn't, and you don't understand what you did differently or how to connect again. I never saw my father with slurred speech, staggering around, really happy or anything. He was always the same person, but there would be this erratic behavior and it was really a total mystery about why one time and not another. My mother was always complaining about his drinking, and she was busy theorizing about his behavior, but none of it made any sense to me. I used to wait for him in the seedy bars on Eighth Avenue, and I couldn't understand what could possibly attract him to this place and these people. It was a complete mystery to me.

PROBLEMS ASSOCIATED
WITH CHILDREN OF ALCOHOLICS

There are at least fifteen million school-age American children with parental alcoholism.[1] For fifteen million children, their parents' drink-

---

[1]Booz-Allen and Hamilton, Inc., *An Assessment of the Needs of and Resources for Children of Alcoholic Parents* (Rockville, Md.: National Institute on Alcohol Abuse and Alcoholism, 1974), pp. 14c, 15.

ing is *the* central fact of their lives. Their feelings, personalities, and behavior, their educational progress, and their social adjustment are influenced more by that one reality than by any other. The great majority of these children do not understand what is happening in their homes and how they are being affected.

Many children of alcoholic parents do not get the nurturance and safety that is needed from families. Instead these children must contend with constant shame, fear, guilt, anger, insecurity, and confusion. The responses and defenses they use to survive in the home become constraining and dysfunctional in the world at large. They go to great lengths to hide their parents' condition and to deny its overwhelming effect on themselves. Children of alcoholics form one of our largest, most explosive, and most remediable populations, yet no one is paying that population the slightest attention. In almost every community it is the exceptional teacher, guidance counselor, social worker, psychologist, clergy, scout leader, coach, probation officer, or other professional who is addressing the specific issue of family alcoholism's effect on children.

The result is that children of alcoholics as a population are at great risk for a variety of lifelong difficulties. Some of the risks associated with parental alcoholism are well documented. Others are only beginning to be confirmed by researchers, but have been consistently noted by clinicians. Much more research is needed, but conclusive data will remain scarce until a broader population can be reached and studied longitudinally with comprehensive, nonthreatening, and reliable instruments. The adverse effects of parental alcoholism on children will be discussed in more depth in upcoming chapters. For the present, we can say that children of alcoholics are at greater risk than other children in the following ways.

Alcohol and Drug Abuse and Alcoholism

Numerous studies over the last four decades have proved definitively that children of alcoholics are significantly more likely to develop alcoholism than other children; some say twice as likely.[2] This may be attributable to genetic or environmental influences, or both; and, in any event, most children of alcoholics are subject to both factors. But a marked propensity to alcoholism is characteristic of

---

[2] Nancy S. Cotton, "The Familial Incidence of Alcoholism," *Journal of Studies on Alcohol* 40 (1979): 99, 111; Donald Goodwin et al., "Alcohol Problems in Adoptees Raised Apart from Alcoholic Biological Parents," *Archives of General Psychiatry* 28 (1973): 242.

these children and not of children who grew up with other kinds of parental deprivation.[3]

Alcohol and drug abuse is strongly associated with problems with the law, school, employment, and social relations. A heightened risk of alcoholism may enhance the risk of such problems. In addition, many children of alcoholics remain abstainers well into adulthood, but when they start to drink, they quickly develop drinking problems.

Psychological and Emotional Problems

Emotional problems are the result of the condition of parental alcoholism itself and also of the traumatic developments it sometimes precipitates. Children of alcoholics are more likely than other children to live through their parents' divorce, to be placed in foster homes, and to have delinquent records.[4] In one study mental illness was diagnosed twice as often in children of alcoholics as in children of schizophrenics or offenders who are incarcerated.[5]

The psychological problems associated with parental alcoholism are chronic depression, psychosomatic complaints, social aggression, emotional detachment and isolation, and suicide. Clinicians also commonly cite poor self-concept and impaired sense of reality.[6]

Even though I was in Honor Society I really felt I was stupid. I thought I had this facade so down that when people thought I was smart I had them fooled. I was popular, active in all kinds of school clubs, but I had no friends. I had an underlying suspicion that I was really an evil and malignant person. If I were to let anyone get close they would know me

---

[3]Sharon Wegscheider, "Children of Alcoholics Caught in Family Trap," *Focus on Alcohol and Drug Issues* 2 (May-June 1979): 8; George E. Vaillant, "Paths Out of Alcoholism—A Forty Year Prospective Study," paper presented at Third Annual Alcoholism Symposium, Cambridge Hospital Department of Psychiatry, Cambridge, Mass., 8 March 1980 (mimeo), p. 1.

[4]James R. McKay, "Clinical Observations on Adolescent Problem Drinkers," *Quarterly Journal of Studies on Alcohol* 22 (1961): 128–30; James R. McKay, "Juvenile Delinquency and Drinking Behavior," *Journal of Health and Social Behavior* 4 (Winter 1963): 282.

[5]Wegscheider, "Children in Family Trap," p. 8.

[6]I. Nylander, "Children of Alcoholic Fathers," *Quarterly Journal of Studies on Alcohol* 24 (1963): 171–72; Patricia O'Gorman, "Children of Alcoholic Parents: Prevention Issues," paper presented at NIAAA Symposium on Services to Children of Alcoholics, Silver Spring, Md., 26 September 1979; Tarpley Richards, "Working with Children of an Alcoholic Mother," *Alcohol Health and Research World* 3 (Spring 1979): 23; Charles Whitfield, "Children of Alcoholics: Treatment Issues," paper presented at NIAAA Symposium on Services to Children of Alcoholics, 25 September 1979; Booz-Allen and Hamilton, Inc., *Assessment of Needs and Resources*, pp. 44a, 49–51.

for what I really was. Most of what I felt, anger and the desire to be taken care of, I felt was wrong.

There were times when I'd come home from college and she just about didn't recognize me. I'd walk in and my mother would stumble up to me and need a minute to figure out who I was. That's how bad it got. But you know what, it was only after the doctor told her she was going to die if she didn't stop drinking that I felt, Hey, I haven't been crazy all these years after all, her drinking really is out of hand.

Physical Health Problems

Research has pointed to a high incidence of hyperactivity among children from alcoholic homes.[7] This finding helps to explain some of the behavioral problems manifested by many of the children in school. Research into fetal alcohol syndrome (FAS) indicates that a pregnant woman's abuse of alcohol can be extremely hazardous to the infant, but it will be some time before possible long-range and more subtle effects can be investigated. The possible relationship between a father's heavy drinking and problems in conception and fetal development is still unexplored.

Medical researchers have identified certain personality constellations, called "Type A's," associated with a significantly higher rate of early and fatal coronary disease. These are the compulsive achievers, standouts in school and in careers, who never really relax or accept failure or seem satisfied with their prodigious accomplishments. What has not been adequately studied is the hypothesis that a sizable proportion of Type A's are children of alcoholics. As we will see in Chapter 4, the compulsive overachiever is one of the common and marked syndromes identified by clinicians in children of alcoholics.[8]

Physical Neglect and Abuse, Including Sexual Abuse

This is doubtless the most sensitive of all topics to research. A study in France in 1971 implicated alcohol abuse in 82 to 90 percent of

---

[7] J. Morrison and M. Stewart, "A Family Study of the Hyperactive Child Syndrome," *Biological Psychiatry* 3 (1971): 192; D. Cantwell, "Psychiatric Illness in the Families of Hyperactive Children," *Archives of General Psychiatry* 27 (1972): 415.

[8] Murray Hecht, "Children of Alcoholics Are Children at Risk," *American Journal of Nursing* 73 (1973): 1767; Sharon Wegscheider, *No One Escapes from a Chemically Dependent Family* (Crystal, Minn.: Nurturing Networks, 1976), p. 11; Life Style: "Kids of Alcoholics," *Newsweek*, 28 May 1977.

reported cases of battered children, whereas a study in 1979 found 69 percent of abuse and neglect cases to be related to alcohol abuse.[9] Three recent studies of incest and sexual abuse reported high incidences of alcohol abuse in incestuous fathers.[10] In light of the marked tendency shown by victims of physical abuse to repeat such abuse with their own children, family alcoholism can be seen to produce not only victims but also perpetrators of this intergenerational damage.

Failure to Complete Schooling

Children of alcoholics have been found in disproportionate numbers among those who perform poorly in school, attend irregularly, and eventually drop out altogether.[11] Certainly the psychological disorders, neglect and abuse, and substance abuse to which the population is prone account for some of the school problems. But while many children learn to submerge themselves in schoolwork as a response to family stress, others are unable to concentrate, attend to their work, and respond well to authority. Needless to say, school problems often translate into subsequent underemployability, with all of the concomitant features of that chronic condition.

Difficulties in Interpersonal Relationships

The relationship children observe between their parents and relationships children develop with their parents and siblings undoubtedly influence relationships they later form with peers and co-workers, and especially with potential or actual mates. The precise nature of the interpersonal difficulties that many children of alcoholics encounter is

---

[9] Milan A. Korcok, "Alcoholism is a Family Affair," *Focus on Alcohol and Drug Issues* 2 (May–June 1979): 4; D. Behling, "Alcohol Abuse as Encountered in 51 Instances of Reported Child Abuse," *Clinical Pediatrics* 18 (1979): 90; *New York Times*, 17 February 1974.

[10] D. Browning and B. Boatman, "Incest: Children at Risk," *American Journal of Psychiatry* 134 (1977): 70–71; R. Rada, D. Kellner, and W. Winslow, "Drinking, Alcoholism, and the Mentally Disordered Sex Offender," *Bulletin of the American Academy of Psychiatry and Law* 6 (1978): 299; M. Virkkunen, "Incest Offenses and Alcoholism," *Medicine, Science, and Law* 14 (1974): 224.

[11] Paul Haberman, "Childhood Symptoms in Children of Alcoholics and Comparison Group Parents," *Journal of Marriage and the Family* 28 (1966): 153; Morris E. Chafetz, Howard T. Blane, and Marjorie J. Hill, "Children of Alcoholics: Observations in a Child Guidance Clinic," *Quarterly Journal of Studies on Alcohol* 32 (1971): 696; V. Lindbeck, "The Adjustment of Adolescents to Paternal Alcoholism," paper presented at Massachusetts General Hospital, Boston, 27 April 1971.

a reflection of the adaptations and defenses they developed in the home as children. Probably the most pronounced pattern involves the choice of an alcoholic spouse.[12]

There are a great many adults being treated for or quietly suffering from the foregoing problems, who could be healthier and happier if they saw the connection between their parent's alcoholism and their own adult difficulties.

As a child, every few months I would just fall apart; I would cry and fall apart. My mother would tell me to go to my room until I pulled myself together. And I would. Then it would be months before I would feel anything at all. It's not surprising that I did the same thing as an adult; not let myself feel anything, then go blooey and be out of commission for a few weeks, without knowing why. I mean, anything could set it off. Now I'm learning that it's OK to cry, to feel, to let things out, and I'm finding people I can let things out with.

I was always a voracious reader. Of course, reading is worthwhile in itself, but I was 34 years old when I realized that a lot of my reading was still trying to lose myself and forget my feelings. And what became especially clear was that I would read late into the night, my eyes closing but I'd keep on reading. I thought it was just because I love books. But one night I was visiting my mother, and I asked myself, "Why am I still awake?" And I knew the answer: I wanted to be *ready* for whatever might happen. There was a lot to be ready for when I was a kid. She fell down the stairs sometimes, or she'd slam into my room and rant at me about God-knows-what in the light of the doorway. But I didn't have to be ready anymore. Once I understood what I was afraid of I could stop feeling the fear.

Adults who grew up in alcoholic homes sorely need more information about how parental alcoholism shaped their personalities. They get precious little insight and support at present. The professionals who work with them rarely receive even the most cursory training in family alcoholism.

But the principal concern of this book is children, including adolescents. If children of alcoholics can be reached early in their lives and helped to understand their own powerful and frightening emotions, their own and their parents' inexplicable actions; if they can share support with others facing the same problem; if they can learn to cope

---

[12]Bernard J. Clifford, "A Study of the Wives of Rehabilitated and Unrehabilitated Alcoholics," *Social Casework* 41 (1960): 458–59; Booz Allen and Hamilton, Inc., *Assessment of Needs and Resources*, pp. 46–48.

instead of to withdraw, deny, or retaliate, then many of the problems to which they are prone may be prevented or at least foreshortened. Only a minuscule percentage of these children are currently getting such help.

> I lived with a feeling that I was shit all my life. If someone had said to me, "You're not causing your mother's drinking, you're not responsible for her actions, you can't control it, you can't change it, and it doesn't make you a bad person," I think that would have made a difference in my relationships as I grew up and, even now, in some of the issues I'm dealing with at my age.

This book does not pretend to be a dispassionate examination of the problem of family alcoholism. It is intended as a plea, a polemic, a blueprint for action we cannot afford to abdicate or postpone. It is primarily addressed to youth professionals because they can make a systematic difference. They are in the best position to help children identify their problem as parental alcoholism and take that first step toward understanding and constructive coping. They may be the only voice of honesty and comfort in a wilderness of denial, blame, and silence.

> You say, "How can a teacher or guidance counselor make a difference when everything in the kid's world reinforces the messages of shame and guilt?" But I think it's like listening to a symphony. There may be an overwhelming amount of sound, but if the person sitting behind you is tapping his foot out of rhythm, you hear it. Even though it's one little voice, it's so dissonant with the message you've always heard that it takes on an importance. One voice speaking when your whole world is shouting something different, it can really make a difference. Especially if what that voice is saying is something it feels good to hear.

PREMISES OF THIS BOOK

This book is based on the following premises:
- Family alcoholism has serious and enduring effects on a great many children and adolescents, including some who are clearly in trouble and many others who seem to be exemplary in every way.
- Children of alcoholics can get meaningful help even if their parents refuse to aknowledge the problems. They can be reached, and they can change, without parental complicity.
- Treatment often consists of a short-term, educational, and suppor-tive experience that leaves children more open to and more likely to

benefit from existing channels of ongoing help: friends, relatives, and self-help groups like Alateen and Al-Anon. Most children do not need sophisticated psychotherapeutic treatment.

● Systematic early intervention with children of alcoholics depends upon a network of trained and motivated youth professionals who have frequent, natural, and nonthreatening contact with young people. All kinds of youth professionals should be trained to help children of alcoholics, but those who can initiate group alcohol education activities may have the greatest potential.

● A limited intervention role with children of alcoholics is consistent with the goals and responsibilities of most youth professionals. All work with these children is compromised unless they are assisted in making sense of a world that seems unpredictable, frightening, and unjust. For example, the most creative or demanding teacher is not apt to get very far with children who are constantly worried about their parents' safety or exhausted because of the nightly 2 A.M. fights.

● To help children understand and acknowledge their parents' alcoholism is to help them live with and love their parents. This help improves the likelihood of the whole family's recovery and reduces the need for more drastic institutional intervention.

● Communities that hope to reduce teenage alcohol and drug abuse, vandalism, school failure, and other adolescent problems must support youth professionals in their attempts to help children of alcoholics and must create resources to which the children can be confidently referred.

● Peer education and self-help groups are the most promising and cost-effective methods for treating children of alcoholics.

Few youth professionals are adequately prepared for an intervention role with children of alcoholics. In fact, many of those who work in alcoholism clinics are insufficiently trained in the children's perspective. This book is organized around the most pressing objectives of such training. Helpers must understand alcoholism and their own attitudes about it. They need insight into the children's experiences, feelings, and behavior. They also need to examine their own fears and biases about the intervention role they might play and develop realistic goals and expectations. They require concrete strategies for raising the subject of drinking and alcoholism and for bringing children to the point where a referral can be made. Finally, they need realistic suggestions for community action in the development of resources to serve the children. And they may need to know and appreciate better resources like Alateen and Al-Anon.

The book is largely based on my experiences with the CASPAR Alcohol Education Program of Somerville, Massachusetts. CASPAR, an acronym for the Cambridge and Somerville Program of Alcoholism Rehabilitation, is a national replication project in alcohol abuse prevention. Its success in providing alcohol education for all children gave rise to a model program for children of alcoholics. The performance and promise of the CASPAR model are reflected in the fact that it is the first program to be funded by the National Institute on Alcohol Abuse and Alcoholism (NIAAA) specifically for work with children of alcoholics; and, perhaps more eloquently, in the financial support of the Somerville School Department at a time when tax cuts are forcing this city and all other fiscally strapped cities to scrutinize their priorities. The approach and the strategies contained in this book are working in Somerville. The anecdotes interspersed throughout the book are the words of some of the more than 250 students and 300 youth professionals who have been involved in a three-year period.

Other programs elsewhere in the country are beginning to meet with success in helping children of alcoholics; some are cited in the Resources section at the end of the book.

Yet it must be acknowledged that the field is new. There is no hard data to prove the contention that early and short-term education and support can really reduce the incidence or duration of serious problems in large numbers of children of alcoholics. And there will never be such proof until we begin to reach and intervene with large numbers of children through programs that can be evaluated.

Do we really need more data to believe that many children of alcoholics are seriously damaged by their parents' illness—or to believe that it would make all the difference in the world if they could be helped when still young to understand the illness and throw off the feelings of shame, guilt, and hatred it engenders? Don't we rightly assume that it is better to acknowledge, get support, and come to grips with a problem than it is to deny and suppress in isolation and ignorance? The handful of programs working with children of alcoholics have documented consistent short-term improvements in most of their young people.[13] Thousands of people have pulled their lives together through Al-Anon and Alateen, though these anonymous organizations keep no statistics. If it takes more than their experience and our own logic and compassion to convince us of the need to make help sys-

---

[13] National Institute on Alcohol Abuse and Alcoholism, program papers presented at Symposium on Services to Children of Alcoholics, Silver Spring, Md., 24–26 September 1979.

tematically available for children of alcoholics, we can be certain that twenty years from now the same negligible percentage of the children will be getting help as do today.

The family is still the most potent shaper of human beings. We may be fond of blaming peer pressure, the school environment, the media, and the general permissiveness of modern society for all that is wrong with today's adolescents. These are indeed factors. But we must also keep in mind that there is a great deal that is admirable about our teenagers. They do not grow up under the easiest of conditions: plenty of leisure, few responsibilities, not enough opportunity, and too many temptations and unrealistic expectations.

Let us not forget that many of the teenage problems we constantly complain about, and others we barely recognize, have their roots in the family; and beyond question one of the most common and destructive family problems is alcoholism. If we hope to reduce teenage alcohol and drug abuse, vandalism and delinquency, early pregnancy and suicide, and the range of psychological problems that keep children from developing into healthy and reasonably complete adults, we cannot continue to ignore children of alcoholics and their special needs.

Chapter 2
ALCOHOLISM: MYTHS, ASSUMPTIONS, AND BIASES

Try to recapture your earliest memory of someone you thought of as "a drunk." Perhaps it was a relative, a friend's parent, a neighbor, a stranger you glimpsed on the street. What did you think? What did the people you were with say? Was the dominant emotion contempt? Fear? Anger? Amazement? You were exceptional indeed if your reaction resembled that of the boy described here by a grandparent:

> My grandchildren, now, the youngest of whom is ten, they know all about it. They can freely discuss it because they get alcohol education in the public schools in Somerville. And the little fellow, well, we have to speak to him sometimes because he counts people's drinks; he's very serious about it. And sometimes he'll see the men who sit on the park benches at the Powderhouse, he'll come home to his mother and say, "There's two unfortunates over there and I'd like to bring them a peanut-butter-and-jelly sandwich."

Most of us don't see people shooting up heroin or popping pills in the street. But alcohol abuse is dramatically encountered by most children long before they can understand what it is all about. Our earliest impressions can continue to color how we regard drunkenness and alcoholism even after we have learned more as adults.

Estimates of the number of American adults with alcoholism range between nine and twelve million.[1] Many authorities believe that the figures grossly understate the number of people who repeatedly hurt

---

[1] American Medical Association, *Manual on Alcoholism* (Chicago, 1977), p. 5.

themselves and others through the abuse of alcohol. In more meaningful terms, there are probably more people who have known and cared about someone with a drinking problem than there are people who have never been touched by alcohol abuse. If that surprises you, ask yourself and ask your friends, "Have I ever been concerned or bothered about the drinking of someone I knew well?" "Have I ever felt about any friends or relatives, 'They drink too much'?" When you think about it, you will probably come to two conclusions: You know more people with possible drinking problems than you ever realized; and quite a few of your friends have been significantly affected by the drinking of someone else.

That people don't think about it and don't talk about it is both a consequence and a further cause of the stigma that surrounds alcoholism. If we have been touched by alcohol abuse, we don't like to dwell on the subject because of the repugnance, shame, and anger it has engendered. If we haven't had much personal contact, we tend to overlook it as a problem and to simplify it in our minds: What is there to know?

Most of us have strong beliefs about drinking, drunkenness, and alcoholism, often based on childhood experiences and assumptions we have made or accepted as adults. Few people examine the attitudes they hold in the light of information that is readily available. And people act according to their beliefs rather than their knowledge. For this reason, alcohol education must help people articulate and examine their own attitudes. Physiological and other objective facts about alcohol and alcoholism may correct some misconceptions without substantially altering the underlying biases that usually determine how professionals behave when confronted with alcoholism.

Each of the statements below touches on important aspects of a perspective on alcoholism. Consider each statement and decide if you generally agree or disagree and with what reasons and qualifications.

● Most people drink because they have acquired a habit that is difficult to break.

● Drinkers who stick to beer or wine run little risk of developing alcoholism.

● "Problem drinker" is just another term for "alcoholic."

● An alcoholic is someone who drinks every day.

● Alcoholism is more prevalent among poor and wealthy males than in other population groups.

● Alcoholism is a preventable, treatable, progressive illness.

● Most alcoholics could stop drinking if they really wanted to.

● You can't help alcoholics until they ask for help or "hit bottom."

We shall discuss each of these statements in this chapter, in the light of a definition of alcoholism adapted from the one framed in 1951 by the World Health Organization. First let us consider the definition.

A FUNCTIONAL DEFINITION OF ALCOHOLISM

Alcoholism is an illness characterized by loss of control over drinking which results in serious problems in any one of the following areas: job, school, or financial affairs; relationships with family and friends; or physical health.[2]

How much and how often someone drinks is not a criterion in the above definition. Apart from being virtually impossible to determine, it is beside the point. Some people are drunk after two drinks; others seem unchanged after four. And tolerance for alcohol changes over time, sometimes from occasion to occasion. Even dangers to an individual's health cannot be accurately predicted on the basis of how much alcohol is ingested. How much someone drinks is nobody's business unless the drinking creates problematic consequences.

How do we know if drinking is creating problems? Suppose a woman complains about her husband's drinking and asks him to cut down or stop. How does a helping professional ascertain whether it is the drinking or the woman's fear, sensitivity, or desire for control that is at the root of the couple's conflict? The drinking and the woman's reaction are contributing in a complementary and cyclical way, and both activities need attention. But it is extremely rare for people to be concerned about someone else's drinking, or their own, without good cause. The woman in this case needs to look at what she brings to the problem; but she is not creating a problem out of thin air. It is safe to assume that her husband really has a drinking problem, one which she may be fostering but did not cause or conjure.

The concept of addiction or dependence is similarly absent from the above definition. Addiction is a physical condition that entails withdrawal in the absence of alcohol. Many people have serious problems because of their drinking long before they become physically addicted. Dependence implies a psychological condition that is practically impossible to verify and suggests daily use of alcohol.

---

[2] United Nations, World Health Organization, Expert Committee on Mental Health (WHO Technical Report Series, no. 42), 1951

A useful definition of alcoholism is one that calls attention to the most critical and observable common denominators. Through discussion of the statements listed above, we can examine in more detail what this definition of alcoholism means, and what it excludes and rejects.

DISCUSSION OF AGREE/DISAGREE STATEMENTS

"Most people drink because they have acquired a habit that is difficult to break."

Two out of every three American adults drink alcoholic beverages, and in some parts of the country, notably the Northeast and Far West, 75 percent of the adult population uses alcohol.[3] Some drink once or twice a year, others virtually every day. The omnipresent and tragic consequences of alcohol abuse can obscure the evidence of our senses: that the great majority of those who drink do so because they find alcohol pleasurable, mildly life-enhancing, and not at all problematic.

America's ethnic and religious heterogeneity has contributed to confused and conflicting attitudes about alcohol. Our forebears brought with them a variety of drinking practices, and if we can speak at all of an American drinking pattern, it is mostly a hodge-podge of contradictory tendencies. Certainly some Americans have liked their liquor, whereas other Americans have deplored the use of alcohol, in every era since the Mayflower landed. Today the cocktail party, the liquid lunch, the happy hour, the tailgate party, the business deal, all are becoming features of an American drinking ethic. And all are worrisome because they are rituals in which drinking is either the central activity or in which alcohol is consumed at the wrong time, in the wrong place, and for unhealthy reasons. Still, the average American neither abuses nor abhors alcohol. Moderate users are in a clear majority. But partly because of our long history of polarizing the subject of drinking, and partly because drinking feels pleasurable to most of us but is so obviously harmful to so many others, many people feel ambivalent, confused, defensive, and even guilty about their responsible use of alcohol.

---

[3]Don Cahalan and Ira Cisin, "American Drinking Practices: Summary of Findings from a National Probability Sample. I. Extent of Drinking by Population Subgroups," *Quarterly Journal of Studies on Alcohol* 29 (1968): 130; *Washington Post*, 10 June 1974; National Institute of Mental Health/National Institute on Alcohol Abuse and Alcoholism, *Alcohol and Alcoholism: Problems, Programs, and Progress* (Washington D.C., 1972), p. 8.

Alcohol is a drug, a depressant that affects the brain and the central nervous system and, through it, the entire body. Does that mean that alcohol, in any amount, damages organs and impairs health? Recent reputable research indicates that moderate drinking does not threaten physical health, and some studies have even associated light but life-long drinking with increased longevity.[4] But whether we regard alcohol as a neutral substance that can be used or abused, or an evil and dangerous entity forbidden by Scriptures or incompatible with "clean living," it should be clear by now that alcoholic beverages have been with us for centuries and cannot be legislated, engineered, or wished away. As long as there are grains and fruits from which to make it, and people to drink it, there will always be alcohol.

The word "drinking," of course, means simply the act of ingesting a liquid, but in modern usage it has come to connote intake of alcohol: a gin and tonic is "a drink," pineapple juice is "something to drink." Even worse, "drinking" is increasingly used to mean heavy drinking, as when someone is described as "a drinker." It is crucial to distinguish between drinking (of alcoholic beverages), drunkenness, and alcoholism.

Most drinking does not result in drunkenness. Alcohol may make light drinkers somewhat more relaxed, convivial, animated, or sleepy than they had been, but faculties and behavior are hardly more modified than they are by fatigue or mood. As one continues to drink, one may reach a stage described as "high," "buzzed," or "mellow." This stage is extremely difficult to define. When people are asked to describe it through drawings, most use pastel colors and wavy lines. They speak of a pleasurable feeling, a mild euphoria, a slight release from inhibitions, without the threatening sense of loss of control. They can still behave appropriately, make good decisions, react to the demands of the situation. Drunkenness denotes the marked impairment of faculties and perceptions, often a radical change in personality, a definite alteration in customary behavior. Needless to say, intoxicated persons are often the worst judges of whether or not they are drunk.

Legal definitions of drunkenness and sobriety, relative to the operation of a motor vehicle, are based on the proportion of alcohol in the bloodstream, which is dependent on three variables: amount of absolute alcohol ingested, time span of ingestion, and weight of the drinker. These objective definitions differ from state to state. In most states a 150-pound person is still legally sober (though not necessarily safe at the wheel) after one and one-half drinks consumed in one hour; and that person could have as many as three drinks in one hour, commit a

---

[4]*New York Times*, 13 November 1980.

traffic infraction, and never be charged with driving under the influence.[5]

Reasons for drinking and the effects of drinking are more important indicators than quantity and frequency. Some people like nothing better than a cold beer on a hot day, prefer wine with their pasta and beer with their fish, wouldn't think of celebrating a special occasion without champagne, use wine in observing Passover or the Sacrament.

"Habit" is a loaded word. It implies dependence, whereas the word "custom" imparts a more positive meaning to a usual practice or established social convention. The daily routine of coming home from work, pouring a drink, putting your feet up and your mind on idle or your nose in a newspaper is in itself no cause for alarm. There is a big difference between enjoying a beer at a ball game, and going to a football game primarily because of the pre- and post-game tailgate parties. Habits, customs, or routines are neither uniformly good nor bad; their purposes and their effects are what count.

Whatever the occasion, whether going out with friends, or relaxing after a hard day at work, there are and must be alternatives to drinking alcoholic beverages. But most people who drink choose to drink, and they do so, in moderation, because it mildly enhances some other primary activity. Such drinking is every bit as responsible, both morally and medically, as abstaining.

On the other hand, there are some reasons for drinking that clearly lead to persistent abuse of alcohol and eventually to alcoholism. Those who use alcohol to escape from their problems or alleviate depression will, like the rest of us, continue to experience problems and depression. Some individuals have isolated incidents in which they "drown their sorrows"; but many, having found alcohol an effective taxi to oblivion, will continue to hail it as problems recur, and will eventually have a surfeit of troubles to forget.

Many drinkers who become alcoholic begin their drinking careers with radically different reasons from those most of us have when we pick up a drink. Like many nonalcoholics, they don't like themselves much when they are sober, and feel acutely insecure with other people. But when they drink they feel more sure of themselves with friends, with the opposite sex, or alone in a crowd. Fears that they are boring, ridiculous, unattractive, or creatively dry vanish. The shy become loquacious, the meek assertive, the self-conscious either nonchalant or eager for the spotlight. Those who look for oblivion in alcohol, or for the personality they wish they had, are likely to drink more on each occasion than they would if they were simply trying to enhance an

---

[5]NIMH/NIAAA, *Alcohol and Alcoholism*, p. 11.

activity that takes precedence over the drinking. And they are going to return to the well for the same reason, time after time.

The reasons leading to the development of alcoholism do not explain the alcoholic's drinking. When people have alcoholism, they are no longer drinking for any reason or choice. They have excuses, but they are drinking because they cannot control their drinking, cannot decide when, where, why, and how much to drink.

"Drinkers who stick to beer or wine run little risk of developing alcoholism."

Nowhere on a can of beer is the word "alcohol" mentioned. This can't be merely fortuitous. The government requires the listing of ingredients, and wine and liquor manufacturers must state the percentage of alcohol by volume. But brewers don't have to, and choose not to tell the public that their product contains alcohol. Perhaps they fear that people would drink less beer if they knew how much, or how little, alcohol they were consuming. On the whole, the omission seems to cultivate an image of beer as being more akin to soft drinks than to hard liquor.

About 5 percent of a 12-ounce can of beer, or six-tenths of an ounce, is alcohol. The same amount is found in a shot of most whiskey, gin, rum, or vodka (the 1.5-ounce shot is 40 percent alcohol), the typical glass of wine (5 ounces, 12 percent of which is alcohol), and the typical serving size of fortified wines such as sherry or port (3 ounces, 20 percent alcohol). My Scotch on the rocks, his screwdriver, her glass of white wine, and your beer are equivalent drinks, each containing a bit more than one-half ounce of absolute alcohol. If you are drinking an imported beer, your drink may well be the most potent of the four; if it is a low-calorie beer, you are ingesting somewhat less alcohol.

People use all sorts of arguments to resist this mathematical equivalency. The most popular one is that beer is more diluted. Unless that statement also means that you drink it more slowly and consequently drink less in a given period of time, the dilution is not very important. It may make the effects of ingestion less sudden, but it doesn't change the fact that the quantity of alcohol consumed is equal to that in a gin and tonic. The second most popular rebuttal is empirical: "Say what you want, but I can drink beer all night, while two mixed drinks have me flying."

Alcohol is a drug, whatever beverage it is imbibed in; and while drugs alter moods, they are also subject to them. If you are elated, alcohol may have the psychological (not the physical) effect of a stimulant; if you are depressed, it may heighten the depression. Just as mood and setting contribute to the effects of alcohol on behavior, so your expectations play a role. If you expect to get drunk on liquor but not on beer, you feel the impact of the same alcohol quite differently, though objectively the same things may be happening.

If you never get drunk (and drunk doesn't necessarily mean boisterous, obnoxious, or withdrawn) you probably can't develop alcoholism. But there are plenty of individuals who drink only beer and are full-fledged alcoholics. "It's only beer" is the same as saying "It's only bourbon."

"'Problem drinker' is just another term for 'alcoholic.'"

"Rose has a problem with her drinking," her friends say. "She ought to cut down; she can't handle her liquor." There are all sorts of euphemisms to avoid the word "alcoholic." In general, a problem drinker is an alcoholic we care about. A woman who drinks because she has problems will soon have more problems because of her drinking. If she persists in her drinking, denying the relationship between it and the trouble it creates for her or for others, she is an alcoholic. An alcoholic is someone whose drinking causes repeated problems.

The term "problem drinker" is not without its value. In trying to get a friend to evaluate his or her drinking, the phrase may avoid the total breakdown of the interaction. But no one has been helped by "Problem Drinkers Anonymous," and sooner rather than later the affliction must be given its real name. It would be less ugly if it were named more often.

If "problem drinker" has any meaning at all, it refers to adolescents who abuse alcohol, and to some adults who are developing new ways of drinking—in response, for example, to radical changes in lifestyle. Ordinarily law-abiding teenagers who steal cars or commit other forms of mayhem when intoxicated may aptly be called "problem drinkers." We don't know if they can ever learn to drink without incident. Some may "settle down"; after all, adolescence is the time for testing limits, proving adulthood, taking risks, experimenting not only with drinking but with drunkenness. Some adolescents pass through a period of riot and ruin and become responsible in every way; they had never completely lost, but simply suspended, the ability to control alcohol and its intake. But many youthful abusers appear to be fairly consistent in their abuse during their teenage years, and are simply alcoholics-in-training, or young alcoholics.

This is emphatically not to suggest that most teenage drinkers are on the road to alcoholism. Most teenagers, with some allowances for testing, are as responsible in their drinking or nondrinking as their parents. If that is hard to believe, it is largely because we make no provisions for teenagers to learn and practice responsible use of alcohol, as is noted in more detail in Chapter 5.

"An alcoholic is someone who drinks every day."

This myth probably constitutes the most common ground for disclaiming and denying alcoholism. Many people now recognize that only about 5 percent of America's alcoholics are Skid Row types, homeless derelicts who sleep on the streets (though people usually incorrectly believe that almost all of those on Skid Row are alcoholic).[6] They know that most alcoholics hold jobs, after a fashion, and participate in family life. But they continue to believe that these people drink virtually every day, and that this is a leading criterion of alcoholism.

Some alcoholics drink only on weekends. Others are binge drinkers; they may have little or nothing to drink for months, then drink excessively for days, weeks, or longer. Their drinking episodes, perhaps spent in dingy bars or hotel rooms far from home, are sometimes completely separate from their nondrinking lives, except for their effect on loved ones and employers. The families of binge drinkers may have no idea where they are, though they know what they are doing. They may comb the city for their parent or spouse, live in fear that some friend or associate will see the person drunk in some alley or gutter, and continually expect the discovery of his or her body to be announced on the radio or in the back pages of the newspaper. Sometimes family members are kept in the dark; they think the alcoholic is on an extended business trip. Employers may be similarly fooled, for a time, and employees for even longer.

Many alcoholics, whether binge drinkers or more consistent drinkers, are not completely sure where they have been and what they have been doing. Some find themselves a thousand miles from home; they had boarded a plane while drunk and "awakened" days later with no recollection whatever of the preceding days' events. This is an alcoholic "blackout." It should be noted that blackouts can last for minutes or days, and may not be discernible to onlookers but are often terrifying to the alcoholic.

Clearly, binge drinkers fit into the definition of alcoholism by virtue of the serious problems their drinking causes. As with all alcoholism, the consequences are usually first and most severely felt (though not necessarily acknowledged) by family members and later by friends and colleagues at work, and usually much later in the deterioration of the drinker's physical health.

---

[6]NIMH/NIAAA, *Alcohol and Alcoholism*, p. 9.

Those who drink sporadically, or "go on the wagon" for extended periods, are often viewed as retaining a certain amount of control over their drinking: "I'm no alcoholic, I can stop whenever I want to." The concept of "loss of control" need not apply to every incident of drinking. Responsible drinkers don't concern themselves with affirming their ability to cut down or do without alcohol. They have no reason to try to limit their drinking. Only people who are worried about their drinking, having seen evidence of its harmful consequences, try to prove their mastery by assembling a period of sobriety. A few days without alcohol convinces them that they are not alcoholic; or they limit themselves to two or three drinks a night. Their fears assuaged, they presently revert to their regular drinking pattern, having satisfied themselves that they drink by choice, not helplessly.

Recovered alcoholics are still alcoholics. With help and support, they can avoid that first drink; but after fifteen years of sobriety, they still cannot have one drink and feel sure that they will drink only as much as they choose. This is the meaning of "loss of control": when alcoholics drink, they do so without the firm capacity to choose how much they drink, a capacity that is taken for granted by nonalcoholics. Many new AA members, after a short period of abstinence, convince themselves that they have licked booze so thoroughly that they can drink once again, with appropriate restraint. Perhaps they succeed—for a time. Then they are back where they started from when they came to AA. Alcoholics who had been sober for ten years or more have reported that in almost every respect their drinking patterns reverted to what they had been in the deepest throes of their alcoholism, almost immediately upon resumption of drinking.

Periods of abstinence, then, are not evidence of control over drinking. On the contrary, enforced sobriety is usually a sign of alcoholism. Again, it is not how often people drink, but what happens when they drink, that is important.

"Alcoholism is more prevalent among poor and wealthy males than in any other population groups."

Alcoholism is a great leveler. It does not respect sex, age, geographic differences, class, educational level, or occupation (some people think that clergy, physicians, business executives, and politicians have, if anything, higher than average rates of alcoholism). Alcoholism may be easier to spot in some configurations than in others, and certainly its impact is influenced by other social and family circumstances, and influences them in its turn.

Alcoholism has always been underestimated in women. In large part, our blindness has been intentional. After all, what is more sacred in western society than motherhood? We don't want to see alcoholism in our womenfolk, largely because we continue to consider it a moral issue, and a far greater stigma for women than for men: "An alcoholic man is a bum, but a woman who is a drunk is a slut." Female alcoholics have gone undiscovered not merely because they were "protected" within the confines of the home, where they could secretly drink and pop Valiums to relieve the boredom of keeping the castle spotless, but also because, for their men as much as themselves, the consequences of their discovery were more deeply dreaded.

As the social mores concerning women's conduct have changed, and drinking has become generally acceptable in women, there has been apparently a real increase in female alcoholism.[7] Women in the workforce attend business lunches in increasing numbers; women who work at home have their own drinking institutions, some of them social, some solitary; and if women are still scarce in the hardcore, sleazy bars, they are certainly plentiful in cocktail lounges that serve the same alcohol with fancier trimmings. A greater percentage of high school girls are drinking today than ever before, and more are drinking heavily.[8] We are seeing more alcoholism in women, both because it seems to be increasing, and because we are beginning to shed our blinders. It now appears to many observers that alcoholism is as prevalent in women as in men.

Some experts contend that alcoholic mothers are most often either single mothers or spouses of alcoholic men. The nonalcoholic wife puts up with her husband's drinking because she is dependent on his paycheck and has been taught to preserve the family at all costs. Nonalcoholic husbands are not as likely to linger. There is little definitive data on the incidence of divorce in families with alcoholism, but it cannot be doubted that a great many marital breakdowns have the alcohol abuse of one or both partners at their roots. The typical alcoholic family may not be a nuclear family at all. But as we look in subsequent chapters at how alcoholism affects the intact family, there is some justification for using as an example one in which the father is alcoholic and the mother nonalcoholic.

The media may sensationalize and exaggerate the scope of youthful alcoholism at times, but clearly there is no age requirement for alco-

---

[7] Edith Gomberg, "Women with Alcohol Problems," in *Alcoholism: Development, Consequences, and Interventions*, ed. Nada J. Estes and M. Edith Heinemann (St. Louis: V. Mosby, 1977), p. 174; Hecht, "Children at Risk," p. 1764.

[8] J. V. Rachal, J. R. Williams, M. L. Brehm, B. Cavanaugh, R. P. Moore, and W. C. Eckerman, *A National Study of Adolescent Drinking Behavior, Attitudes, and Correlates* (Research Triangle Park, N.C.: Research Triangle Park Center for the Study of Social Behavior, 1975), p. 40.

holism, and even preteens who are alcoholic in every sense of the word
are not hard to find. Many people think of alcoholism as a middle-age
affliction, but this belief is also being challenged. We are also becoming
more aware of the elderly alcoholic. Again, it is probable that alcoholism was previously grossly undetected in this age group, but it may also
be on the rise, as seniority in America has bred increasing contempt.

The belief that alcoholism is more prevalent among the poor stems
from the notion that it is caused by poverty and lack of opportunity.
Alcoholic drinking patterns develop in people who use alcohol to forget or escape from their problems and pain; when they are drinking
they feel carefree, respected, the equal of their peers. Certainly, lack
of money, status, and freedom, given little or no prospect of acquiring
these, stimulates feelings of worthlessness and despair, especially when
people are convinced that the fault is their own rather than a principle
of political economy. Some individuals learn to dull these feelings by
drowning them. Whole cultures and underclasses have been encouraged to use alcohol for their pacification. This is nowhere more evident
than in the conquest of the West, in which firewater was probably as
great a weapon as firepower.[9]

On the other hand, people with sufficient money and opportunity
still have feelings they can't tolerate, still want to be different from
who they are. Their problems feel as serious to them as those of
someone living from hand to mouth. There is no shortage of causes for
psychic trauma. Some people, and whole cultures, tend to turn to
alcohol to cope, whereas others turn elsewhere. The Scandinavian countries have probably gone furthest toward reducing the purely economic
gaps in capitalist society; there is little severe poverty, but rampant
alcoholism.[10] Alcoholism is reportedly widespread in the Soviet Union,
and has been identified as a major problem in France, Great Britain,
and Canada. This suggests that it is more a cultural or genetic inheri-
tance than a socioeconomic or political phenomenon.[11]

If it is simplistic to say that poverty causes alcoholism, it is safe to
say that alcoholism often leads to and heightens the effects of poverty.
Many alcoholics descend the career ladders they might have climbed.
They get bounced to jobs that pay less and are less fulfilling, and have
longer periods of unemployment, as their drinking progresses. The

---

[9] Joan M. Baker, "Alcoholism and the American Indian," in *Alcoholism: Development,
Consequences, and Interventions,* ed. N. Estes and M. Heinemann (St. Louis: V. Mosby,
1977), p. 196.

[10] NIMH/NIAAA, *Alcohol and Alcoholism,* p. 15.

[11] Raymond G. McCarthy, ed., *Drinking and Intoxication* (New Haven: College and
University Press, 1959), pp. 130–175.

working-class family may feel compelled to protect the alcoholic's job by lying to the boss; and some nonalcoholic spouses try to control the money supply by having the alcoholic's paycheck sent directly to their banks. Guaranteeing the supply of booze becomes the foremost concern of the alcoholic; money is spent on liquor before it is applied to even the most basic family needs.

> We were up the park, and Danny's brother, who was about seven then, came running up, yelling, "Danny, Danny, come home quick, there's food!" I guess their mother had gotten a bigger welfare check than usual and bought some food with it. 'Cause you'd look in her refrigerator, you'd find a case or two of beer and an old jar of relish or mustard or something. She sends the kids down the corner for subs, that's their dinner every night.

But in important ways money doesn't reduce the impact of alcoholism; it simply disguises it. The underlings who protect alcoholic executives from the immediate effects of their drinking help to prolong it. Corporate officers, professionals, and entrepreneurs may not have to worry about being fired when they are too hung over to work each Monday, but sooner or later their businesses may suffer. Civil service employees may be difficult to discharge, but they are also therefore less apt to confront their problem and arrest it.

Clearly it is easier to be rich than poor, but the children of wealthy alcoholics have their own problems. They may have housekeepers who keep them safe and give them love; they may escape the home to boarding schools and summer camps. But think of the child whose alcoholic father is a prosperous businessman or professional, a pillar of the community, perhaps someone on whom lives depend. How does that child reconcile his or her feelings of distrust or outright contempt with the public respect in which the father is held?

Alcoholic families are often virtual nomads in a generally mobile society. In the denial of alcoholism, both the abuser and the other family members blame their problems on the boss, the neighbors, the kid's friends, the school system. They look for "geographic" solutions: life will improve in a different community, or at least the drinking can be better hidden. Children who are relocated every two or three years (many alcoholic families move more often) are going to have a hard time investing in friendships and feeling stable and secure. They are less likely to find support and guidance outside of the home; the isolation and insularity of the family is intensified.

Some aspects of the family alcoholism experience may also be different in urban, suburban, and rural settings. It is more difficult to hide the staggering drunk or the 2 A.M. fights in a densely populated area or in a small town than in a suburban or rural community. Children who live in housing projects may give up trying to conceal the problem, and may also derive relief from the observation of other alcoholic families.

In suburban or rural areas, the importance of the automobile may color the alcoholism experience. The family members may pressure the alcoholic to drink at home, making them feel both more complicitous and more oppressed. There may be a greater obsession with the alcoholic's safety, an effort to ferry the alcoholic to and from the barroom. There may also be a greater dependence on the alcoholic for transportation; children may have to ride with a drunk parent regularly without showing the slightest sign of fear. How much more likely are these children to mix drinking and driving themselves, or routinely accept rides with intoxicated friends as they get older?

"Alcoholism is a preventable, treatable, progressive illness."

In recent years virtually every medical authority—including the Secretary of the U.S. Department of Health, Education, and Welfare, the Surgeon-General, and the American Medical Association—has called alcoholism an illness and one of our country's greatest public health problems.[12] Nevertheless, most people deeply believe that alcoholism is a moral failing: one becomes psychologically and eventually physically addicted to alcohol because one lacks the willpower to refrain from or control drinking. The alcoholic is either a bad person or a pathetically weak one.

No one can say what causes alcoholism, but many researchers are becoming convinced that both genetic and environmental factors are at work. Some recent studies are mentioned in Chapter 5. But when we look at how individuals develop alcoholism, we have to understand that, at the outset, they are exercising the same choice as most other Americans.

Just as persons who are made to feel like outcasts and failures may seek confirmation by shooting heroin, those who expect to belong acquire the trappings of membership. We live in a drinking society; more people drink than don't. In most parts of the country, more than 80 percent of high school seniors consider themselves drinkers.[13] Now,

---

[12] Joseph A. Califano, Jr., Foreword to *Third Special Report to U.S. Congress on Alcohol and Health* (Rockville, Md.: National Institute on Alcohol Abuse and Alcoholism, 1978), p. vii; Thomas Plaut, *Alcohol Problems: A Report to the Nation* (London: Oxford University Press, 1967), pp. 42–45.

[13] Rachal et al., *Study of Adolescent Drinking Behavior*, pp. 42–44.

no one forces anyone else to drink, or shoot heroin; each individual is responsible for those choices. But many of those who become alcoholics simply elected to use alcohol, like the rest of us. The difference is that they did not have, or soon lost, the capacity to use it judiciously, or the chemical makeup to tolerate *only* small amounts. And for every person who may have warned them of their danger, many more helped them deny the problem. By the time they might have realized that alcohol was the problem, they were no longer drinking by choice. They were drinking because they could not choose not to drink. It is the nature of addiction, and especially alcoholism, that the devotion to the substance precludes the early recognition of its harm.

Some people wink at the illness concept of alcoholism. "Sure, we'll call it a disease because more people will come in for treatment if we do; but we know it's no disease, whatever doctors and lawyers call it." But if it is no disease, what is it? The concept of addiction begs the question: Why do some people become dependent on alcohol or unable to control their drinking? Is it because they are foolish, psychologically deficient, morally bankrupt, socially oppressed?

To begin to comprehend alcoholism as an illness, go to an AA meeting and meet some of the people who are recovering from it. Better still, go to several different meetings. The people you will encounter are different from your friends, relatives, mentors, and children in one respect only: they cannot control their drinking. Sober, they are no more neurotic, selfish, or weak-willed than any other group you could assemble; and the difference between the individuals you see and the "drunken good-for-nothings" you might once have called them is that they have stopped drinking. Psychological tests done on alcoholics with three or more years of sobriety found them to be normatively healthy.[14]

How can these people, now so giving, humble, and responsible, be the same people who abused family and friends and lost all self-respect? And how can it be that people who are so different from one another can have experienced so many of the same things before they stopped drinking? One answer is that alcoholism is an illness with specific symptoms and a definite progression. Alcoholics cannot control alcohol, just as diabetics cannot safely use sugar. For reasons which we don't yet understand, alcohol did different things and produced different results in them, often from the very first drink.

That alcoholism is treatable is beyond question. Alcoholics don't become cured; they can never drink in safety. Alcoholism can only be

---

[14] Vaillant, "Paths Out of Alcoholism," p. 2.

arrested, just as diabetes can only be arrested. We do not speak of former or ex-alcoholics or of reformed alcoholics, but only of recovering alcoholics, always engaged in the recovery process by avoiding that first drink.

If not arrested, alcoholism invariably gets worse. It may progress slowly or rapidly, but it becomes more marked in its effects on family, work, friends, and health; the strength of the denial of the problem; the fear of living without booze. The weekend alcoholic elongates her weekend to include Thursday night, then the Wednesday night bridge game; she isn't worried, because alcoholics drink every day. Then she finds herself drinking every day, but since she never starts until after dinner, and goes a day here or there without alcohol, she has no fear. Eventually she may start drinking at noon, but she's only drinking because people have started picking fights with her and she can't take the tension; and besides, alcoholics are people who need a drink first thing in the morning. In this and countless other ways, her values, her relationships, her thoughts and her behaviors are gradually, inexorably governed by the need to drink and to protect her drinking.

There is reason to believe that alcoholism is preventable. Meaningful alcohol education for all children, education that does not simplistically condemn all drinking but clearly distinguishes between abuse and responsible use would, among other things, help many young people recognize developing alcoholism in themselves and their friends. And such school-based education has been shown to be exceptionally effective in identifying and reaching children who are being groomed for alcoholism by their parents and immediate models. More will be said about this in later chapters.

"Most alcoholics could stop drinking if they really wanted to."

Approximately two-thirds of recovering alcoholics who remain sober for one year recover from alcoholism. They may have an occasional lapse, but for the most part they live as nondrinking alcoholics.[15] This recovery rate vastly exceeds rates reported in mental health treatment. There is ample reason for hope where alcoholism is concerned; and hope is a vital entity, often totally absent in both alcoholics and their loved ones. Recovery is a slow and very painful process. There can be many false starts, and sometimes the beginnings of recovery look like the worst and most hopeless of times.

Most recovered alcoholics would disagree with the sense of the above statement. It implies that the difference between those who stop and

---

[15]National Council on Alcoholism, "Facts on Alcoholism" (New York, 1976); NIAAA, *Alcohol and Alcoholism*, p. 17.

those who continue drinking is a matter of willpower or desire. This notion dies hard in nonalcoholics; after all, we have no trouble deciding when and how much to drink. When we recognize that alcoholics lack that control, we tend to regard those who get sober with great respect. We admire the determination and strength of character it must take to abstain from something that is so central to their lives and so accessible. But we must then also think of active alcoholics as lacking in that determination and desire to stop.

To be sure, alcoholics are susceptible to that same point of view. They may attribute their sobriety to some strength and willpower they never knew they had. If they believe that, they are likely to start drinking again. It was not force of will that led to sobriety, nor is it lack of will that accounts for the failure to recover.

Alcoholics don't want to give up the bottle. They seek or accept treatment because they feel desperately miserable, and have the smallest glint of hope, the faintest sense that they don't have to live this way. "But for the grace of God" expresses the wonder and mystery with which many recovering alcoholics explain why they are sober today, and others are not. "You have to hit your bottom" is another way many see it. People can accept varying levels of misery; when alcoholics can accept no more they may look for help and hope. If it comes far enough to meet them they may get better.

Sometimes we want to shake the alcoholic by the collar. "What's wrong with you, don't you want to change?" But the disease is denial, despair, and worthlessness. To stop drinking is to let go of the parachute. The wonder is not that so many alcoholics continue to drink, but that so many stop.

"You can't help alcoholics until they ask for help or hit bottom."

We often mistake help for the incident that immediately precedes results. Help is a cumulative and often invisible process. Most of us can remember words or deeds that only became useful years later, when we were making career choices, struggling through a marriage, or grieving for a loved one. A friend's observation—ignored, rejected, barely noticed at the time—comes to mind when we need it. Neither we nor the friend know the value of what has transpired. In Chapter 8 the distortions we have built into our conception of "helping" are discussed further.

Alcoholics may have to hit bottom, however deep that bottom may be for each individual, before they can ask for or accept help. But there are many ways in which people help alcoholics reach that stage sooner. Recovering alcoholics are justifiably grateful, not only to the friends who brought them to their first meeting, but to all those who commented on their drinking through the years, and were rebuffed; to the employers who called them on the carpet and ultimately fired them because of their drinking; and to the family members who refused to carry them up to bed each night and clean up their mess. In the end their recovery hinged on their inability to deny the connection between their unhappiness and their drinking. Friends who perpetuate such denial leave alcoholics to get progressively worse, and alcoholism is a fatal illness. It is as if they recognized symptoms of cancer in a friend and declined to mention it because doing so might be impolite, offensive, or fruitless.

Some common signs and symptoms of alcoholism are listed in Appendix A of this book. To be most helpful to alcoholics and family members you already know, and those you may encounter, treat yourself to an AA meeting. Ask the local alcoholism treatment program or a minister to suggest a meeting—different groups may strike you very differently. If you are expecting a depressing experience, you will almost certainly be surprised. There is a great deal of exhilaration and example in a room full of people who spent a long season in hell and came out to find sobriety, fellowship, and acceptance.

Chapter 3
THE CHILD AT HOME

A striking similarity exists among families that have nothing else in common but their alcoholism. Regardless of income or size, or whether it is mom, dad, or both who have alcoholism, most of these families appear to be dominated, in various degrees, by five conditions:
1. The centricity of the alcoholic and alcohol-related behavior;
2. Denial and shame;
3. Inconsistency, insecurity, and fear;
4. Anger and hatred;
5. Guilt and blame.

The above characteristics may not be unique to alcoholic families. Families in which a parent is dying or schizophrenic, or simply violent may exhibit the characteristics in comparable strength, whereas relatively normal and healthy families share some of the tendencies in a much less powerful and destructive form. But what we can describe as the dynamic of family alcoholism is remarkably uniform in most alcoholic homes and significantly different from the conditions which govern most other households.

Children of alcoholics are not victims. They are survivors who testify to the resiliency in all of us. The patterns they develop as children and maintain as adults are comprehensible responses to the conditions in which they were raised. But as we examine the unhealthy dynamics that grip the alcoholic home, we should keep in mind that these families also know love and laughter. The disease of alcoholism, insidious and comprehensive, rules every member of the household; although there is a surfeit of bad memories and bad feelings, there are other moments and intervals in which warmth, pride, and fun predominate, and supply to each member what we need from our families. Every member of the family does the best he or she can, and some families manage to be quite nurturing and supportive in spite of the ravages of alcoholism.

CHARACTERISTICS OF THE ALCOHOLIC FAMILY

The Centricity of the Alcoholic

The scene could be a dinner gathering, an anniversary celebration, a party, picnic, or class reunion. Four friends—Robert, Larry, Sarah and Judy—are having a lively conversation. It might be a heated political discussion or a joyful recounting of shared memories. Then a fifth friend, George, joins the group; and George is quite drunk.

Almost always, the irresponsible behavior that we expect, and to a great degree license in an intoxicated person, becomes the central fact of the group's interaction. If the discussion is serious when George arrives, he may be interruptive, garrulous, unfocused, or rather incoherent, repetitive, inconsistent, and provoking, if not utterly belligerent. If the mood is light, George may be comical, self-deprecating, mocking, tactless and tasteless, maudlin, or nonsensical. Or he may completely change the mood of the group. Even if he stands there, silent and withdrawn, his presence has an unmistakable, chilling effect on the group.

Initially, the four friends try to minimize the interruption and continue their discussion. But their ability to do so depends upon their success in ignoring, controlling, or disposing of George; and that becomes their main task. Each of the friends reacts to George in ways consistent with their personalities or dictated by their emotions and experiences with intoxicated people. Rarely, if ever, does the group agree to a joint course of action designed to restore it to its original activity. Instead, everyone copes differently, and the friends may react strongly to one another's treatment of George.

Robert reacts to George with a sympathy that for him calls for gentle toleration. He listens seriously to George's garbled nonsense, endures his interruptions, laughs at his off-color jokes, humors his verbal violence, flattens his provocations. Maybe Robert regards drunkenness as a relatively harmless, even a humorous human foible; or perhaps he wants to avoid "creating a scene" to prevent embarrassment to himself, George, and George's wife.

Sarah does the same things out of fear. She is terribly anxious and apprehensive, possibly resulting from some past experience with drunkenness. Resenting the intrusion, she is afraid to express or act on her feelings.

Larry is furious, but perhaps he is as angry at his two friends and their meek acquiescence as he is at George. It falls to Larry to dispose of George, to be harsh or cagey, confrontive, or cajoling; and he dislikes having to play the heavy while his friends give George his way. Even after George has been dismissed, Larry may be annoyed at Robert and Sarah and preoccupied with what they may be thinking of his treatment of George.

Judy exercises a fourth option. She bails out and finds another group to mix with. She may not even acknowledge that she has been deprived of anything. In fact, the four friends may not even agree that George is hopelessly drunk. At all events, from the moment George appears, the group does not have the option of simply continuing as before; its primary activity becomes dealing with the drunk. Its members are variously affected, not merely by George, but also by the ways in which other group members react to him.

George's power to dominate his friends in an isolated social situation is a pale reflection, indeed, of the centrality his alcoholism gives him in his family. If George's friends can become so emotionally engaged, so preoccupied with his drunkenness and one another's responses to it, imagine the magnified power of repeated incidents, or the threat of drunkenness, on family members who share with George and with one another bonds and expectations of love, responsibility, emotional and financial interdependence, identification, and daily physical proximity. Every incident becomes part of a chain, with accumulated feelings and past reactions coloring what each family member does and feels on each new occasion. The obsession pervades the family even when the alcoholic is not drinking. Its first consideration is always preventing and preempting his need to drink.

> My father was coming home and you weren't supposed to say anything to get him angry, therefore you said nothing. So the minute you walked in the house you didn't talk. That was it, you went to your room, you stayed in your room, you weren't allowed to watch television until after supper, and then you watched what my father wanted to watch. If he passed out, then the television was shut off 'cause you didn't want to wake him up.

Other family systems are less centralized. They are not organized so exclusively around the real or perceived needs of any one member; there is no one organizing principle or person around whom everything else revolves. Everyone reacts and contributes to the family dynamics in more equal measure. It is common for professionals to undervalue the centrality of the alcoholic in the family, both because family-systems theory emphasizes the confluence of more nearly equal but dissimilar forces and needs and because of a tendency to see alcohol abuse as a symptom rather than a cause of personal and familial stress.

People develop alcoholism not because their problems are more severe or their personalities more deficient than others' but because they somehow learn or are physically predisposed to find in alcohol their principal means of coping with their malaise. At some indeterminate point, probably much earlier than most people assume, reasons for drinking become excuses. Alcoholics do not drink because they are unhappy or persecuted but because they have no control over their intake and its consequences. They drink no matter what else is happening.

> At report card time, my father would line up four drinks, and we'd present our cards one by one. Tommy, the oldest, got straight As, so my father would drink to congratulate himself. Bobby got all Ds and Fs, so he'd yell at him and need a drink out of disgust. Nancy got Cs; he drank to cement a deal with her that she'd do better next time. I got all As, but D in conduct. By that time he barely noticed the As and needed a drink because of the D.

"Driven to drink" is an idiom embedded in our language like a bad debt passed on through the generations. Nagging wives or husbands and naughty children do not cause alcoholism or force someone to take a drink, no matter what all concerned may think. There is no "chicken-and-egg" dilemma here. What we see in alcoholic homes are family members who react to the alcoholics. To be sure, alcoholics respond to their family members as well; if loved ones don't react with hatred or indifference, alcoholics have more trouble justifying their drinking. But their first love, their primary allegiance, is to the bottle. For that reason, they are less subject than nonalcoholic parents to the demands and needs of their families. And the unpredictability and anxiety associated with their drinking give them power over their spouses and children, and make their presence or absence the most important determinant in how their families behave.

In this chapter we will use as a model the nuclear family with a male alcoholic. The justification is that the "intact" family seems most illustrative of the dynamics of alcoholism; and the alcoholic in such families is apparently more often male than female. But as noted earlier, alcoholism is probably equally prevalent in women; and alcoholism in the mother rather than in the father probably dominates the family more completely and devastatingly. First, the mother is generally the primary caretaker, much more central than the father to the wellbeing of children. When children come to school hungry, redolent, dressed inappropriately, or otherwise neglected, there may be a number of explanations, but maternal alcoholism should certainly be considered. Second, an alcoholic mother is more often a single parent than an alcoholic father. And third, the stigma of maternal alcoholism probably has no rival. Boys with alcoholic mothers seem the most difficult children to reach; as soon as they enter the age of locker-room fascination, wet dreams, and "your mother" insults (if not before), the notion of maternal alcoholism becomes unspeakable and unthinkable.

For many children of alcoholics, the obsession with the alcoholic is methodically learned from the nonalcoholic parent, for example, the mother who has been subordinating herself in the interest of security and relative tranquility, or trying to control the alcoholic, for years by the time the children are born. Under the pressures of responsibilities to her family and the exigencies of living with an alcoholic, she becomes as quixotic, bitter, and dishonest as the alcoholic, as important a source of stress, inconsistency, and anger as he is. Far from being a haven and a positive role model for her children, she often becomes the most hated and blamed person in the household. In part this is because all of the limit-setting and disciplining may fall to her. She is the one who has to stretch the money and wait up for the teenagers at night. She thinks the children should be grateful for her self-abnegating efforts to hold the family together. Instead, they are apt to hold her responsible for what is wrong. And small wonder: She has enlisted them regularly in her preemptive strikes intended to control the alcoholic. An account of such a mother's behavior is an example.

> My mother would say, "We're having a barbecue later and the neighbors are coming over. Make your father happy; you're going swimming." "But he's been drinking." "You're going swimming." In our little tire tubes, out in the middle of the Atlantic Ocean, freezing cold water, [we would] swim.

Of course, whether or not this father, or any alcoholic, gets drunk at the barbecue has little or nothing to do with whether the children go swimming with him. It was the mother, not the father, who compelled the children to swim against their will and under hazardous conditions. She is not acting in his behalf; she has her own ends rather than his pleasure in mind; but she is also increasing his power over them. He doesn't even have to crook his own finger; she does it for him.

Naturally, the woman's attitude about wifely duties, transmitted through her upbringing and exaggerated in certain cultures, predisposes her to male domination. The fact that he is alcoholic and irresponsible, if it is recognized at all, is secondary. The nonalcoholic mother in the following example is Greek, but her conception of her role is more similar to than different from that of most women of other backgrounds.

> You were taught by my mother's actions that what my father did, even though it was wrong, was the law. What he said, what he did, [you] just shut your mouth and accepted it. . . . I remember the big thing about not talking in the car. Other kids at Christmastime used to sing Christmas carols when they were riding down the street and everything else. And I remember one time all of us kids decided we were going to sing Christmas carols, and he pulled the car over, got out of the car, and belted us all and told us to get back in the car. My mother did nothing. We were always told, "Your father brings home his paycheck, so you owe to shut up."

Whether she rails against the drinking, tries to prevent it, or silently accepts it, the nonalcoholic parent is often blamed for the drinking. This is most of all a reflection of the responsibility for controlling it which she assumes and passes on to the children. Some children bring their feelings about their nonalcoholic parent into the open:

> I was usually more on my father's side than I was on my mother's. I couldn't stand my mother, the way she screamed. She was a wonderful screamer, an obnoxious screamer, to tell the truth. I couldn't stand her screaming. And I used to think it was her screaming that made him drink, 'cause he used to scream that out in the middle of the place, too.

For other children, it is too threatening to regard both parents as hateful and unreasonable. So they rationalize their mother's most inconsistent behavior, denying her problems and putting her on a pedestal as an example for themselves. They repress their disappointment and rage toward her, and the repressed emotions find indirect expression and continue to be a source of undefined and unresolved feelings.

Sibling relationships can take on added importance when neither parent provides sane and consistent ground rules. If the oldest sibling has achieved some measure of healthy detachment, younger brothers and sisters can get a share. But if siblings are retaliating, retreating, or otherwise reacting most of all to the alcoholism, then they become mediators for the alcoholic's power and influence in much the same way as the nonalcoholic spouse.

Recent evidence suggests that "the protection of holiday rituals apparently constitutes a last line of defense against the general invasion of alcoholism."[1] A study in the District of Columbia found that children whose families had been able to keep their rituals from being dominated by the alcoholic's drinking (actual or threatened) had a much lower rate of alcoholism themselves than children from homes in which the rituals had been disrupted or discontinued. The connection may be associational rather than causal. The study did not explore whether other risks associated with children of alcoholics were also lessened when rituals were preserved. It is possible to speculate that families who maintain rituals (including Sundays, holidays, vacations, family gatherings, even dinnertimes)—during which either the alcoholic doesn't get drunk or the family cohesively rejects his intoxication—keep an identity apart from their more usual sense of continually having to adjust to the alcoholic.

Denial and Shame

> I used to say, "Ma, I wish you'd stop drinking 'cause you don't know what it's doing to you. You know, it's making you nutty." And she used to just swear her head off at me. She said, "You don't know what you're talking about, this stuff is just like Pepsi."

Most people would think this woman is lying. Their judgment reflects an abiding belief that alcoholism is really a moral failing. She may earnestly if not completely believe what she is saying because she desperately needs to believe it. Alcoholic denial is an exaggerated form of a common defense mechanism. It is an unconscious rejection of an unacceptable reality, an elaborate and consistent pattern of selective perception based on profound emotional needs. For the alcoholic, the bottle becomes mother and father, spouse, children and friends; it becomes life itself, and doing without it is too fearful to contemplate. Denial is the defense of the bottle. It protects alcoholics from seeing what drinking is doing to themselves and their loved ones, partly because they couldn't stand the guilt and shame, but at bottom because acknowledging it would mean they have to try to do without booze.
    Denial is extremely flexible and accommodating. Alcoholics can believe their own most implausible excuses and discount lifelong, seemingly incontrovertible evidence, because what is real is less important than what they need to believe. Thus, alcoholics believe their own explanations for why they lost family, jobs, and health, and the ex-

[1]Shirley Aldoory, "Research into Family Factors in Alcoholism," *Alcohol Health and Research World* 3 (Summer 1979): 4.

planations rarely have anything to do with their drinking. Alcoholics may even blame themselves for their misery, but they usually don't blame their drinking. Many alcoholics can be found in psychiatric units all over the country; they would rather be considered crazy than be told they must live without alcohol.[2] The bottle is all things to them, and the bottle must remain blameless.

At some point denial may cease to work for many alcoholics; too much reality gets through, and the dissonance between what they can and want to believe becomes insupportable. Then denial and dishonesty begin to mix and blur. Some alcoholics know that booze is the problem, but are no better able to deal with that knowledge. They lie about their drinking, and they know they are lying; they are now consciously defending against the same fear, guilt, and desperation from which their denial had more effectively protected them.

Denial is equally characteristic of the alcoholic's spouse and children. They too develop an unconscious screening process that keeps out or distorts the evidence they can't bear to face. Popular myths help to support their denial.

> No one in the family recognized the alcoholism as alcoholism. The father was from a family where everyone was an alcoholic, and they were all further gone alcoholics than what he was. You'd hear, you know, "He's not an alcoholic because he can still hold a job. He can wait until noon to drink," those reasons. The mother would see the effects of alcoholism and not recognize it as such. She'd say, "Well, he hadn't been drinking the day that happened," not realizing how the alcoholism can affect their entire life, not just when they're drinking.

The denial of family members also progresses with the illness. The denial of the nonalcoholic spouse often starts before the children are born. It is common, for example, for a young woman to feel keenly worried about her intended's drinking throughout their courtship; but she thinks her love will overcome this and all other problems and he will "cut down." He may beat her occasionally and disappoint her repeatedly, but she loves him and wants all the good characteristics he represents. Devoted to the sacred ideas of what spouses and families should be, she is determined to meet those standards. She vows "to honor and obey." She knows she is expected to "stand by her man"; she is willing to accept almost all of the responsibility for creating a nurturing environment for her children. She doesn't forgive him for what he does; she blocks and forgets. Her feelings fester, but her eyes are

---

[2]NIAAA, *Alcohol and Alcoholism*, pp. 19, 29.

riveted on an idealized image of him because that image satisfies her hopes. The more of her time, love, and future she invests in him, the harder it is to admit that her problems are getting worse, not better. Even when the situation has seriously deteriorated, the spouse is likely to have an assortment of explanations not directly related to alcohol: "He's crazy," "I'm crazy," "We just can't live with each other," "All marriages are like this." Her denial protects her from the truth: The bottle is more important to him than she is.

So the nonalcoholic spouse usually reinforces the alcoholic's denial in overt as well as oblique ways, but for her own reasons. She gets as furious with the children as he does when they comment on his drinking or mock him for it. One young girl remembered:

> I was washing the dishes and he was drying. Only he kept putting the damn dishes back in the dishpan. Finally I figured out that I was washing the same dishes over and over again. All of a sudden I was cursing him out, calling him a drunk and a turkey. I was twelve at the time, and he threw me from one end of the house to the other. But to me that was never violence, that was punishment. And I was told that was punishment by both my mother and my father. "You say those things to your father, you deserve to get belted."

The girl quoted above simply got so angry and frustrated that she blurted out the words even though she knew full well that she would suffer for it.

Children of alcoholics, who have few consistent ground rules and can rarely be certain whether a given behavior will elicit approval or condemnation, learn to be sure of one thing: Accepting their parents' denial is the path to peace and openly rejecting it is the gravest of offenses. Even preschoolers observe the connection between alcohol and their parent's frightening behavior. The words "drinking" and "alcoholism" are either taboo in the household, never mentioned by either parent in spite of alcohol's obvious importance, or they are the most loaded and fearful words, always associated with violent arguments and mutual recrimination. In both cases, the lesson is the same: The children don't just learn not to mention drinking, they learn not to think about it. Alcohol is so freighted with terrifying power that many children cannot tolerate the evidence of their senses. Thus, the children learn denial from their parents, but they internalize and practice it, believing the rationalizations offered to them and creating their own because of their own threatening emotions.

Children need to feel that Mommy is the most loving and virtuous, Daddy the biggest and best, person in the world. They identify with

their parents, especially the parent of the same sex; they feel a measure
of sexual attraction to the other parent; and most important, they are
largely or totally dependent on their parents, and they know it. How
do children of alcoholics face the fact that they do not feel safe, loved,
and respectful of their parents much of the time? How do they endure
their feelings of anger and guilt? Often these feelings are too frightening, so they are suppressed, and each experience that provokes them is
censored. In the most complete form of denial, children don't even
recognize that their parents are hurting them. Probably more often, the
children can't obliterate their pain but develop reflexes that minimize
it. They believe that all families are like theirs, or that their parent is
simply in a bad mood, or that if they behave differently their parent
will too.

As contrary evidence accumulates, they literally cannot see the cause
of the problems and cling more fervently to the beliefs that give them
hope. So when Mom says, " I'm not drinking anymore" or "If you kids
learned to behave yourselves, I wouldn't have to drink," they actually
believe her. Their hope for the future depends on that belief; and
belief, or its gesture, is also the first condition for getting from her
what there is to be had until such time as she does change. But for
many children, the evidence becomes too difficult to rationalize, and
denial, always precarious and imperfect, breaks down. At this stage,
they think of their parent as a drunk; perhaps they talk about it with
their siblings or taunt their parents. However, their dishonesty with
outsiders may become intensified. In addition to the palpable fear
justified by incidents like the dishwashing anecdote, the more subtle
fear is that betrayal and disloyalty will result in the loss of family.
"They're all I have," they think. The children feel worthless and have
already had a taste of abandonment. If their family casts them out for
their honesty, who will take care of them?

The family's interdependence and shared sense of shame increases
its isolation, creating a potent "us versus them" dynamic. Friends are
not welcome and friendships are lost; invitations to family and social
gatherings are declined, usually with flimsy excuses that everyone may
prefer to believe. A secret kept is a secret shared, and a lie they
support becomes their lie too. The children's participation in the denial
and deception increases the sense of shame that provoked the original
deception. They have something else to protect against: their feelings
of duplicity and complicity.

Even children who privately acknowledge that drinking is the problem have ample reasons for denying it to outsiders. But what is more
interesting is the way in which denial can be sustained and even strengthened in children who consider their parents alcoholic but don't fully

accept what the alcoholism means. They understand that their parents must stop drinking, but they continue to believe quite firmly that tearful contrition and promises to quit are signs of imminent recovery instead of symptoms of the disease. They still want to think that they can threaten or accommodate their parents into sobriety. Their hope still rests on "love conquers all," but unless that love is based on a real understanding of what alcoholism is and how family members can support or hinder their recovery, their hope remains largely a groundless self-deception.

The habitual practice of denial and deception has profound consequences for children of alcoholics. They may methodically suppress all threatening feelings; experience a loss of values, because what they feel is right is subordinated to what is necessary and tolerable; retain deep-seated shame, the solution for which has always been isolation; and consistently confuse reality and fantasy.

Inconsistency, Insecurity, and Fear

Dr. Jekyll and Mr. Hyde is probably the outstanding allegorical and imaginative representation of alcoholism in literature. Though the work reflects the highly moralistic view that dominated the Victorian era the book dramatizes, as nothing else has, the extreme inconsistency characterizing the alcoholic. Robert Louis Stevenson's character has two diametrically opposed personalities. Real-life alcoholics are less predictable.

Inconsistency is the hallmark of most active alcoholics, when they are drinking and when they are not. From the beginning, they looked for and found in alcohol an escape from the prison of their circumstances or their skins. Alcohol's very beauty lay in its ability to transform them. When drinking, alcoholics may show mercurial changes: from withdrawn to generous to violent within minutes. When they are not drinking, their lives are still organized around alcohol. They are obsessed with concealing their dependence, protecting the bottle, waiting for the next drink, or struggling against it. In a real sense, everything else in life is an interference, interruption, distraction, or criticism of the main event: the love affair with the bottle. Some alcoholics may be perpetually drunk and consistently uncaring toward their loved ones; but most swing between love, guilt, contrition, and good intentions, on the one hand, and barely disguised indifference or manifest anger on the other.

Inconsistency's offspring is insecurity. Most children are born into the alcoholic situation; the parent's drinking may get worse, or more obvious, through the years, but it usually preceded the arrival of the

children. So for most children of alcoholics, their environment was
more or less inconsistent from the outset.

> Inconsistency, for little kids, is just horrendous. You know, they're just
> beginning to learn what the world is all about. You describe a two-year-
> old like a blind person in a room who goes around feeling the walls to
> see where they are. For a kid, they keep pushing limits to see where
> they are and what they are. And sometimes the wall leaps back on you
> and you don't know what you've done to cause it.

Once the condition of insecurity is established, it becomes a way of
life, a way of apprehending the universe and its uncertainty. Even
when the original cause of the insecurity vanishes and the environment
becomes more consistent and predictable, the children are still tentative and wary, always expecting the unexpected and prepared for the
worst. As one teenager put it, "We learned to walk on eggshells without
cracking a single one."

If the nonalcoholic parent helped soften and explain the alcoholic's
inconsistency to the children, the home and the world would inspire
less fear and uncertainty. Instead, the nonalcoholic parent is often
equally inconsistent. Sometimes the nonalcoholic mother yells at the
father for drinking; other times she pours his drinks. In the morning
she plays up to him to keep him from drinking; in the evening she tells
him she hopes the booze kills him, and she doesn't care if the kids hear.
And the next day, she slaps the child who calls Daddy a drunk. When
she is furious at the alcoholic, frustrated in her attempts to control the
drinking, and distrustful of everyone in sight, she is unreasonably strict
with the children. Two children's recollections:

> I was very overprotected; I wasn't allowed out to play. When I came
> home to the house, I was in the house, period.

> I wasn't allowed to cross the street. And where I lived, you had to cross
> the street to get anywhere. I was nine, ten years old, and the only friend
> I could have was this one girl who lived on my street.

When the mother is full of self-pity, feels sorry for the children, and
is tired of being an unappreciated disciplinarian while her husband is
getting drunk and handing out dollar bills to the children, she turns
overly permissive, letting the children do things she had previously
forbidden, often pretending not to notice. Then the child doesn't know
what to expect from either parent.

If the daughter brings home a mixed report card, and the alcoholic surprises her with approbation and encouragement, her dominant emotion is very likely guilt for having judged him too harshly; so she loses either way. Other times, her hopes are raised and she allows herself to expect consistency and kindness. When she is disappointed, the lesson is hard and thorough: Don't count on anything. And the nonalcoholic parent's denial and rationalization make her an accomplice in the disappointment and the world that much more quixotic.

> You know the situation where the parents are separated and the father's the alcoholic, and he's always promising to come [to visit] and he's so unreliable about coming and doing something with the kids. And then out of his sense of guilt he periodically comes and showers the kids with gifts, being very nice and taking them to a whole bunch of places, and then the next week never showing up. Never calling, and the kid's sitting on the doorstep, you know, all waiting to go with Daddy. And one of the problems I think is how hard it is for mothers to talk to their kids about it. Oftentimes the mother makes excuses for the father and says, you know, "Maybe he had to work," "Maybe the car broke down." And what kind of position is that to put the mother in, when she's not telling the truth either, and the kids know it?

When drinking, many alcoholics are physically violent. The relationship between alcohol abuse and violence, domestic and criminal, is well documented but not clearly understood.[3] One simple explanation is that alcohol weakens or removes the inhibitors that keep people from acting on violent impulses. Nothing contributes to children's insecurity and fear more than recurring violence. It doesn't seem to matter much whether the violence is directed at the children, the nonalcoholic parent, or the furniture. The alcoholic who breaks dishes and walls, always threatening but rarely or never hitting anyone, can be even more frightening. Children who have received severe beatings can become desensitized: They know what parental violence is like and they know they live through it. The children who see furniture shattered beyond repair, but are never hit themselves, can only imagine what would happen if their parent turned that anger on them.

Alcoholic mothers are apparently every bit as violent as fathers. They may not batter their spouses or sexually assault their children, but there is every indication that they physically abuse their children in the same proportion as alcoholic men. One abused child remembered this incident.

---

[3] National Institute on Alcohol Abuse and Alcoholism, *Third Special Report to the U.S. Congress on Alcohol and Health* (Rockville, Md., 1978), pp. 55, 64; American Medical Association, *Manual*, p. 7.

She tried to kill us, actually kill us. We all had our turns fighting her. Everybody used to say, "Ignore her," but you can't ignore her when she comes after you with a knife, you know? One time she choked me, I mean, she was on top of me, choking me, and I would have died; I felt like I was dying. My father came in—this was really great—he had a cigarette in his mouth, he came in and my little sister was screaming—it was just me and my little sister at home. My mother had me and she was, I mean, I was *blue*, I thought I was dying, and my sister was just standing there screaming. My father came in and threw the cigarette on the floor. And 'cause we were in my mother's bedroom, it started a fire and later our carpet had to be thrown out. My father came in and pulled my mother off me, and I just ran out of the house. [When] I came back five hours later, she told me, "Now you're all right, you're all right."

Often the nonalcoholic parent transfers the lumps she receives from the violent alcoholic to the children. Though there may be rationalizations for this ("Once he's hitting them whenever they do something bad, what else can I do? If I just yell at them, it won't even seem like punishment."), the spouse's violence derives largely from her internalized anger and frustration. But even when she tries to protect her children from violence, her efforts often backfire. She becomes so obsessed with preventing violence that its threat grows to be more pervasive and powerful. The children's central concern becomes avoiding conflict, and any act that might provoke violence is as culpable as the violence itself.

There were things we all did just to placate him, like eating together whether we were hungry or not. We were scared a good deal of the time. One time, he demanded his dinner and my mother threw cereal boxes at him. I sat there thinking, "Now that was stupid, why the hell did you do that?" I wished she hadn't done it because I knew I'd have to keep him off her.

And since the violence is gratuitous, the children feel that whatever they do might lead to more harm and destruction:

I don't think my mother ever cooked a meal that he liked. He had a habit, he used to just take the dish like this and go !!! and the dish would go flying. And it was, like, do I stick my hand out and catch the dish, and take the chance of his killing me for catching it, or do I let it go flying and then he's going to kill all of us for letting it hit the floor?

Parental violence can unite the children against a common enemy, but it can also divide them. They save one another's skins, but at great emotional cost; what can be more upsetting than grappling with a parent? They can't control the alcoholic's violence, but they can blame and resent as a provocation almost anything their other parent or siblings do. In this kind of environment, silence can be even more fearful than conflict. A great many children of alcoholics cannot endure long silences or be alone for any period of time.

> I hate silence to this day; that's why I talk so much; I can't stand silence. Perfect silence is awful, especially when there's a lot of tension, 'cause there's no way to release it. My mother still says she doesn't know how my head is still in one piece, because she says I couldn't stand the silence so much, I would get so frustrated, I would go in my room and pound my head against the wall. No one ever came in.

Of all the emotions, outright fear may be the most difficult to cover up. Still, the children's survival depends upon doing so.

> Being the youngest one, I always got to go with my father. Oh my God, him in his blue uniform, cruising down the highway, 95 miles an hour, through traffic, mind you, as I'm praying in the front seat. You don't say a word. We made it from Plymouth, 7:30 traffic on the Expressway, in 25 minutes to Children's Hospital. You talk about being afraid! And you don't talk in the car, you don't say a word, and you don't turn on the radio. If you say, "Eh," forget it, you are out the door.

Relatives, friends, and other outsiders are often mystified about why violence and abuse are tolerated. The children will ask as much of the nonalcoholic parent: "Why don't you get rid of him?" Denial explains part of it, but insecurity may be the key. The nonalcoholic spouse is afraid of the alcoholic, but more afraid of doing without him, or of angering him further with a restraining order she can't believe will work. Insecurity is a condition that takes prominence over and obscures the source of the fear. If a child is chronically insecure, any known quantity may be more acceptable than any unknown. Family members tolerate abuse because of the feelings of insecurity it has already generated. They cannot believe that if they take certain steps, certain other predictable and desirable outcomes will ensue.

Anger and Hatred

Given the family conditions already described, it is not necessary to explain how anger comes to be one of the dominant emotions of children of alcoholics. What anger can rival that of children who are

repeatedly disappointed, neglected, or abused by the people they love
and need the most?

But the children's love, and need for love and protection, lives on;
their hope persists. Because their feelings of anger, even when unex-
pressed, provoke a great deal of guilt and anxiety, many children deny
those feelings altogether. They are genuinely unaware that they have
hatred for their parents. Some turn their anger inward. Others feel a
generalized and helpless rage, a sense that deprivation, injustice, and
cruelty are the rules of life, or, in any event, their portion, now and
forever. Their anger takes shape as chronic depression, self-pity, deep
feelings that life is not worth living. Still other children don't allow
themselves to feel any anger; they withdraw their investment from
everything so that nothing can matter enough to call forth their terrifying anger.

Some children feel the full flood of their anger, but they cannot
directly express it. They harbor bitterness and resentment, and act out
their anger against safer targets: friends, animals, authority figures,
siblings. A seven-year-old boy, a participant in a school-based alcohol
group, knew as much, too.

> He was very disruptive, taking his anger out on his teachers. And we
> talked about that in the group. "You get angry, what do you do when
> you get angry? You yell at people, sometimes you don't yell at the
> people you're angry at." He said, "Yeah, sometimes I yell at my teddy
> bear and sometimes I yell at my teacher when I'm angry at my father.
> And I know she doesn't like it."

However justified it is, anger is not an appropriate emotion toward
people who are sick. Feelings of hatred must be acknowledged and
released before children can consider their parents ill instead of evil.
And if not released, they will continue to be misdirected. One of the
most common and relatively healthy outlets for the children's anger
and hatred is the murder fantasy.

> Come out and say, now, I hate my father. There was a point when I
> was seriously planning . . . well, he used to take pills, various medica-
> tions, and I found out that one of his pills . . . might do him in. I was
> going to drop the pill in the bottle, take care of my father, fix his
> brakes—I almost had someone fix his brakes on his car. I could have
> stabbed him. Thank God, my mother never let him have a gun in the
> house. If he ever had a gun in the house, there were times when, I
> swear, I would have been in a juvenile house because I would have shot
> him. I would have shot him, seriously. One night he was passed out. I

had a knife in my hand. My sister came down the stairs after me. I was
determined to kill him. Sure, I still hate him to this day.

Many children, including honor students like the girl just quoted,
hatch elaborate, cold-blooded, brutal plots. They often feel reflexively
guilty about such thoughts and are not aware how natural the ideas
are.

All the time, I used to lay in bed at night and plot how to kill her
without getting caught and stuff. I was a mean kid.

These are fantasies, not causes for alarm. Actual incidents of violence against parents are as rare as the imaginary incidents are common.
Both the children and the professionals in whom they may confide
need to see the value of such fantasies in releasing overwhelming anger
and hatred and allowing the children to feel more hopeful and powerful.

In some families, one child becomes the scapegoat, bearing the brunt
of everyone's anger and learning to define a role accordingly. In other
families, anger is more diffuse, and most communication is characterized by fits of temper, abrupt and prolonged withdrawal, empty threats,
biting wit, or sarcasm. The rage of both parents and children is so
close to the surface that anything can tap it.

Hopelessness seems to be connected to anger. If the alcoholic is
simply a rotten person, what change is possible? The children, like all
of us, cling to hope; so they resist their anger. It is with this stubborn
hope that they respond, albeit guardedly, when someone they trust
describes their problem as parental alcoholism. But some children cannot respond; their rage is boundless, having eradicated hope as well as
love. Like the bigot's, their hatred has become a kind of refuge from
other intolerable feelings, and they do not easily let go of it.

Guilt and Blame

The more family members deny the alcoholic's drinking problem
and its effects on them, and the more their love and dependence make
them unable to endure feelings of rage and hatred, the more guilt they
are apt to feel about all the problems in the family. Guilt usually
coexists with fear and anger in the alcoholic home. Many adolescents
profess to feel no guilt about the alcoholic's drinking. They say "I don't
care if the drunk lives or dies."

When the teenagers were younger, however, they may well have felt responsible for the constant conflict and tension. Young children believe they are the cause of all they see. The world and everyone in it revolve around them, and even toddlers know when their world is unhappy and strife-ridden. In fact, they usually know that the alcoholic's bottle is somehow involved. Even if they acquire the vocabulary of the situation, no one explains to them what is really happening; so they have no alternative but to believe that they are somehow responsible. And their interpretation is often regularly reinforced by parents and other family members in overt and subtle ways throughout their childhood. Blame is hurled at the children: "Yeah, I'll stop drinking, when you start behaving like you're supposed to. What do you think makes me drink in the first place?" Blame is overheard in the middle of the night, which makes it seem more justified and terrible.

> I was kept downstairs 'cause I was the youngest, so my parents' bedroom was right beside mine. I got to hear all the fights, they were so loud. I used to hear all the shit about, you know, "Well, if we didn't have all these kids, you know—everytime we had problems you had another kid." The big thing at that time [they were talking about] with my father was that my mother got pregnant with me, because they were going to split up.

A sense of responsibility and guilt is conveyed every time the non-alcoholic parent tries, or persuades the children, to prevent the drinking. "Go swimming with him; make him happy," she orders them, or "Play up in your room, Mommy is very nervous." If children have the power to make drinking unnecessary, they must also somehow cause it. And both parents often feel guilty about their childrearing; at such times, they may bestow presents, praise, and special privileges on their children. If the children see this largesse as a response to their good behavior, they may well conclude that their parents' scorn or indifference is a reaction to their misdeeds.

Guilt, too, is a kind of defense: a defense against helplessness and hopelessness. To feel responsible is to feel possessed of power and capable of control: "If I can change, the alcoholic will change too." This belief can be maintained even when children as they grow older understand alcoholism better, and in the face of persistent proof to the contrary. They try to please the alcoholic, or shock her, or threaten her; but the drinking continues anyway. Instead of concluding that they simply can't influence it, they blame themselves for going about it incorrectly. Thus, the children's positive self-concept is damaged not simply by the original feelings of guilt, but by the repeated failure to control that which is most important to them. They feel far more capable of causing problems and pain, inadvertently and involuntarily, than they do of bending situations to their will. They may act as if they are in charge and appear highly confident, but inwardly they are waiting for everything they touch to fall apart.

The children's guilt and insecurity often result in their assumption of the responsibilities abdicated by the alcoholic, and sometimes the nonalcoholic parent. Role reversal is common in alcoholic homes: The children, particularly first children, nurse and protect their parents, clean up their messes, keep them out of trouble.

> I was fourteen, and he was going with a gun to shoot the guy down the road. I just sat in the car and told him I wasn't going to move. And I don't know, I guess I kind of felt above him or something. I don't know what I felt. I guess I felt for the first time that he needed help, you know. Here he was going to shoot this guy and I had to stop him, and I was only fourteen.

Even more typically, they take care of their younger siblings, especially when mother is the alcoholic.

> When Betty was home, she did it. When she left, Donna did it, she took on a real lot. My little brother, when he was just born, she raised him the first year, and she cooked supper every night and she stayed home from school to take care of my brother, she just did all the housecleaning and told us when to be in the house. She was more like my mother than my mother was.

Guilt and blame go hand in hand. If children can believe that their faults cause the drinking and their perfection could prevent it, they can believe the same of their brothers and sisters and their nonalcoholic parent. Some of the anger directed at other family members is predicated on the assumption that we are all responsible and we are all failing miserably.

THE ALCOHOLIC FAMILY WITHOUT ACTIVE ALCOHOLISM

Many people who have lived with family alcoholism or encountered it professionally believe that the alcoholic's attainment of sobriety or removal from the home will drastically and immediately improve the quality of life in the family. Children who were still young when the drinking ended are assumed to have been minimally affected. In fact, the family conditions listed above often persist. The feelings and defenses that began as reactions to the drinking were generalized; they became part of each family member, and they don't automatically go away when the alcoholic does. The three-year-old whose alcoholic parent vanishes, dies, or recovers has lived her most formative years in a home dominated by drinking; and for years thereafter she is still living in an environment reverberating with the dynamics of family alcoholism.

The Alcoholic Is Physically Separated from the Family

The possibility of getting rid of the alcoholic (thereby solving all of the family's problems) is constantly present in the home, as wish, threat, and promise. Both parents repeatedly talk about leaving, and some actually do, for short periods or for good.

In many families the children are expressly forbidden to voice an opinion on the matter, but probably more often they meet with characteristically inconsistent rules. Sometimes parents confide in them, ask after their feelings, solicit their support and complicity, warn them of the hardships. Other times they get enraged when the children suggest a divorce. The children may be even more ambivalent about separation and divorce than the nonalcoholic parent. They still have hopes for family harmony and may blame the nonalcoholic parent for most of the discord.

When the alcoholic is thrown out, and the children continue to have sharp conflict with the remaining parent (as all children must, especially at some stages), they may identify more completely with the alcoholic, feeling more sympathy and guilt, and more anger toward their nonalcoholic parent. This account of a diagnostic interview with a five-year-old illustrates the mixed feelings of many children:

> He started drawing a picture of his father, and he said that his father didn't live with us anymore and he slept on the street, on the sidewalk. So I asked him about drinking, and he said, "Oh, my daddy drinks so much booze!" The parents had been separated since the child was three, and daddy had been abusive to mother. And he described it as "Daddy drank so much booze that he got bigger and bigger and meaner and meaner," and that they didn't see daddy anymore because he might beat up mommy again. And he drew his daddy as a little boy who didn't know what to do, and nobody liked him. I just thought he had such a perception of his father as being an outcast and very unhappy. This kid was in bad shape.

Even when the children are terribly afraid and full of hate, longing for the alcoholic's removal, they may be unable to believe that the separation can be enforced and become more terrified of possible reprisal. They have heard a string of empty threats. The alcoholic has been allowed or even invited back in the house on occasion, rarely without incident. And restraining orders, divorce, or the police have not prevented him from breaking in and wreaking havoc.

Certainly, many alcoholic couples do divorce. The alcoholic is gone, but not forgotten. Children continue to worry about the alcoholic's safety or fear his reappearance; or they know they must see him on the Sundays he shows up to visit. Every phone call is pregnant with possibilities. If the parting was pointedly rancorous, the children often try to proceed as if the alcoholic never existed.

> Tenth grade . . . he was gone for a while. I was sitting in the parlor with, I don't know who it was, one of my friends, who had never seen my father, never even heard of my father, and he walked in through the back door. Talk about me falling off the couch, onto the floor! "Who's that?" and the words would not come out of my mouth. . . . "What the hell is he doing here?" So I was, like, following him around the house, trying to find out what he came back to take. I don't know what I was going to do to stop him, but you could see he had left stuff in the house on purpose, so he could come back. Then he started this big thing when the separation was going through, too. He wanted visiting rights. He wanted visiting rights! My father wouldn't—no, I wouldn't say he wouldn't care if we all dropped dead—actually he might be happy, he could have the house.

The alcoholic who is totally or largely absent can continue to exert a very powerful influence on other family members. But the alcoholic home retains its characteristics because it is composed of a parent and children who still act upon the feelings they have been so long in amassing and suppressing. To get an idea of how resilient are the dynamics of family alcoholism, consider Charlotte's mother. After years of violence and abuse at the hands of her husband, including a fight that ended in a miscarriage and permanent leg injury, she finally divorced him when he broke a chair over Charlotte's aunt's back. Charlotte recalls:

> We all said, "Yes, throw him out, get rid of him!" When I was in junior high she finally did, and then that was a hell of a year! "I got rid of him because of you, and look what you kids do to me!" Oh, I didn't know which was worse, I did not know which was worse.

The Alcoholic Dies

For children who feel any degree of sympathy or identification with their alcoholic parents, nothing enshrines the parents like death. This is particularly true where denial and guilt predominate, as they often do when the mother is alcoholic. All sins are forgiven, entire pasts are reconstructed, reality and fantasy grow increasingly indistinguishable. Bad feelings and bad memories are too painful; the image of the deceased becomes progressively more sacrosanct.

If the children felt more hatred and fear than responsibility, they may actually welcome the alcoholic's death and objectively benefit by it. But after the parent's death their anger has no target and may be that much more difficult to release. And if the children are still young, they may well attribute their parent's death to their fervent hatred. If they invest their anger with such power, how can they allow themselves to feel anger in the future?

Children of alcoholics frequently fear that they are destined to become like their parent. They look back over their shoulders, waiting for the future to catch up with them. Ghosts probably fuel this tendency; a living parent is a mere person, but a dead one has attributes of Fate. We can only speculate on the extent to which this fear of destiny is constructive or self-fulfilling.

The Alcoholic Stops Drinking

Alcoholics who stop drinking are still alcoholics. Their recovery requires total abstinence, which in turn calls for constant and continuing support. But recovery is much more than not drinking; it is reconstructing a life. Booze had been the alcoholics' family, vocation, and only ethical standard; drinking buddies their only friends; alcohol their only recreation; drunkenness their most prized defense. To stop drinking is one thing; to make it through the period when alcohol is no longer the center of creation, and nothing else fills the bill either, is another. During abstinence, the alcoholic's grief over the loss of the bottle is entirely analogous to the grief at losing all of one's loved ones and one's sense of self simultaneously, and to experience that loss in a condition of self-hatred, fear, and outrage. What makes matters worse is that the love of the alcoholic's life is not interred forever in the ground, but calling out from every street corner. The wonder is that so many alcoholics do recover.

Many alcoholics periodically stop drinking, then start again. Neither they nor their children know each morning if they will be sober or drunk that night. In many ways, the period between the first day of abstinence and the onset of an internalized, positive, and holistic approach to a life without alcohol may be even more dominated by the family characteristics cited in this chapter than during the years of active drinking. The children and nonalcoholic parent may be actually more preoccupied with the alcoholic, more anxious and insecure, more determined to avoid conflict, more distrustful and angry. It isn't just that they have accumulated these feelings and learned these responses: They are still living in a condition of alcoholism, but with some of the ground rules changed and unknown.

Four years after her father stopped drinking, one girl reported, "Still the big thing is to please Dad." Another girl spoke of her mother's first months of abstinence:

> She was always edgy and stuff. You had to be real careful not to argue with her. You had to do the dishes when it was your turn without putting up a big fuss. . . . I worry about her all the time. Especially when I know she's in a bad mood or something, like when she's having a hard day, or when my brother died, you know. I just, like, I always think, you know, is she going to be all right when she comes home? Or, like, if I'm arguing with her, and she's having a real bad day and I go out, I say, "Gee, I hope she's all right."

Tension, anger, and distrust continue to characterize the home. Instead of fighting about drinking, there may be fights about how frequently the alcoholic attends AA meetings. If the alcoholic is still neglecting responsibilities (and he or she is certainly in the fragile condition of an invalid), the family's anger may be even greater than heretofore because its hopes and expectations are higher. Conversely, some alcoholics awaken to parental responsibilities with a sudden vengeance, trying to make up for their neglect all at once. They want to take over the checkbook, make decisions, or set limits. But their spouses and children may resent these gestures as intrusions, thinking, "After all I've gone through because of you, who are you to tell me what to do now?" In these and other ways family members sometimes subvert the alcoholic's recovery. They may actually prefer his drinking to his sobriety, since they have already evolved strategies in response to the drinking and are being asked once again to reorganize their lives around the alcoholic's new, and perhaps temporary, wishes.

Conditions within the alcoholic family really begin to change when the nonalcoholic parent and/or the children receive help and support. Only when they consistently put themselves first before the alcoholic do they begin to equalize the real power relationships and reclaim lives of their own. Paradoxically, it is when the family ends its obsession with managing the alcoholic that its capacity to influence his recovery grows.

Chapter 4
THE CHILD'S REACTION

The family is a system made up of individuals who are each genetically and historically unique, and to some degree autonomous, bound together by ties of love, dependence, identification, expectations, and physical, emotional, and social needs. These bonds, this connectedness, are the family's purpose. Familial success depends on the balance the family can achieve between the different wants and contributions of its members. Families functioning well allow members to have their own identities, with each identity compromised just enough so that the whole system works well for everyone.[1] Members may develop, or be assigned, certain primary roles by which they contribute to the family while deriving important and consistent rewards from belonging. But these roles change in different situations and stages of life.

What each person wants from and can give to other family members can change independently of the family and also in response to changes in other family members. For example, a mother decides to take a paying job. The decision reflects her belief that the children are ready to be more independent or that other family members will share some caretaking responsibilities. Members compensate, modifying their roles, contributions, and expectations according to situation and need because they see that other members do the same for them. Healthy families can thus accommodate change, whether developmental or precipitated by crisis.

Judging from the overall health of their children, some alcoholic families apparently maintain a high level of function. It would be a mistake to conclude that their ability to do so depends primarily on how the alcoholic drinks. The dynamics described in Chapter 3 can govern a family in which the alcoholic is a binge drinker who with-

---

[1]Thomas F. Fogarty, "System Concepts and the Dimensions of Self," in *Family Therapy*, ed. Philip J. Guerin (New York: Gardner Press, 1976), pp. 152–153.

draws in silence and depression, as surely as a family in which the alcoholic is a daily and violent drunk.

The success of some alcoholic families is probably more reflective of the nonalcoholic parent's ability to maintain her own identity, and get her own wants and needs satisfied, instead of reacting primarily to the alcoholic. She can promote similar individuation in the first child, and together they teach and encourage later children. Close extended-family members can also help to weight the family balance away from the alcoholic. They broaden the foundation of the family, so that the alcoholic is less of a fulcrum with the power to make the family swivel and sway at every motion.

But probably most alcoholic families fail to satisfy the children's basic emotional needs. Instead, the children are required to adjust to an extremely stressful and isolated environment, often by emulating the behaviors of unhealthy models. The feelings, wants, and contributions of each family member are excessively compromised in the interest of a tenuous equilibrium that really fulfills no one. To understand the connection between the dynamics in the alcoholic home and the development of specific problems in the children, to explain why these children are often so different from one another within a family and so similar to children from other alcoholic families, we can examine briefly how the alcoholic family system is organized differently from other families.

THE ALCOHOLIC FAMILY SYSTEM

The alcoholic family is subject to perpetual and extreme oscillation. All families must adapt to change, but the change is usually gradual and permits a period in which different adjustments can be tested. Family members understand that a drastic change in the needs or capacities of a single member is a crisis, requiring temporary adjustment on the part of all members. Children of alcoholics, however, must on a day-to-day basis accommodate change that is both sudden and sharp, not merely on the part of the alcoholic parent, but usually both parents.

The pervasiveness of the alcoholic's drinking and the nonalcoholic spouse's attempts to preempt it deprive family members of the opportunity to define their predilections independently. The rituals that usually bond family members become instead their most painful battles. Far from developing a secure sense of its own balance and joint purpose, the family views its own existence as increasingly precarious as the alcoholism progresses.

The standard governing the central event of the family, the drinking, and informing all other communication is one that undermines the very notion that words have meaning. The children hear the nonalcoholic father repeatedly threatening to leave, yet he doesn't leave; they hear the alcoholic swearing tearfully that she'll stop drinking, or that she has already stopped; and they listen to all kinds of words said in drunkenness and anger. Words are used chiefly to hurt or manipulate; when they are used to express real feelings, they are discounted or discouraged. Action and silence replace words as the principal medium of communication within the family. Messages are consequently ambiguous and indirect.

The alcoholic family is also cut off from more objective input from the outside environment. When problems begin in nonalcoholic families, their members may turn to friends or relatives to let off steam or get advice. In contrast, children and spouses of alcoholics are sometimes the only ones without complaint when friends start talking about their own troubles. As often, the alcoholic family isolates itself completely to avoid discovery. Family members certainly sublimate, act out, or otherwise bring to the outside world some of the pressures generated in the home. But they rarely bring back into the home insights or advice that may help form a wedge to break into established family patterns. The alcoholic family is too frequently a closed system.

Conflict is virtually unending and always triangulated. Even before the children are born, conflict can never be resolved directly between husband and wife because there is a third member of the family about which the two spouses feel totally differently: the bottle. They cannot fight about anything that is not ultimately connected with the drinking; and they cannot settle their differences about the drinking because the alcoholic cannot keep from drinking and the nonalcoholic cannot keep clear of the consequences. No conflict seems remediable by direct negotiation.

Like all families, the alcoholic family seeks to provide children with an emotional climate that is positive and safe. But the alcoholic's drinking is so contrary to such a climate that the first concern is preventing, limiting, or contending with the drinking. The family tries to deny, deflect, contain, or diffuse its problems in the children's interest. By enlisting each child in this effort from the outset, it drastically curtails their development. The process of becoming an individual is subordinated to that of meeting the family's needs.

Many children are groomed for specialized roles as the outlet, expression, and focus of the dynamics that are creating havoc. Wegscheider identified, and a number of clinicians have since confirmed, four major role structures among children of alcoholics.[2] Like all categories, these four divisions are too neat; many children have traits associated with roles other than the one that seems to describe them best. The roles within alcoholic families resemble those which have been linked to the birth order and gender of siblings in healthy families. The difference lies not in the broad outlines of the roles, but in the reactive and rigid nature of the roles in alcoholic families.

Because many alcoholic family systems are closed, conflict-ridden, inconsistent, inhibiting of direct communication, and convinced of their fragility, children have difficulty initiating new roles that reflect their own desires and physical and psychological changes. The closed systems require the children's reactions to be above all consistent and predictable. The children in most trouble are from the outset so restricted and bound into their reactive roles that they become little more than their roles. Given over to an exaggerated and rigid identification of self with role, so protected by it and at least nominally rewarded for it, children have great difficulty operating outside it.

Moreover, the defenses that comprise each role, though they may be rewarded in certain ways, are never more than partially successful. The defenses help the children fend off threats from inside and outside the family, and defenses do contribute to the family's equilibrium, however precarious and lopsided it may be. But the traits and whole roles have a greater aim, which is usually frustrated: They are intended not simply to withstand what is, but to change it, to make the family more loving and safe and happy. The aim is to stop the drinking; and nothing can be expected to stop the drinking, no matter how much each role is played to the hilt. So even when they most need their respective roles to survive, the children get little real satisfaction from them.

As adults, they continue to adhere to their roles. Role and self are so merged that they create or surround themselves with a reality that requires and reinforces the same role. Many untreated children grow into unhappy and maladjusted adults who can be greatly helped by an understanding of their childhood experiences. Too few are getting such help.

These are the four principal roles adopted by children of alcoholics:
1. The Family Hero
2. The Scapegoat
3. The Lost Child
4. The Mascot

They are presented as though they depend most of all on birth order.

_____
[2]Wegscheider, "Children in Family Trap," p. 8.

This is simplification, useful but perhaps misleading. Clearly there are other potent influences that explain the division of roles within each alcoholic family. In addition, the following schema is based on the progression of the disease. It does not address the effect of the alcoholic or nonalcoholic parent's recovery or other radical changes on the evolution of the children's roles.

THE FAMILY HERO

Also referred to as the superkid, manager, controller, or Goody Two Shoes, Family Heroes are children often regarded with respect and even awe because they have apparently wrested strength, responsibility, and self-esteem from the jaws of adversity. This perception provides a clue about how the role develops and operates within the alcoholic family.

The role is probably most common in the eldest children. When the first child arrives, the alcoholic's drinking is already causing problems, but hope and denial obscure them. Both the alcoholic and nonalcoholic parents make the child the repository of their hope. The alcoholic will drink less and settle down to his or her responsibilities, and the nonalcoholic will be less carping and dissatisfied because of the presence of a child who is exemplary in every way. And this child will prove to the parents and outsiders that all is well. The Family Hero is rewarded by parents and often grandparents for excelling at whatever they deem important and right. The criterion usually differs for girls and boys, and may also depend on the gender of the alcoholic.

The eldest daughter of an alcoholic family is often expected to manage family responsibilities far beyond the capability of her years. She may function as a substitute for the alcoholic mother who abdicates her duties, or for a nonalcoholic mother whose despondency and helplessness in the face of the father's drinking leaves many necessary chores undone, or as an ally and facsimile of a nonalcoholic mother who needs help in order to assume the responsibilities neglected by the alcoholic father. This daughter will also do very well in school, if the family encourages academic achievement in females; if it does not, she is more likely to have a school and work career without blemish but also without particular distinction. Her attendance may be spotty because of caretaking duties. She is the child of whom teachers remark: "She may be absent a lot, but she still does better than the kids who are here every day."

The eldest son of an alcoholic mother may be groomed to assume similar home responsibilities, in addition to being primed for excellence in all other pursuits. Whereas he is rewarded both within the family and outside of it for his scholarship, athletic prowess, and popularity with both sexes, he is likely to feel conflicted about his household role because it is so contrary to socially defined masculinity. If there is no one to whom he can pass on his caretaker role, he may keep performing it with resentment or with what would be called a confused sense of sexual identity. He cannot discard the caretaker role without guilt, for he has been made to feel that the family's survival depends on his enormous contribution.

The eldest son of an alcoholic father is more likely to be excused from heavy burdens in the home so that he can devote all of his time and energy to excellence in the world. The family needs him to bring in from the outside the pride and success that can distract from the problems created by the alcoholic's drinking. The son's mission is to rescue and redeem the family, bring home the praise and envy of others without getting too caught up in the family morass.

Family Heroes usually perform as well in school as their intellectual capacities permit. They do everything that is required of them and more. "I was the only kid in elementary school who did four hours of homework every night, and they didn't give homework in elementary school." A surprising percentage of our class presidents, scholar-athletes, future whiz kids, and most dedicated human-service professionals fulfilled the Family Hero role as children. A faculty member at the University of Maryland Medical School reported, for example, that an estimated 40 percent of his students came from alcoholic families.[3]

Heroes are richly and consistently rewarded by teachers and other adults for precisely the behavior that limits their sound development. Who wouldn't encourage children who are always obedient and eager to please? Sometimes lapses in model behavior occur due to crisis in the family or frustration when perpetual success fails to stop the drinking. School personnel often make ample allowances for the "good kids," perhaps too ample, as one honor student remembered:

When I was in junior high school, my dad was in the hospital 8 or 9 times in one school year, I was out of school a lot and you know, basically no one noticed and no one cared. That year I was so flipped out I could have talked to anyone. I could have talked to a wall, to a drunk on the street. You know, when your dad's in the hospital 8 or 9 times, and every time he goes in they give you less time that he has to live, you sort of flip out a bit. I was also heavy into using drugs, and no one knew. Or they just didn't care because I was keeping up my marks.

---

[3]Whitfield, "Children of Alcoholics: Treatment Issues," NIAAA Symposium.

I graduated second in the class in junior high, so therefore, you know, as long as you're keeping your marks, the problems can't be interfering too much in your life. You have to flunk out, from a straight A to a straight E, before anyone notices that something's wrong. I wanted to get a C so someone would notice, but I couldn't even do that; I was too afraid my parents would yell at me.

And if Family Heroes break through their role enough to show some kind of misdirected anger, they may get, instead of sympathy and understanding, a message like "You know better" or "You can do better than that." As soon as they start to sublimate their feelings in achievement, the praise starts rolling in, and their defense is reinforced.

Because they need to feel in control, independent, and without needs, Heroes cannot tolerate being wrong or slow and have great difficulty admitting that they don't understand something. They may get defensive in the face of criticism or supervision. They feel capable of mending or attending to everything. They like to be challenged, even beset with challenges; but they are constantly fearful of failure and work twice as hard as others to avoid it.

Family Heroes often have admirers but few close friends. They are resented by peers and siblings for their achievement and because Heroes are competitive, perfectionist, and good at getting adult approval. Many Heroes befriend younger children or "losers," people they can take care of. Heroes succeed by pleasing, so they are always giving and never asking, which creates problems in intimate relationships.

Heroes appear to be self-motivated and well adjusted, successfully engaged in the business of detaching from the alcoholic family and making the most of their lives. Indeed, some may be doing just that. But some are simply fitting into a role dictated by the family's need. Task success and detachment from the alcoholic family are healthy when purposeful. When they are the primary defense against and contribution to the family, they can develop a rigid pattern precluding satisfaction of other needs. The Hero's principal and hidden hope is that assiduous achievement and personal selflessness will end the family disharmony and bring about the love and connectedness the family is expected to deliver. Failure of harmony and love does not diminish this hope but is attributed to inadequacy. Heroes become perfectionists, never satisfied with their own work, always demanding more of themselves and less of others. They don't feel entitled to relaxation, to being cared for, to a suspension or abdication of responsibilities.

This syndrome has been called workaholism, and Hero adults are at great risk to develop it. Most observers believe that workaholism is the result of interpersonal difficulties before it is the cause of them. Hero adults submerge themselves in work because achievement is still the measure of their self-worth and the only path they know to what they really want. At the workplace they can garner the praise, respect, and hope they lived on as children. Work is an escape from intimacy and emotion, from the need to trust others, an escape they relied upon and internalized. Devotion to work obliterates the need, or at least crowds out the time, for real relationships. Apart from its devastating effects on personal relationships, workaholism entails dangerous risks. Workaholics are usually classic "Type A" individuals whose behavior patterns have been highly correlated with early and fatal coronary disease. Furthermore, there is an alarming rate of acute depression and suicide among middle-age people whose careers have brought them steadily increasing prestige and earnings. Many persons may be Heroes who have always succeeded, repressing their emotions and leaving gaping holes in their personal lives. When it hits them that they are not at all happy—that they are envied and respected by others but feel empty inside—the direction of their lives is lost, the despair overwhelming, and they don't know how to ask for help.

Heroes are not likely candidates for teenage alcohol or drug abuse. They are too caught up in accomplishing everything and pleasing authorities. But as adults who don't know how to relax, vent their feelings, or refuse added responsibilities and added pressures, these individuals may easily turn to alcohol or tranquilizers. If they are professionals and business executives, their schedules are more flexible, there is less employer supervision, and rituals like the "deal over lunch" or frequent air travel are conducive to drinking. Given their histories and associations with alcohol, and the reasons and needs that may motivate their drinking, many adults who have internalized the Hero role seem prone to substance abuse if they drink at all.

If they marry, Heroes often marry people whom they can care for and manage, including alcoholics. If their spouses are happy being largely dependent, a long, if unequal, marriage may result. But people who want to feel that they are needed, that they are vital to their loved ones, and asked to share their fears, feelings, and decisions are in for some real difficulties in a relationship with a Hero.

The central message these children and adults need to incorporate can be summed up in the words "Let go." They have to learn that they never caused the drinking and could never hope to control it through unwavering excellence. They have to find and express a side of themselves studiously repressed, feelings like weakness, doubt, need, and pain—all feelings that are there in quantity but denied. They must learn to relax, to stop "doing it all." And what they will find is that either others do it or it doesn't get done, and the world doesn't fall apart. They have to begin to accept failure as a condition of life and to feel worthwhile for who they are, not what they accomplish. Heroes who ask for help have already made an important start because they have begun to challenge their feeling that they don't deserve help and mustn't rely on anyone. The problem, of course, is that it is precisely this feeling that keeps many Heroes from reaching help; and to those who are in a position to help, the Hero children appear exemplary in every way. They are engaged in a masquerade, a true confidence game. Youth professionals fall for it every time they equate achievement with healthy adjustment and assume that children who do well academically have fewer critical emotional needs than children whose grades are mediocre or poor.

THE SCAPEGOAT

Scapegoats make their contribution to the family by embracing and expressing each member's anger, disappointment, and frustration. Any child can learn to play this role. For instance, if the relationship between the alcoholic and nonalcoholic spouses is already dominated by rage, overt or repressed, when the first child arrives, that child may be groomed to become the focus of that rage. But the role is probably more common among second children.

Gene was born two years after Joey. His older brother was a Hero from the beginning, who took the family's shame and feelings of inadequacy deep inside himself and brought out praise and proof of domestic health. Meanwhile, the drinking got worse, both parents became more ill, and arguments grew more protracted even though this exemplary child had come on the scene. While his parents continued to reward Joey for achievement and pseudomaturity, and he increasingly measured self-worth by these rewards, neither parents nor child experienced the role as successful. They still felt angry and resentful, and the hope that the eldest child would straighten out the family had been disappointed.

Gene enters a scene that already has firm boundaries. The contribution the family most needs is a safe outlet for its anger. Gene can hardly hope to outdo his brother, with his two years' advantage, and will suffer in every comparison. Gene is set up to disappoint, and in doing so he is identified, and identifies, with the alcoholic parent. What he learns by watching his alcoholic father is that if he causes trouble, shirks responsibility, and upsets people, he gets attention and care. He prefers attention that is consistent, predictable, and all his own to the leavings of his brother or the oscillating reactions of his parents.

Gene's mother and brother are most attentive to Gene through their anger. Though they don't realize it, they almost welcome Gene's behavior problems because he enables them to believe that the family's distress is of his making. Instead of the alcoholic father on whom they depend, he becomes the focus for their anger and disappointment. Joey's position as the object of family pride is enhanced by his brother's wrongheadedness, and the more his brother is to blame, the less Joey has to acknowledge how his father makes him feel. Gene's mother labels him early as "his father's son." Though this notion relieves her of responsibility for him in word only, and not in fact or feeling, it also serves as a stick with which she can retaliate against her husband.

The pattern that is established is invisible to the family members: Gene is encouraged to act out. In part, this is the result of inconsistent limits, or limits that are either more lax or more strict than those applied to Joey. But it is chiefly in the family's reactions that Gene's misbehavior is promoted. The family may try sympathy and understanding, verbal tirades, or physical punishment; all make Gene the center of the family's concern for a time. And frequently, when the collective rage and frustration is temporarily spent, there follows a period of reconciliation and reintegration that tells Gene he really does belong. Mother and brother thus license Gene for conduct that will release their anger upon a safer outlet than its true source. Their innermost hope, and one the Scapegoat comes to share, is that if he is angry and troublesome enough, the drinking will end and the family will unite to save him.

The strong bond of identification between the alcoholic parent and the Scapegoat, who is usually of the same gender, has a number of elements. Gene, for instance, provides his father with someone else to blame for all that is going wrong, and especially for his drinking; and he relieves his father from much of the anger that would otherwise be directed at him. Meanwhile, his father does not have to concern himself with Gene's daily scrapes, since Gene's upbringing was his mother's domain from the beginning, and it grows more exclusively hers as the father abdicates more and more responsibility. To the extent that Gene shields his drinking, the alcoholic father is invested in keeping Gene as the focus for everyone's anger and blame, not in getting Gene to mend his wayward course. In the competition between father and son, Gene is allowed to win the anger, even if he must also be given a share of the family's store of patience and sympathy. Furthermore, Gene's father prefers an ally and facsimile to another child who might identify and collaborate with his wife. From the outset Scapegoats like Gene are taught to identify with their alcoholic fathers, but it often happens that their relationships are nothing but anger, blame, and acrimony. "They can't be in the same room together for two minutes." In other alcoholic families, the Scapegoat gets so much anger and criticism from siblings and the nonalcoholic parent, that the alcoholic parent can lead the way in forgiveness and understanding, assuming a pedestal in the child's eyes and enhancing the force of the identification. Then they really become colleagues, and each successive child must choose between two highly polarized camps.

Scapegoats are usually the most visible children of alcoholics, the known troublemakers. Their grades are poor and don't reflect their capacities. They cut classes, break school rules, talk back to teachers, and may drop out. They choose friends who share or respect their defiance of authority and accomplishment; and with them they abuse alcohol and drugs, get into repeated fights, steal cars, or otherwise violate the law. Often their offenses are so ill-planned that apprehension seems to be the goal, as in the case of one girl who tried to shoplift an entire display case of jewelry. Early and promiscuous sexual activity, and pregnancy, characterize many female Scapegoats. Running away from home is another common Scapegoat practice.

The delinquent behaviors extend into the world the lessons and defenses learned by the Scapegoat in the family and fulfill the family's concept of this child, which has become the child's own self-concept, as a troublemaker and born loser. Whatever else it has done, this role has earned the child a unique and relatively secure place in the family. It can do so in the outside world as well, since authority figures are certain to respond with a blend of punishment, concern, solicitous help, encouragement to change, and a certain vulnerability to the child's threatening conduct. Just as the family did, the world becomes a safer place when it responds to known behavior in a known and predictable way.

Scapegoats internalize the rage and frustration the family vents on them. They have reservoirs of anger, directed not merely against authority, but against peers too. For some children, rage can only be expressed through drugs or alcohol or through sexual abandon. Others have explosive tempers and become violent at the slightest provocation. These are angry children, and that is bad enough; but as they enter adolescence, their anger takes on a social importance for their peers and for adult authorities as well. Just as the family needs Scapegoats to be the expression and focus of its anger, the adolescent and adult authority networks use them as the embodiment and visible symbol of teenage rebellion and its containment.

Limit-testing and experimentation are natural adolescent traits. Some form of rebellion seems central to the process of becoming individuals separate from their parents, and most adolescents rebel in small, daily ways without really challenging or rejecting adult values. However free of rage, however essential to maturation rebellion may be, rebellion is still threatening to authority. The delinquency of Scapegoats is not real rebellion. For them it is not a process of individuation; it is more the acceptance of a very limited role, the fulfilling of others' expectations. But it has all the trappings of the most dramatic adolescent rebellion, the right to define self and break free of arbitrary strictures. Scapegoats find that they earn and keep friends by their misdeeds; and the peers who don't join them often communicate an envy of their apparent freedom. Scapegoats do some of the things other adolescents wish they could do. Less troublesome adolescents sometimes take heart from their defiance, without having to pay any of the consequences. Persons charged with keeping order among adolescents have an easier job because of the Scapegoats. The few teenagers who are extremely fractious can serve as substitutes and outlets for the many more who would like to challenge authority. Authorities and regulations are obeyed by many because of the punishment meted out to the few who reject them.

While many Heroes are bound closely to the home and family, many Scapegoats are spun out of the home early, which may mean large blocks of time in the streets and high levels of loyalty and attachment to the gang. Some Scapegoats get completely cast out: to juvenile homes, military schools, foster placements, the families of relatives, and most of all, in adolescent marriage and parenthood.[4]

It is easy to see how the children's experience predisposes them to behaviors that land them in such places. What is not so obvious is that, just as the Scapegoat role did something for the family from its inception, so does the banishment of the Scapegoat. It is the ultimate expression of anger and blame, and either of two contradictory hopes can be embedded in it: "Certainly this will be enough of a crisis to unite the family in order to save the child." Or more often, "With Scapegoat out of the way, the family will become loving, harmonious, and sober." Like Heroes, Scapegoats are members of a universal mythology, and the magic attached to them in myth is still applied to them in the way many families function.

It is evident that Scapegoats are particularly vulnerable to the assortment of risks described in Chapter 1. As we will see in Chapter 5, their

---

[4] *Boston Globe*, 19 January 1980; Booz-Allen and Hamilton, Inc., *Assessment of Needs and Resources*, p. 44a.

propensity toward alcohol and drug abuse is a studied emulation of their alcoholic parent, the most forceful way of retaliating against the family, and their most comfortable role with peers because it is one way in which they can compete favorably. Failure in school and at work, delinquency, and social aggression are risks concomitant with or independent of substance abuse. It is clear that jails are full of alcoholics; it is likely jails are also overpopulated with children of alcoholics.

The Scapegoat strategy is to unite the family through failure. Some Scapegoats don't break laws and blacken eyes; they simply mess up everything they touch and get written off as useless. They are not troublemakers so much as losers. They appear depressed and suicidal rather than antisocial. It is important to identify and intervene with Scapegoats early before they fully internalize the "born to lose" self-image. By adolescence many Scapegoats have surrounded themselves with friends who are like themselves and written off everyone else. They may also have made choices that are at best difficult to reverse, like pregnancy and addiction. And they have caused other adults to anticipate the worst from them, reinforcing their sense of worthlessness. Preadolescent Scapegoats are sometimes receptive to the attention of intervention.

Intervention with adolescent Scapegoats usually begins with disciplinary procedures once antisocial patterns are established and visible. Schools put a great deal of work into the "bad actors," but rarely do they touch on family alcoholism as a key to promoting change. The same is true of correction and rehabilitation programs. They may acknowledge a high incidence of parental alcoholism in their clients, but they sometimes think of the past as past, rather than a living part of the present.

Many Scapegoats cannot come to terms with their own problem drinking until they see their parents' drinking as abnormal and destructive. They cannot vent their anger constructively until they find its true focus. They cannot change their behavior until they have insight into its sources and consequences.

THE LOST CHILD

Even in healthy families, middle children are thought to get less attention than their siblings and seem to be less certain of their contribution to the family. In alcoholic families this tendency is often exacerbated. While their brothers and sisters suffer from being locked into rigid and exaggerated roles, middle children are often given no role at all, no way in which to make their presence felt in the family. This may have salutary effects for some; they can keep the family at some distance. While everyone else embroils themselves in family conflicts, middle children go about their lives unobtrusively.

Patricia appears to be an example of this kind of adjustment. Throughout her childhood and adolescence, Patricia was extremely quiet and socially isolated. She spent a great deal of time in her room, and on the frequent occasions when conflict and violence reared up, she was nowhere to be found. In all of her affairs she avoided attention and distinction. Now in her early twenties, Patricia seems to be better adjusted than her siblings. She has a good marriage, a few friends, and a solid career—interestingly enough—working with disturbed and autistic children. Without ever having had contact with Alateen, she seems to have lived by important Alateen principles, not by choice but because of her individual traits, her placement in the family, and the complex dynamics that governed it.

But many children, especially middle children, become Lost Children, particularly when the gap between them and younger siblings is small. When Lost Children enter the family both alcoholic and nonalcoholic members are more advanced in their illness and the trenches around each person's position are deeper and more fortified. The family has no interest in another Hero or Scapegoat, since these diametrically opposite courses have not ameliorated conditions in the home and may even appear to have worsened them. In any case, the younger child would have difficulty besting a sibling in either of the roles. The Scapegoat has demanded a great deal of attention and energy and helped intensify conflict within the family. The nonalcoholic parent is exhausted; it is beginning to look as if things will never get better, and bitterness and resignation replace the hope that a very good or a very bad child might bring the family together. The family feels its precariousness, cannot endure more conflict or demands on it. It has lost faith in its own future; it only wants to avoid new pressures that might cause it to explode. The Lost Child is not expected to transform the family but rather to keep from taxing its fragile balance.

The central task of Lost Children is the avoidance of conflict. The high levels of tension and verbal or physical violence, erupting intermittently or constantly threatening to do so, are terrifying. Lost Children conclude that if they cause or contribute to stress, the family they depend on for their survival may crack at the seams. Nor can they help resolve conflicts among other family members; any attempt to do so in a polarized situation constitutes taking sides and adds to the problem. The learned powerlessness of Lost Children results from their experience of any form of participation in conflict as a losing proposition. They adjust silently to every demand and every situation.

Lost Children enact the family's shared sense of insecurity and help-lessness, and the denial with which it tries to mitigate these feelings. Lost Children represent the family's impulse to turn into itself and hide within itself, fearful and without hope.

Lacking a way to contribute to the family through their own distinct patterns, Lost Children tend to withdraw emotionally and physically. They feel lonely, afraid, and unimportant, subject to the whims of every other family member and unable to express their strongest de-sires and fears. In their seclusion they often develop a vivid fantasy life, which serves as an outlet for the emotions they cannot sublimate in action.

Lost Children belong to the faceless crowd, the people difficult to remember. They are quiet and intensely shy, and if they attach to a group at all, it is invariably as followers. They rarely express a strong opinion, qualifying or otherwise undercutting what they say, embrac-ing both sides of any topic, speaking only after recognized leaders have said their piece. They don't volunteer and they don't outwardly oppose; they are above all agreeable. Passive resistance is their mode of assertion; they pretend not to have heard or understood what is wanted of them. And it appears that some Lost Children are more than pretending. With their potent and practiced fantasizing powers, they construct a protective wall that is stronger and thicker than a reflexive stratagem. They may develop somatic and psychological problems to enhance their isolation: hearing difficulties, stuttering, learning disabili-ties, and, in extreme cases, schizophrenia.

Lost Children are often sickly, not only because illness can be a barrier to contact (asthma, for instance, can excuse some children from group games and sports), but sometimes because they only receive attention in the family when they are ill. If Lost Children stand out in school at all, it may be only by virtue of their poor attendance.

> I remember thinking that the only way I was going to get any attention from her was to make myself sick. So I would ask people to cough in my face in the second or third grade. I'd undo my coat on very cold days. I was constantly sick.

Lost Children cannot take themselves seriously, and don't want oth-ers to either. Richie, for example, concluded every sentence with a monosyllabic giggle. He wasn't trying to make people laugh; he was just begging them not to get angry. Richie was a follower rather than an isolate. He had no hopes borne of fantasy; he had no hopes and intentions at all. Responsibility terrified him; he was the child who sits small, and on the playing field he hopes the ball goes to someone else.

Stan was an isolate with other common Lost Child traits. He had elaborate fantasies, some of which would come and go and others that became his obsessions. He longed for a career in show business, though he could neither read nor memorize. He could not take criticism of any kind, and gave up even his most passionate theatrical projects at the first sign of failure, usually by getting sick. He was also extremely effeminate. For reasons that are unclear, Lost Children appear to have a tendency toward gender identity conflicts. In Stan's case, his alcoholic mother was his only parent, and he never acknowledged her alcoholism.

Some Lost Children avoid close contact with adults and peers in order to escape conflict, yet they cannot endure being by themselves. They only know who they are and how to function with reference to the responses and adjustments required of them by others. They hold in their anger and even when it explodes, it is controlled and half-hearted, tempered by the fear that a real outbreak would be devastating, fracturing the family or the delicate terms on which peers accept them. At 19, and after many years of help, Frank had these reflections on his past:

> I had a lot of friends, but they weren't really friends. I hung around with all the tougher kids in school, the kids who were always getting in trouble. But I never got in real trouble. The last fight I got into, this kid was bugging me and I was in a bad mood, and I didn't go to him and say, "Knock it off or I'll hit you," or something. I just did it. And I knew how it was going to end up because the kid was crazy. He started taking a stick and hitting me over the head, and I'm not that violent so I went away. But usually I don't say anything because I feel if I say something it's going to end up in a fight and I'd just rather avoid fights. . . . I can't stand being by myself. I was always like that when I was a little kid, too. I know this is farfetched, but my friend left me his apartment just to watch. Someone had broken into it. I just couldn't sit there. It's a small place, a couple of rooms, but I just couldn't sit there. I was going crazy. I had to call up my friends and they had to come. I just couldn't stand looking at those four walls, I go nuts. Even when I'm with people, I hate it when it's quiet, when no one is saying anything, you know. It feels so serious, I feel like I have to say something.

Lost Children are probably the most difficult of all to identify and reach. They are determined to pass through life unnoticed; they regard this as the safest course and all that they deserve. Schools and other institutions have their hands full with the children who demand attention. Even when they don't assume that all quiet children are doing fine, many youth professionals don't know how to make inroads into the passive barriers that shield the children; or they don't have a sufficient period of contact with them to establish feelings of trust.

Should the family secret of Lost Children become known to a helping adult, referral and intervention are still highly problematic. The children are governed by their fears of conflict and catastrophe, and their hopes may be exhausted. Lost Children may be capable of joining a group for children of alcoholics if a friend or peer benefactor belongs, but it may be unrealistic to expect them to attach themselves to a group of strangers, regardless of the group's purpose.

Some Lost Children adults seek psychological help, often at the urging of someone else, when loneliness, compounded stress, the pressures of change and decision making, and the fear of loss attending every conflict overwhelm their patterns of passive adjustment. These adults are depressed and devoid of enthusiasm; they may speak without affect and use "I should" rather than "I want." They often see themselves as victims, helplessly adrift in the world. Because they choose to remain unnoticed in jobs that are safe and highly structured, they frequently are bored by work that does not challenge their capacities. But they don't know how to take the risk of redirecting their careers. Many Lost Children scrupulously avoid intimacy, engaging in no relationships or in serial failures in which they feel victimized. The ones in more serious trouble live for their fantasies, some at the level of psychosis. Even in therapy, they may be very resistant to using the word "alcoholism" in relation to their parents. It has been the nexus of family conflict, and they are terrified of what might ensue if they mention it.

With help, many Lost Children can capitalize on the positive tendencies that attend their role: independence, creativity, flexibility. But help must be rendered with great delicacy and patience. Children who shrink from attention need time to grow comfortable with gradually increasing doses; too much too soon will drive them away. Lost Children are in need of gentle prodding and low-key support for engaging in all kinds of group activities, where they can discover that others like them and want them around. It is hoped they will also observe examples of constructive and resolved conflict, though it is so foreign to their experience that they will need help to understand it.

Once a degree of trust has been established, helpers can tenderly point out instances of passive resistance and encourage children to feel and express directly their own wants and anger. Simply getting children to take the risk of responsibility, and showing them its rewards, is beneficial. But it is often difficult to transfer the children's trust to other resources. The referring helper often must remain involved during a long transition period, and the acceptance of the referral may hinge upon finding a peer, often a Hero, who can take the Lost Child in hand.

At whatever age they get help, Lost Children need hope. They need a sense of entitlement and a perspective on anger and conflict; a feeling that they are important and lovable, blemishes and all; and confidence in their ability to shape their own lives by knowing what they want and going after it. A tall order, perhaps, for children with their histories. But Lost Children have more strength than their helpless and beaten personas indicate.

THE MASCOT

The Mascot is often the youngest child in a family that knows it is in trouble. In nonalcoholic families it is not uncommon for parents to prolong the immaturity of the "baby of the family" in order to keep feeling needed in the accustomed protective role that the older children are beginning to appreciate less. In alcoholic families additional pressures make faithful adherence to the Mascot role more compelling for the youngest child.

Tension pervades the home and relative tranquility is always precarious. When the youngest is born, direct and honest communication among family members is usually at an all-time low, since the longer secrets and feelings are kept in silence, the more difficult it is to let them out. The air is filled with the threat of divorce; it may provoke fear in children who want to keep the family intact, but is merely infuriating to those who have been urging divorce for years and no longer believe it will ever happen. The alcoholic's drinking may be worse, or it may have become so bad, possibly with medical consequences, that intermittent or continued abstinence has begun. It is entirely possible that the Mascot role is even more pronounced and limiting in families where the alcoholic is in the early stages of recovery.

The family views the Mascot as the immature and fragile object of its protection. Older siblings, even the Scapegoat, subscribe to this idea. Perhaps they are aware of how home has failed them; perhaps they want to experience vicariously some of the care and protection they missed. The Hero welcomes someone to take care of; the Scapegoat wants someone to like and be liked by, someone innocent of their anger; and the Lost Child, though angry and resentful of being supplanted, finds it easier to withdraw with the Mascot around. The alcoholic and nonalcoholic parents may feel guilty and want to redo their childrearing. They are intent not so much on a child who will be successful as a child who is happy.

Children who need to be kept happy and protected can also perform a service the family badly wants: Mascots can dispel the tension. The family tacitly conspires to keep its ugly side from the Mascot. Arguments dissolve when the Mascot enters the room, especially if the youngster does something cute. Ostensibly for the Mascot's own benefit, but actually because of its need for relief from anxiety, family members endow the child with the capacity to make them laugh, or at least, to touch the soft spot. The Mascot becomes more and more of a tool as family members catch on to the child's function. The Mascot is repeatedly called upon to charm, cajole, and otherwise manipulate not merely the alcoholic, but anyone else who is being irrational and intractable.

> I was Daddy's girl, you know. We got a dog; we needed $20 for shots. Amy was elected to ask Daddy for the money, 'cause he would have said, "No, the dog doesn't need shots, she's perfectly fine." So I had to connive: "Dad, hi, Dad, I'm going on a ski trip with school, can I have twenty dollars?" Shaking in my boots. "Bring the coffee to Dad," they'd say. "I will not, he'll throw it at me." But I wouldn't say that, I would just go, and stop in the room and run, "I have to go to the bathroom."

Children may be trained as Mascots, but they can't be made oblivious. They know something dangerous is going on, and usually they sense what it is at an early age. The fact that no one talks about it, that indeed every effort is made to keep them from seeing the family's disorder, only makes it more fear-inspiring. The reward Mascots get for their comic relief is the shortening of the fearful shadows. Their value to the family, and their own greatest need, hinges on their capacity to bring levity into the mysterious tension.

Class clowns are the most obvious type of Mascot. These children show a knack for making everything into a joke. Their humor may be of the obnoxious, spitball variety, timed inappropriately and coming at the expense of others; or it may be the kind that interrupts but still makes people laugh and forgive the interruption. Humor, even self-directed, is the Mascot's trademark. An audience is not always required; the clowning can be a compulsive, preemptive defense.

In addition to actual joking, Mascots, like Lost Children, have a tendency to giggle or make a funny face after any of their comments that they are afraid may be taken too seriously. Children may be nervous, high-strung, and hyperactive for many reasons, and being the Mascot in an alcoholic family is one of them.

The alcoholic home is frequently anxiety-provoking for all family members, but Mascots probably feel the atmosphere with greater intensity. They are kept in the dark about the family's problems, their imaginations free to concoct terrible scenarios and explanations for their parents' conduct. Even more to the point, they are assigned the responsibility for defusing explosive situations. They are constantly attuned to stress and conflict, always ready to douse the brushfires between people before they become conflagrations. Mascots learn to anticipate even the most innocent signs of tension, and to act immediately to dispel it, without the slightest understanding of its sources. To some Mascots, mere silence is too threatening: They need to fill the air with activity and words. Mascots are often unable to concentrate on any one activity for a suitable period. They have difficulty with stress and may avoid competition. Their role and its rewards depend on their immaturity. Mascots may be slow to make developmental transitions at every age, and they also regress when they are feeling most insecure. This compounds their problems in school, both academically and socially.

> I used to let Martin sit next to me because he was very hyper, so I used to keep a hand on his knee or something, just to calm him. He was sent to be at the Resource Room all the time because he was too disruptive. He's socially immature, his behavior is just so different from other nine-year-olds'. He has a hard time interacting, he's like a six-year-old. He likes to play cat, you know, "meow, meow," he likes to be petted, he wants to be chased, I mean, he acts like a six-year-old so the kids his own age feel, "Who is this kid?" He hasn't made it in the classroom.

Some Mascots find older friends to protect them socially. Being the youngest in a street-corner group is a way of re-creating the reality they are most accustomed to and confirms them in this narrow role. Other Mascots associate with youngsters several years their junior because they have more in common and receive more acceptance. In the long run, the latter may practice styles that had been impossible to try in the home.

Mascots are thoroughly schooled in manipulating to get what they want. Often they have actually been told to lie, wheedle, and cajole, and—if charm doesn't work—to whine and pout. This is not to say that they understand why they deserve some of the things they want. They are not likely to insist on their prerogatives but only to use indirect means predicated on their fragility, innocence, and need to be happy.

Untreated, Mascots are prone to perpetual dependence. They are apt to marry strong, silent Heroes and become their child-wives or child-husbands. If their parents and siblings stop babying and protecting them early, they may look for a protector as soon as possible. The same may be true when the older teens who have adopted a young Mascot stop hanging around on the corner.

Sustained anxiety is itself a risk. Mascots are thought to be highly susceptible to abuse of drugs and alcohol, and particularly to the minor tranquilizers, a way of coping with anxiety that is both learned within the family and promoted in the society at large. Hyperactivity also has consequences in school and the workplace. Mascots who cannot sit still, concentrate, and feel comfortable with peers on an equal footing may be frustrated in both settings.

Mascots may not be especially difficult to identify, but their anxiety and hyperactivity can present obstacles to sustained intervention. On the other hand, they have an intense curiosity about what is really going on in their homes. They may be hard to manage in a group, always distracting and rarely serious for long; but an intervention process featuring games and other outlets for tension can tap their desire to explore the family mystery.

Intervention seeks to free Mascots from responsibility for the stress that can crop up in any situation. It isn't that they think they cause it but that they feel obliged to relieve it with an inarticulate fear of what will happen if they fail. Mascots can be extraordinarily ready to believe an authoritative explanation for their families' behavior, and are usually immensely relieved by it because they have imagined worse. By understanding the roots and results of their practiced fragility, their compulsive humor, their constant apprehension, Mascots can, with time, practice slogans like "Easy does it" and "Live and let live." They can learn to take themselves more seriously and others less so. They can feel appreciated, among other things, for the fun and laughter they bring to others when they want to, instead of for the release they must bring whenever tension appears. Many Mascots will always be nervous, compulsively active people, but if they understand this about themselves, they can find satisfying ways to expend their energies and nonchemical ways to relax.

Chapter 5

THE CHILD'S VIEW
OF DRINKING

I remember when I was a little kid I used to go with my father every-where, to the junkyards and every place he went. It was later when I stopped doing that. I went with my friends. But then I still used to go with him drinking and stuff, and go over my cousin's house, [and] watch them all get drunk. We used to think it was funny, and we used to try to get drunk. One of those times, I was 13 and my cousin was 14, I overdosed.

FAMILIAL INCIDENCE OF ALCOHOLISM

There are a great many questions on which professionals in the field of alcoholism research and treatment do not agree. Indeed, the cause of alcoholism remains the subject of heated debate. Is alcoholism attributable to a chemical reaction that can be transmitted genetically or is it the result of a stressful, traumatic childhood in a home in which alcohol abuse is systematically modeled by a parent or older sibling? If and when the causes of alcoholism are determined, they may well include both physiological and environmental factors.[1] But both theories rest securely on one fact no one seems to dispute: Alcoholism runs in families.

About forty studies, most of them conducted in the last ten years, demonstrate the point conclusively: Rates of alcoholism are significantly higher in relatives of alcoholics than in relatives of nonalcoholics. Re—

---

[1]Donald Goodwin, *Is Alcoholism Hereditary?* (New York: Oxford University Press, 1976); NIAAA, *Alcohol and Alcoholism*, pp. 13–16; Vaillant, "Paths Out of Alcoholism," p. 1.

searchers estimate that between 25 and 50 percent of all alcoholics have had an alcoholic parent or close relative.[2] There is reason to believe that the lower percentages are understated because of methodological problems and the probable protection of alcoholic mothers. One researcher has found that children of alcoholic parents are twice as likely to become alcoholics as children of nonalcoholic parents.[3] Furthermore, young alcoholics, and alcoholics who were young when they began to be problem drinkers, are even more likely than other alcoholics to have had a family history of alcoholism.[4]

Some studies suggest that genes are more important in the intergenerational transmission of alcoholism than environment. Research on twins and children adopted into and out of alcoholic homes indicates that wherever they lived, children of biological alcoholic parents were at greater risk than those who lived in a nonbiological alcoholic environment.[5]

On the other hand, a recent and prestigious longitudinal study in the Boston area finds that there are only two significant childhood precursors of alcoholism: growing up in an alcoholic environment or one with ethnic drinking patterns conducive to abuse; and having a number of close relatives with the illness.[6] Children living in either condition became alcoholic in substantially greater numbers than those who grew up with other kinds of problems, such as the death of a parent or mental illness in parent or child. Other studies show that differences in the transmission of alcoholism are associated with differences in the preservation or disruption of family bonding rituals.[7]

Most children of alcoholics satisfy both conditions anyway. They have a biological parent with alcoholism, and they live in an alcoholic environment (whether or not they always live with the active alcoholic). We don't know which, if any, children are born to alcoholism in their physical makeup. If we could know, we might eventually be able to offer them enzymes or antabuse as preventive treatment. But to do so would first require an effective and systematic educative process for informing them, and also those exposed to nonbiological alco-

---

[2]Cotton, "Familial Incidence," pp. 100, 111; Margaret Hindman, "Children of Alcoholic Parents," *Alcohol Health and Research World* (Winter 1975–76): 2; Booz-Allen and Hamilton, Inc., *Assessment of Needs and Resources*, p. 48.

[3]Gerald Globetti, "Alcohol: A Family Affair," paper presented at North American Congress of Parents and Teachers, St. Louis, 1973; Goodwin et al., "Adoptees Raised Apart," p. 242; Hindman, "Children of Alcoholics," p. 3.

[4]Cotton, "Familial Incidence," p. 109.

[5]Goodwin et al., "Adoptees Raised Apart," p. 242.

[6]Vaillant, "Paths Out of Alcoholism," p. 1.

[7]Aldoory, "Research Family Factors," pp. 2–4.

holism, of their risk. That is something we can do now, with our present knowledge. But we are not doing it.

Second to children of alcoholics, the children at greatest risk of alcoholism are those whose parents strictly forbade drinking on religious or moral grounds, equating the activity with damnation. A smaller percentage of these children drank than in the general population; but of those who did, a greater proportion had serious problems.[8] We don't know the genetic histories of these children. But we have little trouble crediting a connection between their earliest attitudes and emotions about alcohol and the development of alcoholism.

Most children of alcoholics learn daily and dramatic lessons about alcohol itself. Whether or not genes are a factor, it is likely that children of alcoholics are at high risk for later alcoholism because their earliest observations lead them to view alcohol so differently from other children that it might as well be two different substances.

These different attitudes toward alcohol can be seen in children at very early ages, and may help us identify children of alcoholics with surprising accuracy. If we are to interrupt the generational cycle of alcoholism, we have to do more than identify attitudes. We have to change them when children are still young, to promote competing images of how one drinks, or, failing that, to help them avoid altogether a substance they may always view with fascination and terror. For adolescents already encountering trouble with drinking, attitudinal change may be impossible. Nevertheless, if they can see the link between a parent's alcoholism and their own development in drinking, they are more likely sooner to acknowledge and work on their own problems with alcohol.

Both children of alcoholics and adults who want to help them need a normative basis of comparison. How do children of nonalcoholics come to view alcohol, and how is the drinking of other teenagers different from the drinking of youngsters raised in an alcoholic environment? In town halls, school committee chambers, and police stations across the country, teenage drinking is described as a grave problem of epidemic proportions. Beneath the oratory and the frequent media sensationalism, some important facts about teenage drinking are obscured.

A PERSPECTIVE ON TEENAGE DRINKING

As noted in Chapter 2, most American adults drink responsibly. They drink because they find it pleasurable; they limit their intake and

---

[8] NIAAA, *Alcohol and Alcoholism*, pp. 13, 16, 25.

do not endanger themselves and others. But a substantial proportion of infrequent, light, and moderate drinkers drink with a modicum of guilt; they apologize for their drinking and believe that we'd all be better off without alcohol, even as they continue to enjoy a cold beer on a hot day. This endemic ambivalence about drinking contaminates the adult community's socialization of its young people and builds contradictions into how teenagers are expected to behave with regard to drinking. As a society, we make drinking increasingly important and attractive to young people.

Regard the "typical" adolescent, a female, for example. Her daily lot is change—subtle, mysterious, uncontrollable. Her body is changing; her wants and needs are changing; others' expectations of her are changing. She wants—is really compelled—to try to build her own identity. She resents the notion that anyone or anything has influence on her unless she desires it. In trying to be an adult, she is constantly exploring the limits set up for her by her parents, other authorities, and society. If she has an island of comparative safety, it is her group of friends; and friends are those who are steadfast, approving, and exciting. With her friends she sifts for values, experiments, tries to figure out what it means to be an adult.

Most of the adults she knows, including the ones she loves and trusts, drink. They enjoy it, but they tell her drinking is only for adults and she must wait until she's of legal age to enjoy it, too. Her heroes and heroines on the television and movie screens drink, and some of them, in the most popular movies, such as *Animal House*, get gleefully and endlessly drunk. Next to these potent images, neither Fonzie declaiming in a twenty-second television spot, "I don't drink and neither should you," nor the formal advertisements for alcoholic beverages on TV or on billboards, probably have much effect.[9] She's not about to wait, and the more she's told by parents and teachers that she must, the more she's insulted and determined to prove that she's ready for this prerogative of adulthood. When she discovers that drinking can alleviate some of her anxieties about boys, it becomes the key to still another forbidden realm. And the same dynamic is at work on all of her friends, so that drinking becomes something of importance to the group and the subculture as a whole: something they are not allowed to do, a risk and an adventure that strengthens the bond between them.

Drinking is a group activity; and teenagers do experience pressure— often unspoken, inferred pressure—to drink in order to win and main-

---

[9]Edith Gomberg, paper presented at New England School of Alcohol Studies, Bristol, R.I., 21 June 1979.

tain peer approval. This is an important factor in youthful drinking, but it is not the overriding influence that adults, especially parents, think it is. Blaming other people's children is a convenient way to exonerate both one's own child and oneself as a parent. Most youngsters have choices in selecting friends, even as adults do, and the choices they make reflect personality characteristics and tastes developed long before the child began to congregate with friends on street corners. Our "typical" teenager's peers may like to drink, but roundly condemn drunkenness. Choosing them as friends is very different from choosing a group that measures stature by volume of alcohol consumed.

Obtaining alcohol is hardly a problem. There are always older siblings, friends who can pass for legal age, derelicts who'll buy for reward of a pint. The illegality of getting and drinking alcohol is part of its allure to adolescents for whom rebellion is natural and even healthy. Barred from drinking in the home, in public drinking places, in discos, our typical teenager and her friends must drink surreptitiously, with no adults present to supervise or model and with no social restraints. They drink in playgrounds, on street corners, or near railroad tracks, and, most of all, in cars—parked and moving. The car embodies for teenagers not only mobility and independence, but privacy, often the only privacy they can get.

Adults arrange it so that drinking becomes a central experiment in the adolescent rite of passage, forcing teenagers to carry out the experiment in places we'd least like to see drinking occur, under the most unfavorable circumstances; and then we conclude that teenagers are too immature and irresponsible to drink sensibly and that the prevalence of drinking among teenagers signals a coming generation of alcoholics. It is an inaccurate conclusion that underestimates both teenagers and their parents.

Children learn more from their parents and close relatives from the time they are infants onward than from other, more remote sources; and most children's parents are responsible about their drinking or nondrinking. It is crucial to understand how teenagers get the values and attitudes toward alcohol they bring with them to their new and changing configurations of friends.

Studies conducted in the sixties of the drinking patterns of different American ethnic groups demonstrate that families from ethnic groups that traditionally had low alcoholism rates (Italians, Jews, Chinese) had radically different patterns of alcohol socialization from the families belonging to groups with high alcoholism rates (Americans descended from northern European cultures, Blacks, and Native Americans).[10]

---

[10] NIAAA, *Alcohol and Alcoholism*, p. 16.

Some cultures with a low incidence of alcoholism, such as Jews, had higher rates of per capita consumption than some groups with high alcoholism rates. Not how much but how and why alcohol was used distinguished the two kinds of cultures.

In the low-rate groups, parents drank in the presence of their children, in conjunction with a meal, a religious ritual, or a family gathering, but they did not get drunk. Drunkenness was consistently and unequivocally condemned. The children were introduced to alcohol when they were very young, just as they were automatically included in the rest of the family's customs and routines. The beverage of choice in these families was generally wine or beer.

In groups with high rates of alcoholism, these patterns were reversed. Drunkenness was tolerated, sometimes even rewarded with laughter, either while the person was drunk or in the stories recounted the morning after. Parents might get drunk in front of the children, but many did no drinking with the family and went away from the family to drink. Often, one parent was a strict teetotaler, so the children had no model of responsible drinking. Hard liquor was usually the preferred drink, and the children were strictly prohibited from drinking until they were of age.

Assimilation is diluting the distinctions between the ethnic groups mentioned, and it is difficult to say whether these cultural differences are the causes of differences in incidence of alcoholism or the reflection in traditional behavior of different genetic predispositions. Still, there is reason to believe that whatever their backgrounds, families approximating the pattern of alcohol education found in the low-rate groups will continue to raise children who view alcohol much as this ninth grader from the Azores did.

> When I first came here I couldn't understand the kids who would sneak out and drink beer near the tracks. In the Azores, we used to go behind the barn and drink Coca-Cola. We had wine and beer at home, it was no big thing; but our parents didn't let us drink Coca-Cola; it was bad for our teeth.

Adolescents will always experiment, but usually the experiments don't get out of hand. Most of us, whatever our present age, had our period of greatest alcohol consumption somewhere between the ages of 15 and 25, in high school, in college, in the service, as a newly independent wage earner, as a swinging single. Drinking styles reflect developmental stages, and they tend to change as people change. This is not to minimize the seriousness of youthful alcohol abuse. Teenagers die in alcohol-related car crashes even if their excesses are experimental. Every youngster needs to think about drinking, and the options in situations involving alcohol, beginning in the primary grades and continuing through high school and perhaps beyond. There is no question that an alarming number of teenage drinkers are forming consistent patterns of alcohol abuse and beginning to suffer the consequences.

There are a variety of estimates of the number of youthful problem drinkers in America, and these estimates vary according to how the term is defined. By one definition, a youthful problem drinker gets drunk at least six times a year or has six alcohol-related problem incidents with school officials, police, parents, or friends. Using this definition, the U.S. Department of Health, Education, and Welfare concluded in 1978 that approximately 3.3 million teenagers are youthful problem drinkers, with females comprising a growing percentage, some say 40 percent of the total.[11]

This highly visible and perhaps growing minority can appear to represent all teenagers, but the fact is that if 20 to 25 percent of all teenagers are having problems with drinking, 75 to 80 percent are either abstaining or fumbling toward responsible adult patterns of drinking. At the tenth-grade level, for example, about 84 percent of the boys and 76 percent of the girls drink. Two out of three male drinkers and three of four female drinkers experience no real problems in spite of the conditions in which they drink.[12] According to one study, a smaller percentage of girls are classified as problem drinkers in the twelfth than the eleventh grade.[13]

Most teenagers stabilize into a pattern of responsible decision making about alcohol, primarily because most have parents who drink responsibly and, hence, teenage friends who drink more or less responsibly too. Of the millions of teenagers who will not gradually curtail their drinking, many are simply drinking as they learned to drink from the time they were very young.

WHAT CHILDREN OF ALCOHOLICS
LEARN ABOUT ALCOHOL

As we have seen, everything in the alcoholic home revolves around the alcoholic's drinking, or, if he is newly sober, his nondrinking. When

---

[11] M. Gunther, "Female Alcoholism: The Drinker in the Pantry," *Today's Health* 53 (1975): 18; J. Fraser, "The Female Alcoholic," *Addictions* 20 (1973): *passim;* NIAAA, *Third Report,* p. xi.

[12] Rachal et al., *Study of Adolescent Drinking Behavior,* p. 118.

[13] Interview with Robert E. White, Program Evaluator, CASPAR Alcohol Education Program, Somerville, Mass., August 1979.

they are three or four years old, most children know, and can articulate, that the fighting, the maltreatment and neglect, the broken promises are connected to alcohol. They may think drinking causes the problems, or they may believe it when they are told that the drinking simply relieves the problems, but they know that the bottle of booze means trouble, sooner or later, one way or another.

Many young children are negative about drinking. A fourth- or fifth-grade class will generally name unhealthy, abusive reasons for drinking before they list positive, socially acceptable ones. Most of these children have seen alcohol abuse somewhere, even if on TV; and the incidents of abuse may have elicited from a parent some kind of simplistic, all-embracing condemnation of alcohol. Many parents feel that children should be told that alcohol is evil, so many children whose parents drink responsibly give teachers the response they think adults want to hear. But if encouraged to think of situations and reasons for drinking not leading to drunkenness, most children can name quite a few.

For children of alcoholics, drinking means getting drunk. They literally may not recognize as drinking any intake that does not have drunkenness as its aim or result. In a classroom discussion on drinking, these youngsters may think drinking is awful; or much more rarely, they may profess to think it's great. But if they are asked to elaborate, it will usually be found that they have in mind always and only excessive drinking. And when asked to name reasons people drink, they can only cite reasons people get drunk.

This equation of drinking with drunkenness is attributable not merely to observation of the alcoholic's drinking, but also to the lack of exposure to adults who drink differently. Very often nonalcoholic spouses do not drink and their criticisms of the alcoholic's drinking are taken by the child to apply to all drinking. If there are older siblings, they are likely to drink abusively when they drink, and their drinking usually occurs outside of the home, anyway, so the child gets no positive examples from them. The social relationships of the alcoholic couple often do not provide the child with responsible role models either. The nonalcoholic spouse, a wife for example, is likely to see what friends she has outside of the home; and if they do come over, she is usually the last person to offer them something to drink. And the alcoholic is losing his sober friends and surrounding himself with people who don't criticize his drinking because they drink the same way. When his friends come to the house, the child can plainly see that all drinking leads to drunkenness.

To the child of an alcoholic, alcohol is at once terrible and fascinating. It has the power to transform peace into chaos and sometimes to restore a semblance of peace again. Drinking presages abuse and neglect, but in the eyes of the child it is also the stimulus for unusual parental kindness and generosity.

> My father drinks the hard stuff. Sometimes he's nice; he'll give you money, you know. "You're nice, here, take ten dollars." Then his attitude changes, you know, sometimes he'll say, "Get away from me, you're no good to me, you just use me," and all this

Concluding that alcohol is responsible for the parent's radical and unsettling changes, many children of alcoholics have at one time or another tried to resolve the problem by dumping all of the alcohol in the house. Sometimes the upshot is a violent and unforgettable scene dramatizing for the child the fact that alcohol is more important to the parent than the child is.

> Once, when I was about nine or ten, I dumped all of the bottles when my parents weren't home. Now I'd drink it all, but then I just wanted to get rid of it. I didn't care if my old man got pissed; I expected him to. But he didn't just go after me, he went after my mother too. "He's your friggin' kid, you probably put him up to it." So my mother started smacking me too. "How could you do something like that? Are you retarded? Don't you know that stuff costs money?" You better believe that was the last time I tried that.

The child soon learns that the supply of alcohol is endless. In fact, six- and seven-year-olds recognize that they don't have enough to eat, or decent clothes to wear, because of the parent's alcohol expenses. So the next question becomes:

> Dear Abby,
>   Why do they make booze? Why are stores allowed to sell it? And why do people drink? I think they should make laws to keep them from selling alcohol.
>   Signed,
>   Booze Is Bad

At the same time children fear alcohol as an evil and uncontrollable mystery, they also believe that alcoholics could stop drinking if they really wanted to. And if they don't want to stop, even though the family is always fighting about it and there's not enough money to go around, then whatever is in that bottle is more than simply powerful, it's desirable. What does it have that makes it so good?

In this play of intense fear and fascination, alcohol, the pivotal object in the child's life, can become as much of an obsession for the child as it is for the alcoholic. Children may notice the strangest details and say the darnedest things, but only a child from an alcoholic home is likely to react as this seven-year-old did.

> There was a play last week and at one point one of the characters picks up a bottle and pours himself a drink, and right away he said, "That's not real booze in there." For a kid to be focusing on that when you're supposed to be focusing on the entire play, the entire idea, and to say, "There's no booze in there." . . . That's his whole focus.

Preadolescent children of alcoholics, then, may have a heightened awareness of drunkenness; an inability to recognize as drinking any intake of alcohol not resulting in drunkenness; a mixture of fear and fascination, probably the greater part of which is fear, which leads them to believe that alcohol is evil and should be banned; and a determination that they themselves will never drink.

THE EMERGENCE OF DRINKING PROBLEMS

The early determination of children of alcoholics to abstain from alcohol is completely justified and natural, but it is often not a desirable attitude. Children who swear never to drink fear that alcohol will do to them what it has done to their parents. An eight-year-old may acknowledge this fear, but most teenagers do not. The need to be an individual separate from the parent leads adolescents to deny that their parent's behavior may influence their own, now or in the future. As one 19-year-old said in retrospect:

> I knew that my father's drinking was affecting my life and making the whole family nervous and unhappy. But when I started drinking at about fourteen, I never thought that my drinking had anything to do with my father's. I drank because I wanted to. I got drunk every time, just like him, but I never said to myself, "Hey, you're drinking just like him."

The fear lies just below the surface, and it can be seen in the body positions of the children of alcoholic parents when a class is asked to respond to the question, "Is alcoholism inherited?" They may be more vehement than their classmates in their disbelief that a parent's alcoholism can be uncontrollably passed on to a child; but they will actually stretch forward in their seats in anticipation of "the answer." From the moment they begin to drink, many children of alcoholics are looking over their shoulders, vaguely, inwardly expecting that some day alcoholism will catch up with them. But the teenager is determined to be autonomous and independent, unique in time and space; and the fear of becoming a drunk like his parent is shrugged off.

Some children from alcoholic backgrounds follow through on their determination to abstain. The ones who succeed best are probably children whose response to family alcoholism has been characterized as the Hero syndrome. Their sole concern is holding things together, as children, as adolescents, and as adults. They become adept at denying themselves any impulses and feelings not subject to their control. In the stages of life in which drinking becomes most attractive, their weakness gives them a kind of strength. They can do without close relationships; they can deny themselves unrestrained elation; but they can also keep away from alcohol and drugs.

More often, the scenario is different. Peter, for example, knew that alcohol was responsible for his father's ill health and bad temper. Peter would not drink, but he found in marijuana the ideal alternative. It was illegal; it helped him make and keep friends; it made him feel good; and it wouldn't make him an alcoholic. At first he smoked whenever he could get it; by 15 he was smoking before and during school. He felt as unequivocally positive about marijuana as he felt negative about alcohol, and apparently transferred to smoking marijuana the lessons in alcohol abuse and problem denial he learned at home.

Jerry's story illustrates the progression from confirmed abstainer to youthful problem drinker. Jerry lived with his mother and his grandparents. His father was an alcoholic and had been a policeman until his drinking got so bad he was fired. He left the house, but Jerry still saw him from time to time. No one at home talked about Jerry's father or his drinking; they were too bitter. Jerry had repeatedly hidden or broken the bottles he found around the house. At age eight, he had outspoken anger for his father, but directed it against teachers and classmates. He was also very clear about drinking; it was bad and he associated it only with barrooms, illness, and death. He said he would never drink, no matter what.

Jerry didn't do well in elementary school, educationally or socially, and spent a good deal of his time outside of the regular classroom receiving individualized attention. His academic problems continued in junior high school, but he made friends with two boys whose attitudes and behavior in school resembled his own. At 13 years of age— the national average for the age of one's first drink—they cast about for sources of adventure and accomplishment and found alcohol.[14] Jerry may have vowed years before never to drink, but he couldn't be expected to live without the approval and sense of belonging that he got from his friends and rarely from his family. For his friends, drinking was experimenting with adulthood, flirting with danger and loss of control, standing up in rebellion, and proving manhood to one's peers. Clearly many alcoholics grew up in nonalcoholic families. Jerry's friends may be among them. The aura we have built around drinking is partly responsible; and their friendship with Jerry may be, too. Jerry's drinking is the only way he knows; his friends may have learned no way at all, always prohibited from even discussing the subject. Jerry is their first teacher. As they began to experiment with alcohol, his friends were participating in an initiation rite, but Jerry was picking up what he still regards as poison with a pretty label.

After years of watching the bottle disrupt his home and his happiness; after endless images of drunkenness and nothing to suggest any other style of drinking; with a daily accumulation of a sense of his impotence to control that bottle and what happens once it appears; and with the fascination that made him wonder as a child just what was in there that his father loved so much; Jerry drinks. Jerry cannot lift a beer to his lips without somewhere inside associating his act with every incident of drunkenness he's suffered from; he cannot grimace at the bitterness of the beer without the internalized understanding that one drinks in spite of the taste, for the power of the alcohol. With his poor self-concept, poorer now because he is indulging in the greatest of evils, what chance does he have to feel control over the magic of alcohol?

Jerry's drinking is inexorably linked to his father's alcoholism and to his own and his relatives' feelings about it. If he has a reservoir of anger, his drinking may become aggressive and violent, in the same kind of indirect retaliation he showed in grade school. Alcohol gives him the courage to strike back at the parent who was always too strong and frightening. If Jerry is depressed, his drinking is intended to obliterate those feelings, and the feelings of guilt that suffuse him because he knows how his mother and grandparents would feel about his drinking. If he is most of all clinging to the unspoken hope that he can still push the right button and bring the family back together, then his drinking may be designed to attract attention. And if he has made his friends his family, and relies upon their approval, then he desper-

---

[14]George L. Maddox, "Teenage Drinking in the United States," in *Society, Culture, and Drinking Patterns,* ed. David J. Pittman and Charles R. Snyder (New York: John Wiley and Sons, 1962), p. 233.

ately wants to excel at this group activity; and equating drinking with drunkenness, he drinks more and gets more drunk than anyone else.

Jerry has learned to use alcohol abusively as certainly as he's learned to use a fork to eat spaghetti and a knife to cut his meat. It may be that, like the recovered alcoholic, Jerry cannot drink in safety; he can't simply pick up an innocent drink without calling forth his whole unresolved relationship with alcohol. Small wonder, then, that a great many alcoholics of all ages vividly recall having gotten drunk the very first time they drank.

Alcoholics and teenage problem drinkers are usually very different when they are drinking from when they are sober. Teenagers pick up on the differences and can be astute at recognizing drinkers among them who can't control their drinking. Sometimes they express it under a veil of good humor. The teacher starts a unit on alcohol and someone says, "Ralph knows all about alcohol, don't you, Ralph? Ralph's studying to be an alcoholic when he grows up." Ralph takes up the playful tone and appears to disregard the core of seriousness: "Yeah, I'm an alcoholic. I love to drink. Let's go have a few beers and talk about it."

Many young people are more active in their concern than adults. Teachers repeatedly tell of incidents like this:

> This girl was having trouble with her drinking, and some of the kids who knew her were really worried about her; it was getting very serious. In fact, one night she got so drunk that she didn't come home at all. She was about 13, and she was drinking every night. They were talking about it in the locker room one day and I didn't let them know I had overheard it because the girl was having a lot of problems—truancy— and her mother was up to school a few times, and I didn't think it was right of me to bring it up to her at the particular time. But maybe they were hoping I'd overhear them, because soon afterwards they came to me and said, "This is what's happening, can you do anything?"

Sometimes youngsters use alcohol to adopt a new personality, to become the happy-go-lucky, fun-loving extroverts they can't be when they're sober. Again, this is often a result of watching the Jekyll-and-Hyde changes that an alcoholic parent undergoes, and drinking with the expectation that alcohol can produce the same changes. If this new personality meets with peer success, and the girl likes herself better drunk than sober, she will become increasingly dependent on alcohol as the key to her happiness and sense of worth. As long as she is comical without being obnoxious, her friends are not likely to complain.

The drinking of children of alcoholics probably more consistently expresses the anger, hurt, and depression they've held inside for so long. If they are abusing alcohol, and their friends, while getting drunk occasionally, are mostly experimenting with drinking, then a parting of the ways is inevitable. Everytime Bobby and his friends got together, Bobby put up a fourth of the money and drank half the beer. He was constantly talking, repeating himself, interrupting everyone else, and making no sense at all. Sometimes he was insulting and picked fights with passersby. Or he tried to pressure everyone into stealing a car or getting some money. Finally the group had a run-in with the police, and two of them got arrested. "It started to be a drag to be with Bobby when he was drinking," one friend remembered. So his friends started leaving the corner earlier, or not coming at all. It was a gradual process, but Bobby felt the distancing and began to look for new friends. He usually met them in drinking situations, and he chose them for the way they drank.

Bobby was not aware that he had lost friends because of his drinking, nor did he think his drinking was problematic just because he'd gotten in legal trouble a few times. In part, his ability to overlook the relationship between his drinking and his problems was attributable to his adolescence and the culturally shared expectation that teenagers are by definition mercurial. When a girlfriend commented on Bobby's drinking, she was ditched without delay for a dozen other reasons that suddenly appeared; teenagers may change girlfriends every week. His father was bothered by Bobby's drinking, but he usually thought he was "a kid drinking, like every other kid." And like most other teenagers Bobby discounted his father's criticism along with his countless other admonitions. He lost a job or two because he was hung over once too often, but it wasn't a remarkable occurrence to him, his father, or his friends; teenagers change jobs with frequency. Drinking affected Bobby's schoolwork, and he was constantly being hassled and chastised in school; but he found plenty of company in classmates who, for one reason or another, had no use for school.

There was a much more important reason that Bobby, the child of an alcoholic, couldn't see what was happening to him. When he was five, his mother used to tell him that she'd stopped drinking, but he would find bottles hidden in the toilet tank. When he was ten, he was made to tell neighbors that mama had the flu. Not surprisingly, he became a 15-year-old with a great deal of confusion about what is real and what is not. He had learned and internalized the habit of denial, and had it firmly in place as the evidence of his own drinking problem began to pile up. He was not simply lying when he said he could control his drinking if he really wanted to; he needed to believe his lie and had a long-standing habit of protecting himself with a blindness to the actual events of his life.

MAKING THE FAMILY CONNECTION

Whereas the majority of young problem drinkers solidify their abusive patterns without having to confront their life consequences in a serious way, an increasing number of young alcoholics are identified through the juvenile justice system, which then has the leverage to compel attendance in some kind of alcohol program. Too often, by the time the youths are thus identified, they have been having alcohol-related problems for several years; and girls tend to be overlooked entirely and returned home instead of being booked for their offenses.

In working with youthful problem drinkers, the goal is to begin to overcome their denial and help them examine their drinking in the light of its effect on their present and their future. In this process, understanding the physiology of alcohol and the exact blood alcohol content that legally defines drunkenness counts for very little. Teenagers probably cannot come to terms with their own drinking until they understand something about the drinking of their parents, since this standard has been their own from the time they first saw drinking occur.

Ron and Steve were in the same court-mandated alcohol group, but they appeared to be from different planets. Ron, at 17, was only beginning to accumulate a record of criminal charges, but every few weeks there would be another incident. Before his misbehavior, Ron had been protected; he lived in an affluent suburb and his father was a respected local businessman. Handsome and well-built, Ron played halfback on the football team and was extremely popular with the most sought-after girls. He would laugh without any trace of joy, he was sarcastic, distrustful, almost never sincere: he was "cool." He began to get arrested, first for driving under the influence, then for joyriding in stolen cars and driving without a license. After each arrest he would be mandated to an alcohol group and fail to complete the attendance requirements; then he'd be arrested again and referred to another group. At each group, he maintained that he didn't drink and didn't belong in the group.

Steve, on the other hand, had a face that no one could trust. Only 16, he looked like a derelict of 40. He had lived all his life in the city's worst project, and his first arrest occurred when he was about 11. His older brothers had constantly been in trouble, and one had died of a

drug overdose. His friends had similarly notorious predecessors, so the
police were looking for them from the beginning. Steve and his friends
did not disappoint their expectations. Steve dropped out of school at
14. The feelings of anger and deprivation that he, like Jerry, took out
on his teachers and on classmates toward whom he felt a vague envy,
contributed to a process leaving him undereducated and unemploya-
ble, a failure at 16. His overflowing rage found targets in all forms of
authority; his bitterness condemned achievement. He and his friends
did whatever they could think of to get money, and spent all their
money on alcohol. They would get drunk and make a mess of their
careers in crime, getting arrested for breaking and entering, extortion,
and, of course, being idle and disorderly. Assault and battery on a
police officer was a common charge; the cops would try to move them
off their corner after they had been drinking since five o'clock. Among
his friends, Steve was the butt of jokes, but he joked back and took it
all for affection. They would blame one another for getting into trouble, but they always took the punishment together.

Ron and Steve had a great deal in common. Ron's mother was an
alcoholic, as was Steve's father. Neither had ever discussed alcoholism
or ever heard it discussed in a dispassionate, knowledgeable way. They
both denied their parents' alcoholism. Ron talked about his mother all
the time, but he never saw her or talked to her; he said she lived in
Chicago. His father had been awarded custody when they divorced
when Ron was nine. Ron vehemently blamed his father and stepmother
for his separation from his mother and for some of his subsequent
problems; he had only the strongest profession of love for his mother.
In Ron, and in many other boys with alcoholic mothers, the overwhelming need was to protect the mother's integrity and reputation; he
could not tolerate thinking of his mother as a drunkard and, therefore,
a slut. The need to deny the feelings of abandonment, lovelessness,
and disgrace created a defense against all feelings of pain and intrusions of reality. Ron was incapable of being honest about his own
drinking until he began to be honest about his mother's.

Steve considered his father a heavy drinker, not an alcoholic. Even
after he described his father's drinking and it was seen to fit within the
definition of alcoholism, and after a muted comment or two from his
friends in the group, Steve held to his assertion. He freely described his
older brother as a bum, but would not use the word alcoholic. He
didn't want to talk about anyone's drinking because he didn't want to
confront his own. His drinking was no problem because he drank like
everyone else, and his father's drinking was no problem because it had
never bothered him. If he had to think of his father as an alcoholic, he
might have to think of himself as one, too.

What affected Steve most during the court group was a prolonged discussion of how a young person learns to drink by watching a parent. Other members of the group made jokes to lighten the atmosphere; Steve sat sullenly. His life had been nothing but trouble; he didn't want to be dragged into court every few weeks with the threat of jail over him. He wanted a car, money to spend, someone to be close to. Some people had these things, but none of these was on the horizon for him, when he thought about it honestly. He could see that he had been born to lose and born to be a drunk. If he felt like a victim and blamed his parents for the way he drank, he was largely justified. That conception of his drinking will never get him sober; but it is the first step toward admitting that he is unhappy with what drinking is doing to his life and unable to control it.

Young people like Ron and Steve don't want to examine their own drinking, but they have an involuntary need to understand, and feel better about, the drinking of their parent, no less at age 17 or 27 than at age 7. The youthful alcoholic may resist talking about family alcoholism and deny its effect on him, but inside the hard offender is a hurt, bitter, and frightened child who often undermines the denial and lets what he needs through the facade of impermeability. The young alcoholic needs to know the specific signs of alcoholism and to be forewarned about the tricks of denial that will enable him to blame his problems on everything but his drinking. He needs to believe that there is help and to know where to find it. He needs hope. For these seeds to be planted, the old dirt must be dug up and turned. He can't come to terms with his own drinking until he has put his parent's drinking into perspective. And if he doesn't come to terms with his drinking he will become the exemplar of drinking for his own sons and daughters.

Part Two

HELPING

Chapter 6
OVERCOMING OBSTACLES FOR PROFESSIONALS

> I was always getting into fights and acting bad, and people, teachers and social workers, they'd warn me to straighten out, but no one helped me. And some of them would act as if there was nothing wrong with me, everything I was doing was normal. But it wasn't. But I guess I have to say that I didn't let anyone help me, either. I couldn't.

Many children from families with alcoholism, like Terri quoted above, leave behind them a trail of signs forcefully declaring that a problem exists but not specifying its nature. For other youngsters, the clues are much more subtle, easily overlooked by professionals throughout the child's long school career and sometimes prolonged contact with social service and recreational agencies. With early assistance, these children could learn better ways to cope with their family situation and the emotions it engenders, and increase their chances of healthy development of personality and education.

Some of the obstacles to assistance come from the children themselves. Adolescents in general are notoriously difficult to work with. At an age in which confusion, irresponsibility, and rebellion are the rule, in which independence is the watchword and rationality often the fool of hormones, the adolescent repeatedly proves reluctant to ask for or to accept help and hesitant to use that help in a sustained way. Professionals who expect the same level of cooperation that they might get from adults or younger children are often frustrated, as was the instructor quoted below, who switched to the tenth grade after years of teaching about alcohol at the seventh-grade level.

> The junior high kids show more of a reaction on their faces, whereas these kids, it's like trying to read a stone wall. There were lots of times

95

when I felt I was getting through to them, but they wouldn't come right out and say it. In the seventh grade some of them couldn't control their emotions enough *not* to talk about [family alcoholism]. These people can. They want to talk, you can see it, but they put on a front that there isn't a problem.

Young children and preteens, on the other hand, may be more accessible emotionally, but they are less available physically and ethically. Work done with children at this age must be done with the parent's consent and cooperation, or, in a very few extreme cases, with the goal of confronting (threatening, restraining, replacing) the parent.

Perhaps the most accurate generalization about young people's attitudes toward help is that, like adults, at all ages there are some children who can't keep their problems in; others who contain them only until the first good, trustworthy opportunity; and still others who resist any and all attempts to glimpse into their lives and feelings.

Children with family alcoholism, however, are a great deal less likely to seek help than other children, for all of the reasons described in Chapters 3 and 4. They are ashamed of their family secret and isolated by it; they feel anger and guilt; they are taught to deny the existence of the problem itself and their own feelings about it; they feel an intense loyalty that would make any revelation a betrayal; and they feel hopeless. They are usually discouraged or even prohibited from getting help by the alcoholic or nonalcoholic parent. Even when the parent is in treatment and supports the child's seeking help, the child's anger and need to rebel may render the parent's urging counterproductive. By the time they are in their midteens many children of alcoholics are so bitter and resentful that they refuse to concede that their alcoholic parent's drinking affects them and profess not to care what happens to their parent.

But many of these children are also generally so unhappy and anxious that, if there is any kind of path through their resistance, particularly at early ages, their desperation will find it—provided that the path meets them right outside their door. This chapter concentrates on the reasons so few helping professionals are traveling up the path and knocking on the door.

Most youth-serving professionals—be they teachers, guidance counselors, social welfare workers, therapists, employment counselors, youth outreach workers, recreation workers, probation officers, or clergy—start out with some attitudinal or practical obstacles that have kept them from taking on an aggressive intervention role with children of alcoholics. They have real and valid fears and reservations, not mere excuses for avoiding further involvement. These professionals are dedicated people who have classes and caseloads that are much too large; they need to know something about almost everything in order to meet widely disparate needs; they are paid too little, sometimes trained too little, and supported and praised too little. They are people who rarely see the results of their best work.

In outlining the professional attitudes most often inhibiting aggressive intervention with children from alcoholic families, we in no way disparage the understandable fears of people who are too often undervalued. Once these reservations—many of them difficult for dedicated professionals to express to colleagues or admit to themselves— are raised by a trainer and discussed as perfectly valid concerns, the professionals who hold them can examine them more openly and more dispassionately and eventually overcome them.

Fears and inhibitions of the helpers usually occur in combination and reinforce one another. They can be dealt with in five somewhat artificial groupings, represented by statements like these:[1]

1. Only a handful of my kids are affected by family alcoholism.
2. It's the parent's problem, not the child's.
3. The children who really want help will ask for it.
4. It's not my job.
5. It's really a personal matter.

"Only a handful of my kids are affected by family alcoholism."

> If you didn't live with alcoholism you usually know nothing about it and don't see it as a problem. If you did live with it, you feel hopeless (as a helper) or you want to avoid the subject altogether.

Virtually every American adult knows that alcoholism is considered a major problem. Even if they don't know an alcoholic personally, most people have seen alcoholics—or persons they assume to be alcoholics—on the street, in subways, in bars. Most would not be able to define the term accurately nor would they agree upon the signs and consequences of alcoholism; they know little more than that there are alcoholics, and not just a few of them. But large faceless numbers are meaningless to people of all ages. People may be shocked to know that there are ten million alcoholics or at least fifteen million children of alcoholics in this country. However, abstractions neither deter nor motivate, and abstract knowledge of a problem is not usually translated into an active awareness of the problem's existence in daily interactions.

The first goal in training youth professionals in family alcoholism intervention is to create an immediate awareness, a presence in the

minds of those who work with children, that a good many of these
very children live with family alcoholism and are profoundly affected
by it. This goal addresses itself to two distinct biases: The first is that
alcoholism is not itself the cause of family dynamics damaging the
child, but is rather a more or less incidental accompaniment of more
complex dynamics. The drinking is thus viewed as a result of family
problems and a convenient excuse for the child's behavior, rather than
the cause. The second bias is that alcoholism, however widespread it
may be in the general population, is not a significant problem among
the families of children with whom the professional has close contact.

In the absence of an awareness of family alcoholism as the major
cause of problems in the lives of many of the youngsters an agency
serves, it can be extremely difficult to persuade the staff of that agency
to allocate time or money to training that might create that awareness.
While there are many reasons that agencies fail to recognize the need
for training on alcohol and alcoholism (not the least of which is that the
key person in the agency is unresolved about his or her own drinking
or experience with family alcoholism), the principal obstacle is that
most people who don't look for something never see it.

The history of CASPAR's relationship with the DARE Girls' Multi-
service Program illustrates this phenomenon. DARE offers counseling,
advocacy, and crisis intervention services to preteen and teenage females and their mothers. To qualify, girls must be referred by the
court, the welfare department, or the special education division of the
schools. DARE's initial request for training was the result of the director's exposure to a brief interagency exposition on CASPAR; she had in
mind a two-hour workshop focusing on teenage drinking. As with
many youth professionals, there was a great deal of justified distress
about the drinking of the girls, and almost no cognizance, in spite of
frequent family contact, of its precursor—alcoholism in the home.

CASPAR refused DARE's request, the reasoning being that staff
should get ten hours of training or none at all. A few hours' training
confuses more than it clarifies, and still allows participants to consider
themselves "trained." Probably because the director of DARE believed
in the importance of ongoing training rather than in the need for specific training on alcohol and alcoholism, she agreed to allocate ten
hours.

With the training, and a monthly case consultation set up immediately afterward, came a change that was astounding both in its magni-
tude and speed. The DARE staff had been submerged in disastrous
family situations. So much existed in these situations that was destructive and unhealthy that, when staff members noticed drinking at all,
they relegated it to a minor role, something family members did be-

cause their lives were so miserable. In a way, the staff members viewed their clients' drinking much as they did their own and that of their friends. It was something people did, and occasionally overdid; it could complicate a bad situation but not create one. For the cause of the families' problems they looked to the sophisticated psychosocial theories in which they had been schooled.

In a matter of months after CASPAR training, the same workers saw that 50 to 75 percent of their cases *revolved* around family alcoholism. The families were not behaving differently; the workers were simply seeing the drinking in a new light. It became a presence, something they actively looked for in assessing any situation, whereas prior to training even the most blatant clues were somehow overlooked or inappropriately interpreted. And this new consciousness has been passed on to successive staff members and colleagues at new jobs.

While it did not happen in the case of the DARE program, lack of awareness of the problem can create not merely indifference to training, but outright resistance. Many times CASPAR is called upon to train people compelled by their agency director or department head. Some trainers balk at that situation; they don't feel they can get anywhere with people who don't want to be there in the first place. Whether resistance is a function of being too close to or too distant from the subject at the outset, it is certain that unless we get people in the same room with us, they don't get trained and we don't have a program. Almost all manner of coercion, incentives, coaxing, and wheedling can be useful in getting people to the point where a dramatic and pertinent workshop can overcome initial resistance.

Even professionals who think of alcoholism as the pivotal problem, rather than an incidental symptom of a larger problem, often make a variety of erroneous assumptions that allow them to discount the problem for the actual children they see. The most pervasive, perhaps, is that alcoholism is primarily a lower-class phenomenon. Another assumption is that children who do well in school are not likely to be suffering serious emotional damage at home. In the best "ostrich" fashion, many communities that exclude bars and liquor stores maintain that they have eradicated, or at least greatly reduced, the local alcoholism problem.

While the origins of these myths are understandable, there are reliable data that repudiate them. As noted in Chapter 2, alcoholism may be better hidden from outside view in wealthy families, or in middle-class suburbs or dry communities; but all indications are that it is just as prevalent as in any congested working-class district.

While it was once true that alcoholism rates in Jewish or Italian families, for example, were significantly lower than in other American ethnic groups, assimilation and intermarriage seem to be diluting the mores that may account for the difference. Professionals from these ethnic groups, having had little acquaintance with alcoholism as children, are often unaware of it in their work.

In an academically proficient class of 25 children from a middle-class, ethnic neighborhood in a dry town, there is still every reason to believe that four to six children are being affected by family alcoholism.

To be persuaded (and at best that means emotionally persuaded) that family alcoholism is widespread and causing problems for people they know, professionals need proof that is both dramatic and safe. Regardless of the degrees they hold, most people have never examined alcoholism as a course subject or discussed it with friends or colleagues. A round-robin interchange in which workshop participants recall their first contact with alcoholism is one of the simplest and most effective techniques in the CASPAR training repertory.

CASPAR's Basic Alcohol Education course begins with the trainers relating the circumstances of their first drink, its effects, the setting, and other details, and briefly describing their present tastes in drinking. Then each participant is asked to share the same reminiscences in turn. While people often understate their present drinking, most are willing to talk at some length about their drinking experiences. The exercise is instrumental in helping participants focus on the pleasurable aspects of drinking and their own attitudinal and behavioral development, giving them a context for what they will learn and a better sense of the distinctions between drinking, drunkenness, and alcoholism.

A few sessions later—after hours spent on the subject of drinking— the topic of alcoholism is introduced, and it is introduced in much the same way. Familiar now with the technique, and considerably more comfortable with one another, participants who might otherwise have been threatened are asked to comb their memories for their earliest recognition of someone who was alcoholic, whether or not they were thought of in those terms. Responses typically vary in personal proximity, depending in part on the trust shared between group members and on the bursting need of individual members who have never before had the opportunity to discuss alcoholism openly. In every group stories are told about uncles, aunts, family friends, in-laws, present intimates, and even parents. This activity functions as a wonderful springboard for examining ingrained biases about alcoholism and arriving at a definition of the term. But this can be achieved in other ways. The main purpose of this roundtable discussion is to dramatize the sweep of alcoholism, its hidden prevalence.

A junior high school teacher told this story almost three years after her training workshop.

> One girl came in with a black eye. She'd been beaten up. I asked her what had happened, and she told me she fell or gave me some excuse. I knew it just wasn't possible. And then I overheard her, or eaves-dropped—that's what I did—talking to her friend, and she said her mother hit her. That's all she said to her friend. Then after class I asked her what had happened again, and I said I was sorry that I overheard her, but did her mother really do that? And she admitted it. And I said, "Does your mother drink, by any chance?" She said, "Yes." Then I gave her CASPAR's name, and she went. She was very willing to go. In fact, she was just hoping, looking for something to grab onto at that moment. She went either that day or the next day. . . . Before the black eye, I had no idea there was a problem at home. I never would have known that unless I took the course. I probably would have believed her ex-cuse right away, because I never ever thought . . . . I mean, I went to a school where you never heard anything about alcohol and alcoholism. And I never was exposed to alcoholism amongst any of my friends' parents, or even my parents, I just never knew of it, and even through college I never knew. When I took the course, *then* I started to realize what was happening, and then I realized some of *my* relatives and some of my parents' friends were alcoholic. In fact, about two weeks before I took the course I had found out that someone who was an administrator at my high school had gone from the top, back in the days when I was in high school he was a big wheel, and by the time I finished college he was kaput. And then I realized, someone happened to mention him at the CASPAR workshop, not by name of course, but someone said they had this friend, and described him; and then I thought, wow, was I stupid, I never realized! He was a well-educated man, and I would never ever suspect alcoholism.

It is surprising how frequently people respond to this exercise by sharing, sometimes for the first time, recollections of their own child-hood in an alcoholic home. It shouldn't come as such a surprise. Adults, like the children we encourage them to help, are relieved to hear the subject discussed openly and supportively, and it's easier for many to let it out than to continue to suppress their feelings and experiences.

"It's the parent's problem."

As workshop participants examine alcoholism, its definition and par-ticularly its signs, they begin to identify additional people in their acquaintance whom they never before thought of as having alcohol-ism. The net effect is to heighten attentiveness to alcoholism's occurrence in participants' lives. But there is a large step to be made from a greater awareness of alcoholism to a consciousness that many of the children one sees every day suffer in various ways from the effects of family alcoholism and need help. To promote that consciousness, a training program must put professionals directly in touch with the *children's* pain: both its breadth across the youth population and its depth for each individual child.

But the pain, though poignant, can scarcely seem relevant to people who work with children if they consider alcoholism to be the parent's problem. The common misconception is that, while a parent's alcoholism certainly affects a child (and those effects tend to be underestimated), the only real help consists in getting the parent sober. Anything else is beside the point. Subscribers to this myth can be found in teachers' rooms, mental health centers, probation offices, and the highest echelons of policy planning and dissemination. William A. Horn, editor of the United States Office of Education's *American Education,* wrote in response to an article on the teacher's role in helping children of alcoholics:

> How can one really help a child from a family afflicted with alcoholism without reaching the parent responsible for the problem? And with this in mind, is it a teacher's or a school's prerogative to counsel an alcoholic parent?

Who would argue that a child whose parent is dying can only be helped by the doctors who try to keep that parent alive? The argument is even more absurd when applied to alcoholism. The self-hate, the confusion, the resentment that a child accumulates through twelve years of a parent's drinking don't simply vanish when the parent stops drinking. No one knows that better than the recovered alcoholic. One knowledgeable teacher described:

> A woman at PTA [who] had a problem, and she's still got a problem but she's done something about it, you know. And evidently one of her teenage kids either resented her or whatever, but she said that she had moved into this district so that her son could come here and have alcohol education in school.

The child's problem is the result of the parent's alcoholism, but the child's receiving help cannot be contingent upon the parent's treatment. Alcoholics need to·stop drinking; children need to understand the drinking, the feelings it creates and the unhealthy ways in which the children react, while the drinking is still going on, as well as once it has ended. Children who understand alcoholism can help their nonalcoholic parent and younger siblings change the family's response to the alcoholic, and, in this and other ways, contribute to the alcoholic's recovery. But the children's need for help is itself independent of their own, or anyone else's, effort to help the alcoholic.

For teachers at all grade levels, and others working with groups of children in educational settings, CASPAR has developed a technique that rarely fails to demonstrate dramatically that family alcoholism is troubling a significant number of their own youngsters. At about the midpoint in the teacher-training workshop, participants are asked to assign their students an exercise called "Dear Abby," based on the syndicated newspaper column. Children are familiar with newspaper advice columns. The teacher brings in a few sample letters on any subject except alcohol and alcoholism. Some are problem-ridden, others written to obtain information. The teacher reads them aloud, with the anonymous signatures and the responses. Then, as part of what is usually described to the children as the beginning of a unit on alcohol and drinking, the class is asked to write a letter about alcohol to Abigail van Buren or Ann Landers. Minimal directions are best. "It can be about information you want, questions you want answered, a problem concerning alcohol, whatever. It can be as long or as short as you want. And don't forget to sign it with a made-up name so no one will know who wrote it."

The teachers take the letters home and read them, show them to a colleague or friend, then read them in the workshop. In virtually every class at every grade there are several letters like these:

Dear Abby
I have a problem. Everyone in my family hates my father, and I do too. My older brother says he's not an alcoholic but I say he is. He comes home drunk and acts real stupid. I really couldn't care if he went out and killed himself with the stuff. He really isn't hurting me, but it's my mother he hurts the most. When he's not drinking he acts smart and I wouldn't mind being his daughter, but when he does I wish he were dead! He was going to get help before but he really doesn't want it. Please help!
                              A girl with two fathers

Dear Abby
My mother has a drinking problom and I will like to asek you about it. She gos out with men that I don't now. She cams home drink and she gats verey sick. My opinion I think drinking is anuthe way of death. Sum peaple drink because thay wont to fall [feel] kool.
                              Sincerely,
                              Sam Anonymous

Some teachers are quick to point out that children may bring to this assignment, as they do to others, a vivid imagination. The great majority know that the most poignant letters are absolutely sincere, regardless of who may have written them. Teachers may need help to notice other kinds of responses: The children who normally write long and well whose papers, if they can be recognized, consist of one or two innocuous lines; and the opposite, those who never write who turn in comparative books; and finally, the papers relating alcohol problems of an uncle, aunt, or friend, some not to be taken at face value.

The "Dear Abby" letters make it viscerally real to teachers that *their* children come from families with alcoholism in no inconsequential numbers and that the children's need for openness on the subject is profound. For people who work with youngsters individually or in noneducational settings, assessing the extent of family alcoholism in a nonthreatening way is more difficult. If a low-key discussion of drinking makes a child unusually restless and evasive—or unusually attentive—or if, as described in Chapter 5, a child equates drinking with drunkenness and concedes that his or her parent "drinks now and then," the professional should be alert to the probability of family alcoholism.

To demonstrate to professionals that children getting help with family alcoholism can make dramatic improvements in their lives, nothing succeeds like the young people themselves. Films and books carrying the voices and images of such children help fill this need, but the most lasting impression is created by an Alateen speaker. Hearing a child talk about painful personal experiences in a candid and understanding way is a revelation, especially to those who know they couldn't do the same and never suspected young people of such insight.

A young lady came and talked with the students here at the school. That girl, that she could stand in front of this group and relate all the incidents of her life, and what she went through, that was so motivating! She had a handicap and a slight speech impediment, and initially the kids would mock her. But as she went on they stopped and listened in awe. They had to.

Many teachers expect, and want, the compleat rags-to-riches "My father is sober today and we're living happily ever after" story. In many ways it's important for them to be exposed to children who are "together" in spite of the fact that their alcoholic is still drinking.

CASPAR's teachers have the opportunity to see firsthand the changes that occur in students who were once the pariahs of their school. Young people who had been nothing but trouble are displaying their CASPAR affiliation, helping other kids, and getting better marks. Teachers even start calling on them as resources. There can be no better advertisement for the capacity to turn children of alcoholics around without reaching their parents.

"The children who really want help will ask for it."

The Alateen speaker, and especially the "Dear Abby" letters, helps professionals see not only that children of alcoholics need help, but also that they want help and rely on them to provide it. To some teachers, the way in which a student discards anonymity in the "Dear Abby" letter, signing "Sam Anonymous" when there is only one Sam in the room, is a clear cry for help. In most workshops, at least one incident demonstrates even more dramatically that the teacher's intervention is desired and efficacious.

> I assigned the letters to begin the (7th grade) unit. I hadn't even looked at the letters yet. One student came up after class and asked me how soon the letters would be answered. Apparently she expected a simple answer about how to get her father to stop drinking. I told her we would be doing the unit, and maybe her question would be answered in it, but if she wanted to talk it over now she could. Boy, did she start to talk! The following night, I think it was, the school social worker took her to an Alateen meeting. She had been seeing this girl once a week for several months, but she had never suspected alcoholism in the family.

Such incidents are motivating, but they can also be misleading. They can create in youth professionals the expectation that the children who really want help come forward to ask for it; and the ones who don't ask for it would resent and resist any offer of help. In part, this expectation is based on deep-seated and unrealistic assumptions about what helping is. In preparing people to deal with family alcoholism, it is crucial that they develop a sound sense of what they can do and what they can expect in return. This is the subject of Chapter 7.

Most children of alcoholics cannot be expected simply to come forward with their tales of woe. Professionals who initiate the helping process will miss various positive responses if they are looking only for an immediate, unequivocal outpouring of gratitude and relief. To reach the children who want help but can't ask for it, the helper must create fluid, natural opportunities that make it easier for the child to ask for help and easier for the professional to offer it. And during these opportunities, the professional must be alert to the subtle clues children leave instead of a blatant invitation.

The above is precisely what we mean by "aggressive intervention."

If we can postpone briefly the consideration of how such intervention with children from alcoholic families fits within the role of a teacher, employment counselor, or recreation worker, we can examine the necessity of intervention for the child. Very few children of alcoholics go off on their own to an alcoholism treatment program or mental health center to talk about their parents' drinking. Someone must bring them for help, and it's a gradual, sometimes an imperceptible business; but it is the business of the people the child sees regularly, develops a trust, affection, or respect for, and has the opportunity to share secrets with. Intervention means, literally, "to come between." The youth professional's role is to connect children who have family alcoholism problems they usually have never revealed to an adult with the person or persons who can provide prolonged help with that problem.

Youth professionals working with relatively large numbers of children—usually in groups—within a more or less fixed role, tend to hold counselors and therapists (whose job it is to work intensively on whatever problem the child may present) responsible for helping children of alcoholics. Nowhere is this tendency more apparent than in the schools.

> I feel that a guidance counselor is better capable of approaching them on the subject because they can really sit down and talk to the kid on a one-to-one basis. And I think most kids know they can go to a guidance counselor, realize why the guidance counselor is there, to help, and they're not going to be threatened.

Some teachers actually think guidance counselors will resent the teacher's exploration of the student's problems. In fact, most counselors share this junior high school counselor's opinion:

> The more a teacher knows about alcoholism, [the more] it's helpful to me as a guidance counselor because they can channel things through me. Actually, the classroom teacher's the best screen as far as the counselor is concerned. You sometimes don't pick up a problem until it's too late. Some of the kids who have become problems by the end of the year, probably there were some things I could have done earlier in the year if I had known or had some input. That's particularly true of seventh graders. We get very little information fed up from the elementary school, and we don't really get to know them until the end of the year. But the teacher sees them all year. Anything a teacher can make known to me is beneficial to me, and also to the teachers themselves.

Specialists—be they guidance counselors, child therapists, alcoholism counselors, or Alateen members—may be superb at talking to the child once the child acknowledges the problem and a desire for help. But they often can't do what the teacher can do: Help the child understand alcoholism well enough to indicate, directly or obliquely, "That's my problem and I need some help with it."

A teacher initiates help in a nonthreatening way that no guidance counselor can because a teacher talks with thirty children and singles out none. A teacher offers alcohol education as a subject for everyone; a counselor responds to it as an individual problem. And, of course, many of the youngsters most in need of an opening are those who never trouble their counselors: the Goody Two Shoes kids and the withdrawn children.

Children may know the guidance counselor's role is to help with problems; but they sometimes have little relationship with the person in that role because they see the counselor sporadically at best. Since the children are fearful of betraying their families, they generally won't raise the subject of drinking; and the best the trained guidance counselor can do, playing a hunch or picking up on a rumor, is to say, "Johnny, does your father's drinking bother you?" Johnny shakes his head, and the conversation is pretty much closed.

Teachers, on the other hand, by teaching about alcohol and alcoholism as part of their curriculum, create fluid and nonthreatening opportunities for learning and for acknowledgment of the problem. They get across some vital things for Johnny to think about, even if Johnny's head never leaves his desk. And because teachers raise the subject of family alcoholism in full view of everyone, not cloistered in a cubbyhole, Johnny learns that it's not just his problem and that it's OK to talk about alcoholism and not joke about it.

As often as not, it isn't the teacher at all who first raises the issue of family alcoholism in class, but the children themselves, which is even more valuable. One seventh-grade teacher, in the middle of his unit on alcohol, found himself with extra time in the period.

I started doing the Word Search, pretty much as busy work. I handed out the sheets, they started asking questions about what to do. Before I knew it, I don't know what brought it about, but the first two people in the first row just started saying, "Well, my father's an alcoholic, he's been to AA" (I think that's what started it, the first word was "AA"), and then they started explaining what Alcoholics Anonymous was, and then another girl said, "My father's an alcoholic too," and before I knew it there was a discussion going.

As the result of experiences like this, Johnny learns invaluable lessons which, if they don't help him confide his secret immediately, build toward the point where he can. He gets dramatic evidence that family alcoholism affects other homes besides his own, that other youngsters are not ashamed to talk about it, and that there is hope that the alcoholic may recover. And he learns all this without ever opening his mouth.

As for guidance counselors, far from being supplanted, they are empowered.

> A lot of the kids had gotten alcohol education through the science classes, and it opened up a new avenue, because a lot of kids would come down and want to talk about it with me. I'm getting people coming in that aren't afraid to discuss it now.

The same dynamic applies to settings outside of the school. The recreation worker, the employment counselor, the probation officer—instead of expecting troubled children to get help on their own or trying to promote that help through indirect methods—can make it a great deal easier for children to learn about alcohol and alcoholism, and to reveal their problems, by mounting nonthreatening group approaches to the subject as part of their work with children.

The youth professional who can generate these kinds of natural opportunities for children to discuss family alcoholism must also be able to recognize the variety of ways in which they respond to those opportunities. Many children neither seize the chance to ask for help openly and unequivocally nor remain stolidly silent about their problem. They are more reticent: They want a better sense of how the teacher will relate to their confidences, and they want to reduce their sense of betrayal by sharing with the teacher the responsibility for the revelation of their secret. The youth professional must learn to recognize the subtle comments and actions by which the child hopes to be drawn out of cover. A number of these covert signs have been documented by CASPAR. They are illustrated in the scenarios in Chapter 8 and listed in Appendix A.

"It's not my job."

Youth professionals can come to feel strongly that much more should be done for children of alcoholics and equally strongly that it's someone else's responsibility to do it. One need only look at all that is expected of the teacher to sympathize with such a reaction. The elementary school teacher is charged not merely to contain but to channel constructively the immeasurable energy of 25 children, each of whose wants and needs are magnified in the presence of the other 24. The teacher is expected to construct a safe learning environment in a room filled with the most disparate and elemental drives, fears, and fascinations, and is expected to do so five hours a day, five days a week, and forty weeks a year, year in and year out. The teacher at the junior high or intermediate school level, and at the high school level, is asked to stimulate intellectually, and in a real sense protect emotionally, not 25 but 125 youngsters whose fragility is only differently disguised than when they were in grade school. No wonder teachers and other youth professionals feel overwhelmed!

Not bad enough, but currently teachers and school systems are incessantly criticized for failing to equip students with basic reading, writing, and math skills. Administrators authorizing annually shrinking school budgets are gradually creating an atmosphere where anything not directly contributing to higher scores on uniform competency tests is suspected of subverting the school's purpose. The result is that teachers express, and administrators articulate or are assumed to share, the following sentiment.

> My job is to teach English. I have to try to create a classroom environment that will maximize learning for all of my students. Anything outside of that classroom environment is beyond my control and responsibility. It's the concern of guidance counselors, social workers, and outside agencies. They have the authority, the time, and the structure to get involved in something like family alcoholism. I don't.

The issue here is not whether youngsters want and can benefit from the intervention of trained youth professionals, but whether professionals have the responsibility and the right to function in that capacity. To answer that question, youth professionals must ask themselves if the principal goals of their work are impeded by family alcoholism for a sizable number of youngsters.

The teacher, for example, may have creative and exciting ways to present interesting material, may indeed work for hours at home devising stimulating lessons, but the student who is expected to benefit from this hard work is guilty, depressed, sleepy, and worried. As one teenager put it:

> Lots of times I just wanted to say, "Hey, if you knew what it was like for me! I get it at home, and then I get it worse in school." I wanted to say, "How smart would *you* be if you had to lie awake in bed at night in case your mother got it into her head to beat up on you? How much homework would *you* get done? Could *you* concentrate in school if you were wondering what you were going to find when you got home?"

Youth employment counselors are an equally apt example. They want to place teenagers in jobs that will be instructive and fulfilling, to provide them with a meaningful and positive work experience. They know their role doesn't end with the placement because all sorts of things in teenagers' lives may prevent them from sticking to their jobs. If a teenager's abuse of drugs or alcohol created problems at the work-site, counselors would see it as an integral part of their job to raise the subject with the trainee and to offer some kind of assistance. The same obligation holds for family alcoholism, which, even when it doesn't lead to abuse of alcohol, often results in the same kinds of behavior, though for very different reasons: frequent tardiness, irregular attend-ance, irritability, resistance to authority, and drowsiness.

In order to fulfill their stated job goals, youth professionals must try to ascertain the precise barriers in the children that interfere with those goals. It may be someone else's job to deal with the barriers once they are identified, but no one but the youth professional can spot them. The teacher's role in referring children with special perceptual, read-ing, speech, physical, and *emotional* problems has become thoroughly routine and accepted. Since family alcoholism is the central problem of so many children and affects them so totally, it certainly falls within this same purview and the teacher's responsibility for catalyzing help is the same.

Batteries of tests have been designed to diagnose reading and per-ceptual problems, hearing and coordination disabilities. No test cur-rently exists for diagnosing family alcoholism; it is most readily identi-fied through integrated activities. But those activities have their own intrinsic value. The subject of alcohol and drinking holds great interest for children beginning in the lowest grades, and their enthusiasm makes it an ideal vehicle for practicing and reinforcing language arts skills. The content, of course, could not be more important. If children are to make responsible decisions about drinking, they must be taught early and often, not left to learn haphazardly in the streets and in the home. Even if recurring alcohol education units did not lead to the identifi-cation of children of alcoholics, such units would be essential parts of a child's learning experience.

In every 10-session CASPAR unit, family alcoholism is discussed only in the last two or three classes. It is a mistake to think that even this subsection is relevant only to students affected by family alcoholism. We can be certain that some of the children not involved with the illness know, or will know intimately, someone who is. A friend some-where along the line will be depressed, hostile, or self-destructive; a spouse will be terrified by or worried about a parent without knowing why.

Dear Abby,

I have a friend whose mother is an alcoholic. When she is drunk she beats on my friend for the littlest thing. So instead of letting her get beat I always let her sleep over my house when her mother is drunk, sometimes 3 times a week. The other day my mother asked why she always sleeps over and I did not know what to say, please help.

Signed,
Sleeper

Dear Abbey

My brother have a problem, he always gos out with hes friends, he gos plasses like a bar, he drings beer and wiskey but my brother thas not want to tell me. So one day I follow him with my bick, I follow him so far that I was tayerd, so after a few minute he stoped and went into a small bar. So I went off my bick and I looked inside the bar and there was my brother dringing wiskey and beer. After a few minute I went home but I did not now if I had to tall to my mother or not. [Sic]

Young people are increasingly taught cardiopulmonary resuscitation and other first aid measures, because anyone may encounter a situation where intervention can save a life. The same is true of family alcoholism. Children are in key positions to help friends or siblings, and teaching them about family alcoholism in the context of an overall unit on drinking is a life preparation they will get nowhere else. Chapters 8 and 9 show how trained teenagers account for a great deal of CASPAR's success with children of alcoholics.

For youth professionals to include within their role definition alcohol education activities and the consequent intervention with children of alcoholics, they need administrative sanction. Such support would be essential in any case, but it takes on added importance in light of the helper's most frightening nightmare: confrontation with an angry parent. Such nightmares almost never occur. What parent desperately hiding alcoholism is about to come into school and challenge a teacher or administrator on the subject? But reticence on the part of an alcoholic parent, justifiably, is not enough to ease the teacher's mind. Some mandate is needed; for the teacher, it would be an authorized curriculum or the express support of the school administration. Within that framework, all the teacher does is help youngsters articulate their own needs and take the first step in seeing them satisfied. As one intervention veteran put it: "The key element here is if you can reach a child and the child can admit that he wants help, *nobody* is going to block that" (italics his).

The other necessity in support of the youth professional's intervention role is the availability of helping resources. Ideally, there should be a choice of resources to which children of alcoholics can be referred, each of them appealing, nonstigmatizing, confidential, and convenient. All-purpose youth counseling centers are sometimes inappropriate; young people think of them as only for problem kids, and too often staff members know nothing about family alcoholism. Alcoholism-treatment-program personnel are more expert on the subject, but few of them work in a setting that the child will find attractive and fun and devoid of stigma.

Oftentimes treatment resources must be developed side by side with the capacity to intervene. To create the resources, one needs children who will use them, and to get the children to the services, intervention agents need resources they can count on. Alateen is an excellent resource, but it is not sufficiently widespread. Also, young people sometimes need help to start attending, and professionals themselves have certain biases about it, which discourage referral. Chapter 9 describes a successful and cost-effective resource model for children of alcoholic families, and Chapter 10 takes a closer look at Alateen and Al-Anon.

Communities and institutions wanting to help their most troubled youth and reduce the incidence of youthful alcohol abuse must authorize youth professionals to teach about alcohol and intervene with children of alcoholics. And they must provide trustworthy referral resources. Under such conditions, the help so vital to the children becomes a fluid and integral part of the trained youth professional's total job.

"It's really a personal matter."

> It's the role we were brought up in that you don't interfere, that it's personal family life, and you stay out of it. Just knowing this in the back of your mind, even though you want to help, is a real deterrent.

When some helpers say that family alcoholism is a personal matter for the child, what they really mean is that intervention is a personal matter for the helper. There can be no doubt that many youth professionals have strong fears, reservations, and biases that are quite independent of their feelings about their role and its limits. This is most obviously true of those helpers who are themselves children of alcoholics.

Once they have examined their feelings about their own childhoods— whether in Al-Anon, therapy, or even in training—adults who grew up in alcoholic homes are almost always more sensitive and sympathetic to their younger counterparts than are their colleagues. But for the many more professionals who never resolved their own emotions about their experiences, the subject is often too close to the raw nerves. The same is doubly true of recovering alcoholics. The last thing these professionals want to see is the destruction alcoholism wreaks on children. The number of people who balk at a professional role in family alcoholism intervention because of personal proximity to the disease is easily underestimated. It is no mere handful.

Many of these people, and a great many others with lesser contact with alcoholism, are inhibited by their strong biases about alcoholism, as demonstrated by a workshop participant.

> At the workshop they asked us what our attitudes were, and we talked about them. I'll have to admit that my attitude toward alcoholism was kind of slanted. I had some real strong feelings. Especially I had problems dealing with alcoholism as an illness. I felt some moral kinds of things about it.

For this reason, CASPAR's training workshops spend much more time on attitudes about alcoholism than on physiological information. The helper who believes that alcoholism is a moral failing, or that "You can't help an alcoholic until he asks for help or hits bottom," or that sobriety requires nothing more than reasonable willpower, is ill-equipped to talk to the child of an alcoholic in a compassionate way.

But aside from these common helper biases about alcoholism, there are feelings about privacy and emotion that keep professionals from intervening.

> He never came to me and said, "I'm having a problem." He probably wouldn't want to admit it. I probably didn't want to confront him with it myself, I'd be passing lines or barriers that maybe I shouldn't. . . . I'm always willing to listen to anything and I've always said that. But I'm glad in a way that they won't open up everything because I don't want to hear all the sadness. I have enough problems of my own to contend with. With friends, too, I don't want to delve into their private affairs if there's something wrong. In my own family sometimes I don't . . . my wife will confront more than I. She's great, she sees something the way she sees it, she'll say so, and I wish I were myself, but I'm not a confronting type person.

In the end, this is the most formidable obstacle of all. People who are very private about their problems and emotions assume that others want and need the same privacy, and no training workshop or dramatic proof to the contrary will enable them to adopt a style in their professional life different from that in their personal life. Some people are governed by this reluctance to "pry," but virtually everyone shares to some extent feelings about the privacy of one's own problems. They may be afraid that raising the subject of family alcoholism will cause a child to cry, as if seeing pain is causing it or making it apparent is making it worse. The whole realm of the emotions can appear to be a Pandora's box that won't close and won't empty. They may worry that children will be publicly, lastingly embarrassed by an outbreak, instead of viewing the outbreak as a request for help and, really, the first sign that they are getting the relief they need.

Sometimes the helper is afraid that aggressiveness of any kind will close off the avenues that have been painstakingly opened up. This is a valid concern for a time, but often that time persists. Some workers spend years supporting a child, helping with 3 A.M. crises, and going bowling and canoeing; and even after they see that the child is being devastated by her mother's alcoholism, they are afraid that raising the issue directly will drive the child away. Sometimes it will, but much more often, the worker's value to the child makes her the only person who can get the child to deal with the problem. What's the purpose of building all this trust and affection if not to reach the point where the child will accept difficult help along with pizza?

One way to address this issue of "politeness" is to roleplay talking to a friend about her drinking problem. The situation is derived from the participants' actual experiences with close friends or relatives. The intervener hesitates; the feeling of delicacy about invading the private life, even of someone close, is palpable. And this is someone who is, literally, killing herself, and scarring others, with her uncontrolled drinking! If we are polite enough to keep silent while a friend ruins her life, what will we do for an enemy?

Even helpers who are embarrassed by emotion can be extremely valuable when trained. Some youngsters, particularly boys at certain ages, relate best to strong, silent men. In revealing themselves, they may sound as if they're bragging, not asking for help. This is an interchange the helper finds more comfortable, the emotion well below the surface. In fact, his opportunity to intervene comes precisely because the boy assumes that the worker will allow him to underplay his feelings. The helper can say some important things, do some critical listening, and suggest resources, while keeping the interchange comfortable for himself and for the child.

Most of all, what helps professionals feel at ease in discussing family alcoholism with children is simply intervention experience. One child who is forward and unequivocal about asking for help, and who shows that she or he feels better as a result, is the best incentive a youth professional can have, and does the more tentative children who may come afterward a great service. As one teacher said:

In my experience, as soon as you've had the opportunity, and not every-one gets the opportunity, to help one person, then you know it was all worthwhile.

Armed with an immediate awareness of the prevalence of family alcoholism and its impact on the children they see, and a clear sense of the importance of the intervention role they cán play within the limits of their jobs and their personal styles, youth professionals can make an immeasurable difference in the lives of children of alcoholics. After they are motivated to create or take advantage of opportunities for intervention, their final need is to set realistic goals and expectations for their helping role.

Chapter 7
EXPECTATIONS AND GOALS

In becoming committed to the intervention process with children of alcoholic parents, youth professionals can easily fall prey to a final obstacle that often prevents them from sustaining their helping role. The compassion that has been touched in them, and the new realization that their limited intervention can be crucial and is part of their professional duties, may give rise to a zeal that can carry dangerous hidden baggage: unrealistic expectations and goals.

What happens then is simple. The motivated helper is watchful for opportunities to aid children of alcoholics, with a distorted, often unarticulated picture of what that help will look like. Her goal for the child is acceptance of a referral, and on its heels, improvement in the child's behavior or emotional state. She may even be ultimately satisfied only when the alcoholic parent has begun to recover. If she structures her intervention attempt according to those kinds of goals, she may not only sabotage the help she is offering, but also make the child less open to subsequent help from others.

Even if the helper's unrealistic goals do not result in an intervention strategy that backfires, they will still inform her own perception of what she has accomplished. She may have been extremely helpful to the child, but fallen short of her high standard of success, and in the end consider her intervention a failure, frustrating to her and, she believes, probably harmful to the child. She will become increasingly reluctant to raise the subject of family alcoholism with subsequent youngsters.

The long-range goals of all work with children of alcoholics are emotional and behavioral. We would like children to feel better about themselves and their families; and to make choices, at home and in the world, which reflect and promote these feelings rather than feelings like shame, anger, and fear. Some children begin to show dramatic changes almost immediately, but many more do not. Helpers cannot sustain themselves looking for such changes. They need concrete and realistic expectations, attainable yet meaningful objectives, and a clear sense of their own limitations.

WHAT IS HELP?

Much of what must be understood about helping children with family alcoholism applies to all intervention, regardless of the specific position of the helper or the problem of the person being helped. As basic and as evident as these principles of helping may seem, they are easy to lose sight of in the trenches, amid the cries of people in need. The result is often the erosion of the helper's sense of efficacy and, ultimately, a loss of appetite for the helping profession.

It requires delicacy to remind people of the fundamental precepts under which they are working. In practice, many youth professionals reaffirm during their training on helping children of alcoholics five principles essential to their survival and self-esteem as teachers, nurses, psychologists, social workers, probation officers, and clergy.

The five principles of helping, elaborated below, are:
1. Help is a process.
2. Help is often invisible or in disguise.
3. Help is not necessarily a dialogue.
4. Tone is more important than content.
5. Helpers' responses are more than what they say.

Help Is a Process

This is an age that values product, not process. There have doubtless been other eras in which people were more attuned to the intrinsic value of the gradual, incremental steps that went into achieving an end. Today, theoretical science and pure mathematics seem to be two fields in which the builders of stepping stones are still accorded great respect. The stock-and-trade of human service professionals is the stepping stone, but as the larger society increasingly emphasizes only the end point, helping professionals can forget their true calling.

The helping process readily lends itself to metaphor. One metaphor is the planting of a seed, and it is the comparison to helping most often heard at meetings of Alcoholics Anonymous, Al-Anon, and Alateen. The seed is planted, sometimes purposefully, sometimes accidentally and randomly. The planter can do nothing more at that moment, yet unless the seed is planted somehow, nothing grows. The seed may need to be watered and otherwise nurtured, or it may require only the passage of time. It may grow and bear flowers, or it may never take root at all. Until the shoot begins to appear, there is no way to know if anything is taking shape beneath the soil. Help is sometimes more, but never less, than planting a seed and hoping that it gets whatever it needs to grow and flower. Planters do not castigate themselves if the plant doesn't appear soon enough, or at all.

Another metaphor is to picture a huge boulder sitting at the top of a mountain. A boy comes along and, with great effort, nudges the rock; it hurtles down the slope, a mighty force that changes the face of the mountainside. The boy congratulates himself on his handiwork, forgetting that before he was born that boulder was being shaped and moved, imperceptibly, by every gust of wind and storm of rain or snow, and by every human predecessor who tried to push it and gave up exhausted and frustrated. Without those prior forces the boy's strength would have appeared puny indeed; and it may be that the rock had already been dislodged enough to roll downhill from the mere alighting of a bird upon it.

These metaphors may leave images in the mind that will be easier to recall than a more verbal formulation. Help is a gradual and often imperceptible process, and the helper can only give what the child being helped is able to receive. The child can receive something today and not be able to use it until next year. Help is incremental, in that one person's small contribution today increases the opportunity and the effect of another's effort tomorrow. And it is cumulative: It all adds up, and there is no way and no need to measure the relative importance of all the little steps along the way.

Help Is Often Invisible or in Disguise

As often as not, neither the helper nor the helped knows when a major contribution has been made. A nineteen-year-old girl recalled, five years later, the events that led up to her pivotal acknowledgment of her mother's alcoholism:

> I got into a lot of trouble in school and one teacher, Mr. C., I had him for first period and every day, like, I'd just come in there and some days I'd be real happy and other days I used to sit there and be depressed and I wouldn't open my mouth, and other days I'd be yakety-yak. He always knew something was wrong, and a couple of times he asked me if I wanted to talk to someone, and I always said, "No, no." And then one day, I did my homework and so he was real happy. But I wasn't in too good of a mood, so he asked me to read it, and I said,

"No." And everybody just looked at me, and he said, "Read it," and I said "No!" He said, "Why not?" and I said, "'Cause I don't want to," and I started crying and I got all upset. I walked out, and he came out in the hall and he said, "You want to go down and talk to Miss T?" Because he knew I was really into gym and always used to hang out down there. So finally I just had to talk to someone and I did, I talked to her. But I will always . . . I mean, I say "Hi" to Mr. C., like, we don't have conversations or anything, but I will always, you know, have a deep respect for him and thank him. You know, he doesn't know exactly what he did for me, but he helped me a great lot. 'Cause at least he cared enough to think that something was wrong, instead of other teachers who just said, "She's just a wise little bitch."

Helping professionals must live with the sad reality that they rarely see the results of their best work. They owe it to themselves to recognize, and derive satisfaction from, the certainty that much of their help contributes a great deal, even or especially when it is unacknowledged. As has been said earlier, teachers who bring the topic of family alcoholism out in the open get visible responses, and often immediate results, from some students; but they can't tell which students with heads on their desks, or hiding behind impassive masks, are being brought considerably closer to asking for help. The same is true of individual interactions; trained counselors have learned to be undaunted by the child's silence, blithe denial, or seeming indifference. They have done what they can for the present, and they know they can't judge the effect of their words on the basis of the child's immediate reaction.

In fact, an immediate demonstration of relief and gratitude is not so rare with children of alcoholics. Many are desperate, particularly before adolescence. Instances in which children jump at the chance to talk about their parent's drinking encourage the helper in the intervention role, but may ironically set up the expectation that children who are *really* being helped will respond in the same way. The helper must be equally ready to accept denial, anger, or withdrawal.

Anger can be the greatest problem for helpers. They often think they have gone too far, loaded the child with more than she can handle, and jeopardized their relationship and any chance to help her later. This is a shortsighted view inconsistent with the nature of the helping process, and it misinterprets the anger, which is not directed at the helper at all but at the truth he or she is trying to help the child confront. In the words of a CASPAR peer leader trained to help other children with parental alcoholism:

I'd rather have the kid get angry and kind of throw things around. That's a lot easier, I mean, someone not to say anything, you just, you have to stick with it and that kind of stuff, but for them to get angry, I mean, that's a good sign.

Help Is Not Necessarily a Dialogue

This point, again, is anything but profound, and is related to the above discussion of help as being difficult to recognize. It deserves special emphasis because many helpers place inordinate value on the give-and-take of dialogue. A meaningful interaction consists of words between two people, spoken and heard, even if one person is doing all the talking and the other person is doing all the listening.

Help is often a monologue. Sometimes it is the child simply giving vent to all that he has been holding inside. If the helper feels that her own intermittent comments and suggestions were lost in the deluge, she is probably right, and it doesn't matter at all. The child's need at this point is to release; there is plenty of time to channel that release later.

More often, it is the helper who is doing all the talking. That can be the extent of the interaction, yet it may make all the difference for the child. One typical intervention tableau consists of several helper monologues over time, culminating in the child's outpouring and the beginnings of a conventional dialogue. Some children need to hear more than others before they can open up, and if any one subgroup can be singled out for this particular need, it is the adolescent sons of alcoholic mothers. A CASPAR peer leader described one participant in an after-school group for children with family alcoholism:

> The first meeting, this kid Joe, he didn't say anything, but we were all talking and he turned white as a ghost, I mean, I thought he was going to get sick. OK, so he didn't say anything at all. But M. [the other peer leader] and I figured he wouldn't have had that reaction unless something was going on in the house. It didn't matter how many times we asked him, he wouldn't say anything. It was because he had an alcoholic mother, and the last all-day session everything came out. It was, like, you get so used to him saying nothing, that when you pulled and he gave. . . ! You could hear a pin drop, and he talked for an hour nonstop and nobody moved. He was just at the point that he really needed to talk and it was the right time and right place.

The hardest form of help for a professional to come to grips with is neither dialogue nor monologue, but a complete break in communication. This is not an uncommon result when dealing with alcoholics or their family members. Helpers who work hard to build trusting rela-

tionships are terrified that their sole effect will be to drive the child
away and close off any further opportunities; and when it happens,
they describe their intervention as an utter failure.

It is not a desirable outcome by any means, but the child's withdrawal testifies most of all to the importance of the nerve that has
been touched rather than to an incompetent helper. Some children will
admit to being bothered by a parent's drinking only after they have
lost something or someone valuable because of it. For a number of
reasons these children may never get back to the professionals from
whom they pulled away. But many are closer to the truth of their
problem, and to acknowledging it, because of the rupture. Regardless
of how the professional goes about raising the issue of family alcoholism, some people will flee immediately. It is all the help they can take
just then, but it is still help. The following anecdote, related by a
trained consultant to day-care and preschool programs, illustrates the
professional's dilemma and its realistic perspective, in a situation involving the spouse of an alcoholic.

> In one case I remember, it was an only child, middle-class family,
> middle-class day-care center, and what they were concerned about was
> the little boy kept getting hurt. And they didn't think the parents were
> abusing the child, but what was keeping them from being able to keep
> this little kid safe? The parents were saying that the little boy would
> wake up very early in the morning and the parents just wouldn't hear
> him. I said, "Possibly there's a drinking problem?" When I first men-
> tioned it the teachers said, "Oh, no, it couldn't possibly be," but the
> teacher who was on duty late in the afternoon said, "Well, I don't know,
> the father's come in here looking a little tipsy to me a couple of times."
> And they said, "Well, so, well, maybe he was at a party at the end of
> work," that kind of thing. And I said, "You don't show up tipsy to pick
> up your kid at a day-care center without a drinking problem. I mean,
> sure people have a drink at the end of a day, but you don't come
> staggering in to pick up your kid. . . ." But the massive denial on the
> part of the staff, I had to talk with almost every one of the teachers for
> close to an hour, individually, including the director. We had so many
> go-rounds of talking about it, and they sort of hoped that we could give
> this child some kind of help or see the family without having to mention
> what they were concerned about. I said no, they had to confront it.
> Finally, the director was able to say something to the mother; the mother
> got very angry and denied it and removed the child from the center. I
> think that's what they were afraid of, and I think their feeling was that
> they had done no good. And I said, "It might take a couple of people
> saying this to mother, at a couple of centers, or whatever, in the com-
> munity, before they can hear it. But if nobody ever mentions it then
> there is no possibility of them hearing what it is."

Tone Is More Important than Content

Throughout the helping process, and especially at its beginning, what gets communicated is less crucial than establishing a pattern, with expectations and ground rules, for safe and open communication. This is another obvious truth, but some professionals' fears that they lack sufficient knowledge and expertise attest to how readily it may be overlooked. Helpers needn't have all the answers. They must be able to convey concern, a willingness to listen to whatever the child cares to say, and a guarantee of complete confidentiality. Their first goal is to keep the door open to a safe place to talk. This is not always easy, in part because of space limitations and time constraints. How many helping professionals have a private room to which a child can come unobtrusively and as needed?

One guidance counselor cited the difficulties faced by teachers and students in a secondary school setting:

> In years gone by, when I was a student here, the homeroom teacher was someone you could talk to because they spent time in the morning, in midday when they took attendance, and at the end of the school day. You got to know your homeroom teacher, I was one myself, you got to talk to kids informally, and that's missing.

Nevertheless, a will finds a way, and helpers who are sincerely concerned about their students still find the space and time to offer help. For some youngsters, a busy hallway can be as good a place as an enclosed cubby.

> Some kids, you can get them in the corridor and put your arm around their shoulders and say, "What's wrong?" and they just blurt it out. They need the right person at the right time, more than the right place.

More will be said about establishing a caring atmosphere in this and the following chapters. The point here is that helpers are first and foremost concerned and compassionate listeners. Unless that is successfully communicated to the child, they may have a universe of expertise in dynamic counseling techniques and a thorough knowledge of alcoholism issues, and never get to use it.

Helpers' Responses Are More than What They Say

Children who are asking for help are concatenations of raw nerves. Every part of the helper's response may be taken in, whether consciously or not. If helpers are shocked, frightened, or skeptical, children are apt to sense it, and may well elaborate and exaggerate such reactions in conformance with their worst fears. The helper may say all the right things, but the children don't come back. Here is a blatant example:

> A lot of them, they'd give you an opening, but when you brought up alcoholism would all of a sudden, like, freeze up and that was the last time you wanted to talk to them. That happened once in high school before CASPAR, that happened twice in junior high and it happened in elementary. In elementary they just did not want to deal with anything. When they asked you what was wrong, I guess they expected some simple, everyday problem, like a headache or something.

Helpers may find themselves listening to some very alarming things and they need to be prepared for what children may say so that their prominent reaction is neither horror nor disbelief. For instance, we saw that many children of alcoholics have elaborate plans for how they will murder their parent, complete in every detail and sometimes discussed with the icy detachment of a maniac. This is a fairly safe outlet for their anger and a way of fantasizing release from their family situation. Helpers who know that this is a natural and common characteristic of children of alcoholics will not have to hide their shock or alarm because they will not feel it; and children will be able to see that this, too, is a feeling others have had, of which they needn't be embarrassed.

Tales of physical and sexual abuse are too often met with skepticism. Many helpers *want* to believe children are exaggerating, seeking attention, spiting their parents; anything to avoid the necessity of dealing with the actual and indeed disgusting problem. Helpers read into the children's way of relating the account some justification for their rather large grain of salt. They may, for instance, think the girl in question is something of a coquette, and indeed she may be. But they prefer to think they can therefore discount her story, instead of attributing her manner to her need to survive in a home she is explicitly describing as sexually dangerous. Children have been known to invent innocent lies and serious lies, but our readiness to presume that they are exaggerating is a product of our needs and hopes more than our experience. Most children do not lie about such matters; and recent studies have shown that physical and sexual abuse of children has always been much more common than we have liked to recognize.

In their demeanor and their attitude, not merely in their words, helpers must say, "I believe you, I understand and care about you." And they must mean it.

REALISTIC GOALS

There are five distinct, more or less sequential goals in what can be called a complete intervention process for children with family alcoholism.

1. Expressing concern and a willingness to listen in complete confidence
2. Raising the subject of drinking or family alcoholism explicitly
3. Communicating key ideas about alcoholism
4. Helping the child acknowledge the parent's alcoholism
5. Facilitating ongoing help

They are presented in a logical order, but this order is not inviolable because children may be at different stages, and ready to accept different notions, at any one intervention point. Yet each individual intervention is usually a microcosm of the whole process, beginning with the first goal and proceeding as far as the child is able to go.

The goals are the helper's goals. Accomplishing them depends on the helper, not the child; and each goal has intrinsic value from which the professional can take satisfaction, regardless of the child's immediate and visible response.

Expressing Concern and a Willingness to Listen in Complete Confidence

Two salient things need to be said about this goal: First, it is indispensable; second, the helper who gets no further has still accomplished a great deal.

Everyone has different thermometers, and one person's fire is another's ice. Like Goldilocks, a child may find one adult too warm, another too cool, and a third just right. Conversely, the same professional may seem smothering to one child and motherly to another. We all have our styles; each style attracts some, and no style attracts everyone. Whatever we do to convey warmth and concern must be genuine and natural. But we can still evaluate and practice the ways we establish a caring atmosphere in order to be both comfortable and effective.

The biggest asset in projecting understanding and readiness to listen is the relationship that grows out of natural contact. In the development of this relationship, the little asides and three-word compliments, the smallest jokes and smiles in the hallway are just as important as the actual experiences shared. It is this quality, or its absence, to which one junior high school teacher referred:

I've had kids come back from the high school and say, "God, they don't listen to a thing you say down there." They say that the teachers don't joke around and talk to them. They feel the teachers up there are so impersonal that they don't even bother to try to communicate with them.

Some people go to great lengths to build an informal relationship and create the attendant opportunities: One teacher asked her adolescent boys for suggestions about dealing with her car. Such situations gave her the chance to meet the student person-to-person instead of teacher-to-student. But in every working day the professional has dozens of occasions in which to communicate interest and caring in word and gesture, and the smallest expression does not go unnoticed.

Even if professionals have this kind of relationship as they sit down to try to talk about family alcoholism with children, it is essential that they clearly convey concern, openness, and patience, and refrain from pushing too hard and too fast. Children need the right to choose their own time and place, for their own reasons. As one teacher put it:

They're very honest with you if you give them that freedom to tell you what they want and not push too much. Kids come to me and say, "I don't want to talk with my counselor anymore, she's getting to the point where she's asking questions that I don't want to answer."

One child with parental alcoholism characterized the helper's main job as "listening and handing out tissues." The scenarios in Chapter 8 illustrate how a supportive and encouraging atmosphere may be created. But even the best display of concern and acceptance will not itself enable most children to talk about parental alcoholism: They need more help. Professionals can feel confident that, having created a warm and safe atmosphere for the child, they can move on to their second goal without misgivings.

Raising the Subject of Drinking or Family Alcoholism Explicitly

The point of gaining children's trust and confidence is to be able to help them deal with their problems and bad feelings. If their problems stem from their parent's alcoholism, there comes a time when it must be confronted squarely, if little by little. Children may talk freely about their conflicts with friends, siblings, or teachers; but what they most need to talk about is still shrouded in secrecy, in spite of their trust in the helper.

Professionals can't assume indefinitely that children will bring the subject up when they are ready. On the contrary, they may assume that many children rely upon the helpers to introduce it. It may be raised obliquely: "I know this kid—I won't tell you who—but his father drinks a lot and it makes him so angry and upset that he takes it out on his teachers and friends. Maybe like him, you fought with Tommy because you were angry about something else?" One way or another, the subject must be raised, in a manner consistent with the helper's personal style and relationship with the child.

By mentioning parental drinking, helpers tell children that this too is a topic that is permissible, one they are prepared to listen to with understanding and confidentiality. To those children who have not yet actively associated their bad feelings with their parent's drinking, helpers give a name for what is troubling them. They help them make the connection, at that moment and countless times afterward, in media and other messages that might otherwise go unattended.

> At five o'clock all my girlfriends go in and have supper, but five o'clock I go in the house and there was no supper. What could I make? Twelve years old, you know? All I knew was spaghetti, and you boil it. I felt hurt inside. I felt, Wow, my mother never pays attention to me; she's always drinking with her brothers. I never really knew about it until I talked to Mr. G. about it. Until I started hearing things on TV too. There wasn't that much until Mr. G. told me about it, then I started hearing about it.

Perhaps most important, by raising the subject of drinking, helpers relieve children of the sole responsibility for what they perceive as an infamous betrayal. They break the taboo. If the child supplies hints, and the helper *doesn't* call the problem by its name (not necessarily using the word "alcoholism" at first), the taboo is reinforced. The helper says, by eloquent omission, "This is too sensitive [shameful, unnatural] a subject for us to talk about."

Helpers who talk about parental drinking in a comfortable, non-threatening environment make it a universal rather than an individual problem. Here is a social worker's account of a five-year-old girl's progress:

> The little girl's behavior played out a lot what was going on at home, but she could not talk about the drinking. Even as mother became more sensitized through going to Al-Anon for close to a year, still, to try to talk with the little girl, when we'd say we can talk about this she would start every kind of diversionary tactic, running around the room, just really falling apart. She picked up a lot of taboos in talking about it.

Mother would be uncomfortable talking to the daughter about it because what if she said something to the husband, she was afraid he would accuse her of putting ideas in our daughter's head, this kind of thing. But the year I saw her, they did some training in the public school system. The following year I only worked with the mother, and the little girl was seeing someone in the public schools. The counselor told me that the little girl still did not talk about it, until one day the program had done some training in the classroom, and they talked about drinking and alcoholism in the first-grade classroom. The counselor said she was like a different child when she walked into the therapy room. She walked in and said, "You know my daddy is an alcoholic," and proceeded to talk about all the effects of his drinking, how it scared her, what the problems were. I mean, it was just being allowed; the program in school just made clear it wasn't a taboo subject, she could talk about it. None of us could make her feel that.

Communicating Key Ideas about Alcoholism

When the helper mentions parental drinking or alcoholism and the child remains within earshot, the helper can take it as evidence of a receptivity to more information. There are five basic notions that the child inwardly wants to believe and needs to hear in order to proceed any further. All five can be mentioned, very simply, in about a minute's time, but giving the child any one can help immensely.

The five notions cannot be ranked in any order of importance: They are all important. Children will fix on, and cling to the one or two that are most meaningful to them.

"You are not alone."

Children of alcoholics are ashamed of their families, and the more they struggle to keep their secret, the more ashamed of it they become. They prefer isolation to the risk of having that secret discovered, and they never imagine that their own friends and classmates have the same problem. They describe a relief bordering on exhilaration when they meet, or even just hear about, other children who share their predicament.

"It's not your fault."

We have seen how these children, through the natural self-centeredness of their childhood perceptions, as well as through both the alcoholic and nonalcoholic parents' explicit blame, accumulate deep-seated guilt. This guilt contributes to low self-esteem, and, in terms of the specific objective of intervention, can keep children from feeling worthy of help.

"It's not the alcoholic's fault either."

Given daily and dramatic proof that the bottle is more important to their parents than they are, children build hatred and anger toward their parents while they blame themselves. The anger is often much too dangerous to express, or even acknowledge, and it comes out in harmful, indirect ways. Children who hear that their parents are sick, not evil, may argue vociferously, and it may be a long time before they really believe they are good people who love them; that they don't *choose* to hurt those they love by drinking. Not many children subjected to it can readily accept that alcoholism is a disease and the alcoholic a sick person. But each time someone trusted presents alcoholism in that light, most children feel more open to further discussion because they would dearly like to believe it.

"Alcoholics can and do recover."

Often a child's initial reason for seeking help is to help the alcoholic stop drinking. While it is true that children and other family members who understand alcoholism can increase the chances of the alcoholic's recovery (just as members who don't understand it can diminish them), the child can no more stop the drinking than cause it. But the child's earliest disclosure often relies on the hope that the parent can get better, and that hope is to some degree justified and must be nourished. As the children begin to feel better as a result of the help they themselves receive, that initial goal of helping the alcoholic is put into more realistic perspective.

"You need and deserve help for yourself."

Some children find it more difficult than others to admit that their parent's drinking disturbs and affects them profoundly. Anger and resentment contribute to that denial; so do the adolescent need for independence and the male's facade of invulnerability. Many children with family alcoholism have in common with untrained professionals the attitude that the only thing that will really help is the parent's sobriety. Short of that, they fail to believe that they *can* feel better. It is useful for the helper to present examples of the kinds of coping behavior children can learn from one another, and how they help the child remain sane and happy whether or not the parent is drinking. The children don't know what they have to learn: how to vent emotions constructively; how to stay out of pointless arguments; how to keep the drinking from interfering with things that are important and pleasurable to them, as some examples. They need to define the problem as their problem and see that the means for addressing it lie within their grasp.

Helping the Child Acknowledge the Parent's Alcoholism

Many children of alcoholics know, deep down, the name of their parent's affliction. The pivotal moment, the step that makes it possible for them to begin to shape their own lives, is the moment they use the word out loud. Earlier in this chapter was the grateful account of how a 14-year-old girl was helped by a classroom teacher who turned a potentially conflict-laden showdown into her crucial intervention. That teacher, Mr. C., sent her down to her favorite gym teacher. What happened next is recounted by that gym teacher.

> She came down and sat in my office for maybe an hour and a half, and did not open her mouth. I said, "S., you can stay here all day if you want, I'll make you a cup of tea and you can sit here, and when you're ready to tell me whatever it is you want to tell me, then you can just spit it out." I had an idea what it was, but I didn't want to be the one to say anything. Because I think that was S.'s most important step, when she heard herself say, "My mother is an alcoholic." She couldn't say the word, she would start, she would say, "My mother . . ." and I'd say, "OK, you have a problem with your mother," and she'd say, "Yep," and then clam up for a little longer. And then I'd say, "OK, don't rush, whenever you're ready." It took her an hour and a half just to say the words "My mother is an alcoholic." Once she got it out, then everything was easy. Then any suggestion I made was accepted wholeheartedly.

More often, and particularly at younger ages, children don't really know that their parent has alcoholism; they simply know that drinking is a problem in the household. For these children to understand their parent's alcoholism as illness, they need both to learn more about the disease and to work through their own emotions about it. That is, they must learn enough about alcoholism's symptoms and effects to recognize their parent in the definition; and they must feel better about the term (less emotional, less stigmatized and ashamed) in order to apply it to someone they love and depend upon.

The girl described above went on to become a trained group leader, conducting extended workshops, some composed exclusively of children with family alcoholism, others open to any youngster and focused more generally on alcohol education. (These workshops are described in detail in Chapter 9.) Below is her account of a seventh-grade boy who participated in one of her basic alcohol-education workshops:

> When we were just beginning, talking about alcohol, he started talking about one time, he was in Revere, and his father was shitfaced and he was driving down the street and he hit a telephone pole, and the cops

pulled the whole family in. He said, "But that's just only because my
father was drunk that one time." And then he started talking about
other times his father got shitty. "He sits down at home at night with his
beer, and you know, he just sits there and drinks. He doesn't cause no
trouble and stuff." The kid was worried about it, but I don't think he
thought that his father was an alcoholic. At the end of the group I just
said, "If you want to be called for another group, just write on a piece
of paper what kind of group you want to be in." He wrote that he
wanted to go into a group for children who are worried about someone's drinking. In that group, he wasn't afraid to talk, but in the beginning he still didn't think his father was an alcoholic. He got along good
with his father, they never fought or nothing, but his father did drink a
lot and got into quite a few accidents with his drinking, and whenever
he went out for an occasion or something he'd always come home
shitty. At the end he just said, "Hey, my father is an alcoholic, you
know?"

Very often helpers are reluctant to introduce the word "alcoholism."
At the outset, when children are just starting to open up about their
parent's drinking, it may be acceptable and even appropriate to avoid
the term. Doing so is simply recognizing that the stigma attached to it
can threaten continued help, and that children may need time before
they can call a spade a spade and begin to face the problem. But
professionals sometimes prolong this period of delicacy, at bottom
because they themselves still attach a great deal of shame and aversion
to the word and fail to think of it as an illness. Would anyone hesitate
to use terms like "heart disease" or "diabetes" in helping a child understand his parent's condition?

Just as an alcoholic's recovery depends on his saying to others, "I'm
an alcoholic," so the children must be able to call the disease by its
name or they cannot hope to deal with it satisfactorily. And the professional, far from shrinking from the use of the word, must help the
child to say it. Only when that happens will the word lose its power to
shame and stigmatize.

Facilitating Ongoing Help

The ultimate goal of intervention is to prepare children to accept
ongoing help suited to their needs and capacities. In most cases the
intervention agent has neither the time nor the training to provide that
help. Tragically, in many communities resources that directly address
family alcoholism are scarce or nonexistent. Chapter 9 covers strategies
for building such programs. Alateen, the resource par excellence, is
one of the subjects of Chapter 10.

Generic counseling or recreational resources are important as adjuncts to, and too often as substitutes for, programs specifically structured for children with family alcoholism. The staffs of these agencies would greatly increase their effectiveness if they had thorough training in alcohol and alcoholism; but even without it, they offer youngsters a place to talk, activities to enjoy, and the opportunity to make friends. They afford the child a modicum of structure, stability, and praise the family is not providing. Thus, the professional who helps a child join a program at the Y, the drama club at school, or an athletic team has contributed to the child's effort to live a happy and fulfilling life even while the parent is drinking.

At this stage, too, helpers must remain realistic. Sometimes the most they can hope for is the chance to expose children to resources and outlets they may not yet be ready to use with consistency. If it is difficult for any teenager (or adult, for that matter) to join a new group or try a new activity, imagine how much more frightening it can be for a child with the insecurity and self-deprecation that comes from having a parent with alcoholism. Helpers are wise to anticipate a negative reaction to the referrals they make: "That counselor is off the wall" or "The kids down there are too straight and serious."

Professionals must be sympathetic to children's fear of failure and rejection, but it is essential that they help them understand and overcome it. The child who finds every option and every resource unacceptable is simply afraid. She can't be allowed to cling indefinitely to the one person she has been able to trust so far, for the most important thing she must learn is that she can find and use her own lasting supports.

Chapter 8
HELPING SCENARIOS

Roleplay is a fundamental part of the training process for intervention agents because it enables professionals to test, practice, analyze, and refine their strategies, and to experience in safety their own and the children's emotions at all stages of the interaction. This chapter approximates in writing some of the features of roleplay, though the script is better used as an adjunct than a substitute. Professionals who do not have a training workshop to prepare for intervention would be wise to ask a colleague or friend to help them simulate situations they may face.

Five scenarios are presented in the following pages. Each scenario begins with trained helpers who are committed to a limited and realistic intervention role with children of alcoholics. In each scenario, family alcoholism is *not* the presenting problem. The child has not openly requested help with a parent's drinking. Instead, each scenario represents the first attempt to discuss parental drinking on the part of a youth professional or other helper who has an existing relationship with the child. That relationship may be warm, marginal, sporadic, or even adversarial, but it has a context that has little or nothing to do with drinking or alcoholism. Furthermore, these are situations in which the helper has reason to speculate on the presence of parental alcoholism, but no hard data. Family members are assumed to be actively denying the problem and discouraging the child from seeking help. In other words, these scenarios illustrate the most difficult part of the intervention process: the first direct offer of help.

The scenarios are based on recollections of individual incidents or composites of interactions, as related by children and professionals. Each is presented with its antecedent details: the helper's role and relationship to the child; the indicators to which the helper is responding; the setting of the interaction; and the child's family circumstances and feelings at the outset of the conversation. Each scenario is followed by a discussion of what occurred and a summary of likely variations.

THE CLASSROOM TEACHER

Mrs. Hoff is a sixth-grade teacher. She tries to balance firmness and a structure of daily routines and classroom rules with her own rather motherly disposition.

Kenneth is eleven. His father has alcoholism. In the past year, Father has grown increasingly abusive toward Mother, but not yet toward Kenneth or his two older sisters. Mother threw Kenneth's father out of the house for a short time, then "took him back." But the situation didn't improve in spite of Father's promise to "cut down," so Mother recently threw him out again. Both of Kenneth's parents have always regarded him as "his father's son." He tends to side with his father although he has been repeatedly disappointed and hurt, and lately frightened, by him.

Kenneth's style most closely resembles that of the family Mascot. He tries to make the family laugh to reduce his anxiety and fear, and the family uses him for that purpose. He is hyperactive, unable to concentrate for more than a few minutes; consequently, he is a poor achiever and requires regular discipline in school, where he plays the role of the class clown. He desperately wants his father back in the house; but when he is around, Kenneth is on edge, always ready to try to defuse an explosive situation. He is starting to experiment with drinking, and sometimes fantasizes about joining his father wherever he is living.

Mrs. Hoff has a natural but not special relationship with Kenneth. He requires a great deal of attention; often annoys her, and she sometimes shows it; and besides, she doesn't believe that he should be rewarded for being so demanding. She began to suspect family alcoholism in his case when she taught the first five sessions of her alcohol education unit early in March. It is late April and she has almost finished the second and final week of alcohol education.

As often happens, Kenneth's reactions during the unit were revealing, and Mrs. Hoff is quite certain he has an alcoholic parent. While he still made jokes from time to time, he was noticeably more attentive than usual. He thought drinking was "great," and spoke admiringly of older friends who drank, always equating drinking with drunkenness. He seemed to know more than his classmates about the varieties of alcoholic drinks.

The day before, the unit turned to alcoholism. One girl spoke up about her father, who "stopped drinking and went to AA." Kenneth avidly listened to her and to the ensuing discussion, then began to joke and fidget, became disruptive, and asked to go to the bathroom.

Today, Mrs. Hoff showed a short animated film, *All Bottled Up*, narrated by several teenagers with alcoholic parents. She left the lights off for several minutes after the film. Kenneth kept his head on his desk, most unusual for him. Yet when the discussion started he was unable to sit still, distracting his friends and paying no attention whatever.

Mrs. Hoff knows that Kenneth will have about fifteen minutes after the final bell before he must board his schoolbus. Following her custom, she waits until just before the bell and quietly asks Kenneth to see her after class. She knows that anyone who might overhear would see this as her typical way of dealing with students whose behavior has been unsatisfactory. And that is how Kenneth himself sees her order; he expects to be reprimanded for his behavior as he approaches her desk in the room in which they are now alone.

> *Mrs. Hoff:* You had kind of a rough time today, didn't you, Kenneth? *(He shrugs.)* Any particular reason? *(Shrugs again.)* Is there anything going on at home or anything else I can help you with?
>
> *Kenneth:* No, everything's okay. I was just bored, I guess. Besides, everyone was talking, not just me.
>
> *Mrs. Hoff:* How about the alcohol unit? You seemed to like that.
>
> *Kenneth:* It was okay. I'm a little tired of it. Is it almost over?
>
> *Mrs. Hoff:* Tomorrow's the last day. What did you think of the film?
>
> *Kenneth:* It was okay. I thought it was a little dumb.
>
> *Mrs. Hoff:* Really? Why?
>
> *Kenneth: (He shrugs.)* I just thought it was dumb.
>
> *Mrs. Hoff:* I'm sorry you didn't like it. It would help me if you could say what you didn't like about it. Maybe I shouldn't use it anymore?
>
> *Kenneth:* It was okay, it was just a little weird. The colors were nice. I liked the part when the girl goes up the chimney.
>
> *Mrs. Hoff:* Yes, I liked the scene where the parents are arguing and the roof is coming off the house, and the kid goes out and finds someone to talk to. *(Pause)* I show that film because it's important to know about alcoholism, to know it's an illness and that it isn't anyone's fault. Because it's so common. I'm sure there are four or five kids in this class who have this problem in their families, and lots of other kids who have friends who do.
>
> *Kenneth:* I know this kid, his father gets drunk and beats up his mother, so she threw him out. But he wants her to let him back.
>
> *Mrs. Hoff:* But is he afraid of his father when he's drinking?
>
> *Kenneth:* I don't know. That's all I know, he doesn't talk about it much.
>
> *Mrs. Hoff:* Sure, it's hard to talk about, because he loves his father.

That's why the film kept saying, find someone you can talk to, instead of letting it all build up inside you.

Kenneth: I have to get my bus.

Mrs. Hoff: I know. I just wanted to tell you . . . well, I have to tell you I didn't like your behavior today, but mostly I wanted to say that I understand that sometimes there are reasons for it, reasons you might be in a bad mood, something you're worried about. And I want you to know you can talk to me about whatever's on your mind. Just between us. Maybe it would help. Okay? *(He nods.)* Okay. *(He leaves.)*

Discussion

Mrs. Hoff set out to establish a helpful, understanding, sympathetic tone. She wanted to give Kenneth the opportunity to confide in her, but from his behavior in class she correctly foresaw his unwillingness to do so. She succeeded in conveying her concern and future availability; took advantage of her alcohol unit to raise the subject of drinking and alcoholism; and briefly mentioned some of the key ideas about alcoholism that Kenneth needed to hear. In doing so, she also presented herself as someone who is knowledgeable about alcoholism and comfortable with talking about it. And she did it all in about five minutes.

She might have approached Kenneth at his desk, or sat side by side with him in the two front seats. But Kenneth was expecting to be reprimanded by his teacher, not comforted by a caring adult. He might well have been made more uneasy by such an immediate and abrupt change in the familiar ground rules. As it was, he doubtless caught on early that this was not to be a typical disciplinary session and may have preferred one. And Mrs. Hoff probably did not need to underline her desire to help by choice of a different seat. The contrast between what Kenneth was expecting and what he found served to increase the impact of her tone and her words.

Mrs. Hoff didn't push. She didn't hold Kenneth longer than he could stand. She didn't subject him to lengthy silences. She asked questions meant to be inviting but not demanding, and though she surmised that he was talking about himself when he mentioned "his friend," she allowed him the safety of the third person. Still, Kenneth couldn't wait to escape from her. Yet he felt so hurt and desperate about his family situation that he couldn't resist the chance to get her reaction.

Afterward he tries not to think about it but he can't help himself. He's not sure whether or not Mrs. Hoff knows his family secret. He fervently hopes that she will continue to treat him as she always has and is relieved the next day when she returns to form. But without knowing it, he begins to think about her differently and behave accordingly. In the ongoing weeks, he finds casual occasions to test her sincerity and her concern. Does she believe him when he explains why he forgot his homework? He begins to like it when she asks him how he's doing. And perhaps, some weeks later, after a particularly frightening night or a bitter disappointment, he waits for her after class.

Variations

The helper in this case was a sixth-grade teacher, but might easily have been a teacher at the secondary level, or someone involved in recreational groups (a youth program worker or scout leader), even an employment counselor—anyone who can initiate group alcohol-education activities. The many advantages of such activities in identifying and approaching children, discussed in Chapter 6, are manifest in this case. Chapter 9 also describes peer education methods. Trained peer leaders can conduct structured alcohol education workshops and be every bit as effective as teachers in identifying and reaching children of alcoholics.

It happens with surprising frequency that children are willing to talk in class about a parent's drinking, as one child did in Mrs. Hoff's room. The children who do are worth their weight in gold and twice that when they can talk about how their parent is recovering.

THE GUIDANCE COUNSELOR

Mr. Dorr is the guidance counselor for almost two hundred junior high school students. With that kind of caseload, he can manage only a couple of visits each year with many of his students; the ones who are regularly in trouble receive most of his attention. Then there is the paperwork. Somehow, though, he keeps his zeal in spite of these constraints. He knows, and remembers, how hard it can be to be thirteen years old.

Mr. Dorr receives a note from an eighth-grade English teacher: "Martha L.'s work has really fallen off this quarter. She says her Dad's in the hospital. Could you talk with her?"

He checks with two of her other teachers. They say that Martha, an A student in academically advanced classes, owes a science project and an important history paper. She has assured them she will get her work in soon. When one teacher asked, she said, "My house is a little crazy right now, that's all," and made an exaggerated, almost comical gesture, and rolled her eyes.

The guidance counselor schedules an appointment with Martha. He wants to help her vent her anxiety and distress and make himself available during this crisis. He also wants to relieve her of some of the pressure she must feel about her schoolwork and is confident that her teachers will cooperate. He does not suspect family alcoholism. However, from his training, he is familiar with the pattern of assiduous achievement, unswerving responsibility, pseudomaturity, and a desire to please, which characterizes some children of alcoholics.

Martha's father was hospitalized because his drinking aggravated his stomach ulcers. His blood pressure is also alarmingly high. He is being treated as a medical patient; the hospital staff did not diagnose and Martha's mother certainly did not describe his problem as alcoholism. Martha feels little love for her father; she thinks of him as a drunk who bullies and verbally abuses her mother and brother. His only physical violence consists of breaking dishes and furniture, but that is more than enough to create a constant threat of harm. In a way, she is relieved to have him out of the house, and has even fantasized that he might die, though these feelings make her feel extremely guilty.

But her mother is so upset and anxious that Martha ends up spending more time than ever catering to her needs and fulfilling her responsibilities. Because her mother is at the hospital virtually every afternoon and evening, Martha shops, cleans, and looks after her younger brother. A few times a week, she also has to visit her father. And she has to be ready to comfort and calm her mother. Between the emotional strain and the physical overexhaustion, she can't meet her school responsibilities or participate in the extracurricular activities to which she is committed. These added worries keep her from sleeping soundly.

She approaches Mr. Dorr's office with trepidation. She barely knows him. She feels inadequate and self-critical because of her poor schoolwork and expects him to castigate her. But she also knows she has a legitimate reason for her recent grades, and is almost confident that, with minimal disclosure (and certainly no mention of her father's drinking problem!), she can enlist his help with her teachers.

Mr. Dorr: Hello, Martha. Have a seat. You know, you do beautiful work all year and no one calls you in to pat you on the back, say "Keep up the good work." Then as soon as your marks fall a little, Mr. Dorr calls you down and says (*with exaggerated severity*) "What's going on here, Martha?" (*He smiles; so does she.*) I don't want it to be that way. I'd like it if you'd stop by when things are going well, too, tell me about all your As, or just to chat. You don't have to wait for me to send for you, you know.

Martha: There won't be any As to talk about at the rate I'm going. I guess you know I'm behind in just about every subject.

Mr. Dorr: Yes, so I've heard.

Martha: I told my teachers I'd get the work in before the end of the marking period.

Mr. Dorr: That's fine, if you can get it done.

Martha: I think I can.

Mr. Dorr: But if you're under a lot of pressure at home, we might be able to make some allowances. You know, give you more time, then go back and change your marks or something. Your grades are so good, no one wants to spoil them because you're having some kind of problem.

Martha: It's just that my father is in the hospital, so everything's a little crazy at my house.

Mr. Dorr: I'm sorry to hear that. Is he all right?

Martha: I guess he's getting better. He's got high blood pressure and bleeding ulcers. He's supposed to come out next Tuesday, but he'll have to stay in bed. I don't know how long.

Mr. Dorr: It must be really hard for all of you.

Martha: It is. My mother's pretty nervous as it is. Now she's really jumpy and worried. And she spends a lot of time at the hospital, so I have to do a lot of the chores in the house.

Mr. Dorr: Like what?

(Martha describes in detail a typical day.)

Mr. Dorr: It's a wonder you can keep your eyes open. Does your mother know what kind of strain you're under? Does she know what's going on in school?

Martha: She must know. I don't know. She doesn't need to worry about me on top of everything else.

Mr. Dorr: I think she does, Martha. Even though you help her so much, she's your mother and you need and deserve her help too. Maybe she can take some of the pressure off you.

Martha: I don't know; she's so freaked out. But I guess she'll find out sooner or later.

Mr. Dorr: If you mean your grades, don't worry about them, please. *(He emphasizes again that Martha has her own legitimate needs in this situation, but no one can help meet them unless she expresses them.)*

(Martha nods and says, "I know" in an unconvincing way. Mr. Dorr tries to return to the subject of her father.)

Mr. Dorr: I guess your father will need to be on a very strict diet?

Martha: Yeah, but I doubt he'll stick to it. He's used to doing whatever he wants. This isn't the first time he's had these problems. I don't know. *(Long pause.)*

Mr. Dorr: What don't you know?

Martha: No, 'cause my father is a very intelligent man, but when it comes to this—Sometimes I think he just doesn't care. But maybe it'll be different, maybe he'll really be scared this time.

Mr. Dorr: Oh, I'm sure he's scared, I'm sure he doesn't want to be sick again.

Martha: No, I think he doesn't believe it. He thinks he can just go on the way he does and nothing will happen.

Mr. Dorr: Maybe he believes it but he can't help himself. *(She makes a skeptical and disapproving face.)* Look at all the heavy smokers who keep smoking after the doctor's told them their lungs are shot. Look at all the heavy drinkers who keep drinking—the doctor tells them their stomach's going, their liver's going, they're in pain, their families are miserable about it—but they don't know how to live without alcohol.

Martha: I think that's just an excuse. Like my father, my mother cooks him special meals and everything; he throws them in the garbage, calls it slop, the whole bit. He's really hard to please.

Mr. Dorr: But your mother keeps trying.

Martha: Sure she does; what else can she do?

Mr. Dorr: Does your father drink at all?

Martha: No, he's not allowed to.

Mr. Dorr: I know he wouldn't be allowed to drink, but you said he doesn't stick to his diet anyway, so I thought I'd ask.

Martha: Well, mostly he does. I mean once in a while he'll take a drink, but my mother flips out on him. You should see what happens when he brings home greasy hamburgers and french fries, 'cause he loves them but he's not supposed to eat them. . . .

(Martha follows with a long anecdote, fleeing from the subject of drinking. Immediately thereafter, she talks about making up her schoolwork, praises her teachers, and talks about her swimming team activities. Mr. Dorr has long since abandoned the thought of bringing up her father's drinking again today. Their time draws to an end.)

Mr. Dorr: I'm glad we talked today, Martha, and I'll talk to your teachers about the work you owe. I don't want you to worry about it right now. We all want to help you get through this rough time. Let's make another appointment, okay? How about this time next week? You don't look too happy about it. *(She shrugs and smiles faintly.)* If I made you uncomfortable, I'm sorry. I just think it's important that you let out some of your feelings when so much is going on, and I try to help you do that. But next time, just say, "I don't want to talk about that," if I bring up something that you don't want to talk about. I won't force you. Okay? And in case I've never said it before, nothing you say here leaves here—ever. Now you have a good day today, okay, and please, don't worry. See you next week, or come in sooner if you feel like it. Take care.

Discussion

Martha is the type of child who has a very hard time asking for or accepting help. Her tendency is to disavow her problems. On the other hand, she respects authority and order, and is worried and guilty about her schoolwork. She responds somewhat reflexively to her counselor's role and function and less to his personality and style. She sees his role in narrow terms: to straighten her out in school.

Mr. Dorr's task is to use his office and his manner to broaden these terms. He recognizes that, in all likelihood, Martha has no one to whom she comes for comfort and understanding. Above all, he wants her to begin to like the experience of release and support. From that perspective, he may regret his direct approach on the subject of her father's drinking. So great was her need to talk that her perpetual guard had been dropped until he raised the subject. Since he has the authority and opportunity to see Martha regularly, he needn't be so direct in the first interview.

However, there are also good reasons for proceeding as Mr. Dorr did. The risk he took can be easily overstated. Martha has strong defenses, and can be trusted to protect herself if she has to. But her need to talk may outweigh her need to deny, particularly during times of crisis. If she had responded to his mention of drinking with an outpouring of words or tears, no one would fault him for being direct. It should be noted that he asked about the drinking casually, in the same spirit as his other questions. He didn't take a deep breath first to indicate that this is a really sensitive subject.

It was chiefly her reaction to the subject that sustained his suspicions about family alcoholism. In particular, she said that her father drinks in spite of his condition, that her mother "flips out," and that this is apparently a recurring problem. Her flight from the subject was also significant. Prior to this, alcoholism was just one possible contributing factor. Now Mr. Dorr can back off a little, try to build her trust and her appetite for sympathy and support, but now he also has a clearer sense of his long-range goals.

Mr. Dorr tries not to take personally Martha's reluctance to see him next week. He knows it would be difficult for her no matter who he was or what he said. He trusts his perceptions of what she needs from him. He accepts that she will resist, albeit with ambivalence, his effort to help her talk about her father's drinking and its effect on her family and herself. He may avoid the subject for a brief time, but he knows it is his responsibility to find ways to address it.

In this case, Mr. Dorr is justified in relieving Martha of some of her academic pressures. But sometimes this can be overdone. In some instances, when school personnel learn of a child's family problem, they are reluctant to place any demands on him (or her). Less work is expected of him, and he gets excused from class whenever he wants to see the nurse or counselor. One of the skills many children of alcoholics learn is the ability to manipulate people through their sympathy and concern. The child is not being helped when he is allowed to take refuge in his problem. At some point, it is only by insisting that the child meet reasonable obligations that the school helps him to overcome his turmoil.

Variations

Alcoholism can be expected to create crises making it impossible for even the most stoic of children to proceed in their accustomed ways. The helpers to whom the child is somehow accountable—such as a work supervisor, employment counselor, probation officer, or coach— are ideally situated to notice the signs of disruption and explore the possible reasons. Obviously, many problems may underlie the child's behavior; the helper is simply obliged to consider alcoholism among them.

Some children, instead of merely neglecting their schoolwork, react to the strain and lack of attention in Martha's situation by acting out in delinquent or self-destructive ways. They may stay out late at night, skip school, fight with their friends and siblings, or find sanctuary in sleep. Young children may show marked regression.

Others for whom some aspects of the above scenario might apply are child therapists and hospital personnel. If a parent is hospitalized, nurses, social workers, or physicians might see it as their duty to "steal" time during a child's visit to offer an encouraging word. If the patient's symptoms are often associated with alcohol abuse, they might find that a question analogous to Mr. Dorr's question about Martha's father's diet will be helpful to the child as well as the patient.

THE CLINICIAN

The language of a small child is difficult to reproduce, and particularly in play therapy nonverbal communication can be the most important form of intercourse. In order to illustrate constructive approaches in working with young children (ages 4 to 7), it may be best simply to relate some case histories recounted by Suzanne Pratt and Karin Schaeffer of the Cambridge-Somerville Mental Health and Retardation Center's Preschool Unit.

I had a little girl, she was five. The referral problem was that the child had a poor self-image and put herself in situations with other kids where she was always the victim. When she came to diagnostic nursery school, the intake had said nothing about drinking. The parents were separated. In diagnostic, the little girl drew a picture of Mommy and said her worst dream was that Mommy threw up in the bathtub. That turned on a red light for us. In doing the interpretation, we asked the mother about drinking and she said, yes, she had had a history of alcoholism but she didn't drink anymore. She's a bartender and sometimes she is tempted, and in fact did stay after work once or twice and had a drink with the waitresses.

The little girl came in to see me again, and at one point started drawing a mask that she put up in front of her face; and it included a throat, which is unusual for children, to draw in a throat. So I asked her, "What goes down that throat? Could it be milk, juice, booze?"

She immediately held the mask out in front of her face and said, "Yes, booze goes down that throat."

"Well, what do you do then? What happens when booze goes down there?"

"I can only sleep when I drink booze."

"Can you take care of your little girl?"

"No, my little girl has to take care of herself, and she has to take care of me." She put down the mask. "You know, my Mommy drinks."

We talked about what that was like, and she said that she was scared, that her mommy couldn't take care of her; she had to comb her mommy's hair. I said I needed to talk to her mommy about that and she said, "Fine!" I said, "What would you like me to say?" She made up a whole list of things to say to her mommy:

1. Mommy, what does it feel like to drink?
2. I worry about being safe. There are lots of scary things I don't like to be scared of.
3. When you bring friends home they scream and wake me up.

I asked her if she wanted to be at the meeting and she said she did. We met the next week with her mother. I said, "Do you want me to read the list or do you want to?"

She said she wanted to, and turned immediately to her mother and said, "Mommy, what does it feel like to drink?" And started crying.

"I don't drink anymore," her mother said.

"Mommy, what does it feel like to drink?"

I had to help the mother answer. She said, "Well, it doesn't feel very good." The little girl went through the whole list of questions, sitting in her mother's lap, crying.

I asked her mother what it felt like, and she said, "I didn't know that she knew I drank."

That comes up a lot with little kids, that the kids know what's going on and it's a big, dark secret. The parents know that they're drinking and it's a problem; the kids know it; but the parents don't know that the kids know, and the kids *know* that the parents don't know that they know. Part of the time they just need someone to help them communicate it. It turned out that this girl was desperate because at one point, when the little girl tried to wake her mother up one morning and she couldn't wake her up, she started playing with matches and set fire to the bedroom. And that had been really terrifying for her, that her mother had not been awake and had not been able to stop her. This kid was one of the strongest kids I've ever met; she just needed someone to facilitate the communication between them. And [her] mother [later] was able to hear it and bear it and respond to her.

There's a four-year-old boy that I see whose mom had been abused by [his] alcoholic uncles, her brothers. The kid had witnessed a great deal of this, and was very, very frightened. And I saw the child. He had nightmares about his mother dying, and his feeling was one of total lack of control. There was nothing he could do about it. He wished he were a big, strong superhero so he could protect his mother, and he was very afraid she was going to die. As she got her life together and got an apartment, and finally got with a boyfriend who didn't drink, he said, "You know, I'm really safe now—Mommy's safe and I'm safe." But the kids don't say it without help. When they start saying that one animal beat up another animal, you usually try to say, "What is wrong with that animal that he keeps beating up on other animals? I wonder if she's been drinking?" More often than not, that's the answer. And if it's not, they just go on. Really, if you're wrong they just ignore you! If you're right they think, well, this person knows what's going on and it's okay to talk to her.

Discussion

Children are easy to underestimate. It is common for parents to tell one another, somewhat wishfully, that their children can't possibly understand something, particularly when they take pains to keep them from understanding it. Some helping professionals doubtless begin their careers with a share of this bias, but experience teaches them that most children know—and with help can verbalize—much more than they had imagined.

Three- and four-year-olds know when drinking is the problem. They can be fooled on occasion, but they have ample opportunity over time to discover and rediscover the discrepancy between what the alcoholic or nonalcoholic parent says is going on and what really seems to be the case. Parental denial can damage the child's grasp of reality with enduring and tragic consequences, but it cannot completely obliterate the child's perceptions.

Not every child would have the courage to persevere in spite of the mother's denial, as did the girl in the first anecdote. But most children would still know what they know, and continue to know it in secret. The sooner the child can receive confirmation of his or her private interpretations of the mother's behavior, the less the child's sense of reality may be impaired.

Many helpers tend to agree when a parent says, "Well, Philip was only three when my spouse stopped drinking, so he really wasn't affected." As noted in Chapter 3, families often continue long after the drinking has ended to behave as they did at its worst. Besides, the three-year-old has already seen and felt a great deal.

> My brother Tommy was only a baby when she was drinking real heavy and stuff. And when he was starting to realize what was going on she stopped, you know, she went sober. He was about three and he still knew, like, when she broke out, she was sober for a year and then she broke out. He knew, you know. "Mommy's drunk, Mommy's drunk," he used to say it all the time. And one time my mother went to the hospital, she had her teeth taken out and she was on medication, so when she came back she was all blurry, and Tommy said, "Oh, what are you, drunk, Mommy?" You know, he thought she was drunk.

One common assumption professionals make about small children, on ethical, legal, or pragmatic grounds is that they are too young to be the first or only family member to apprehend the truth of the family's situation. Some programs accordingly limit their services to children with one parent in treatment. Some even work with children only in the presence of their parent. This approach excludes most children and enormously restrains those it includes.

The child therapist's ultimate goal is to enable children to express their fears and needs to their parents in a constructive and useful way, and then to help the parents fulfill those needs. The clinician knows that these needs must sometimes first be expressed privately, in a very safe place, especially where family alcoholism is concerned. But their responsibility and their legal grounds are vague when the child's rights and needs conflict with those of the parent. Educators, as noted in Chapter 9, are more protected from legal risk. Clinicians need parental consent and sanction. But if they can assure parents that children's talking about drinking is vital to their interests, and is best done apart from their parents at first, permission may be granted.

To be sure, it is a difficult and critical task of the professional to keep the child from becoming too much the focus and agent of the family's change. But very often the young child is the only one who is honest about the role of drinking in the home. In many cases, it is the family's dedication to the safety and protection of the child that leads to a concerted effort to change, once the child has introduced the subject of alcoholism through a counselor.

Variations

The school remains the most promising setting for systematic intervention with young children. In the lower elementary grades there is less equivocation about the school's responsibility for emotional development, and a more consistent effort is made to diagnose impediments to learning. Children evaluated as having special needs receive individual and small-group attention, and the parent is required to be involved in the educational decisions and corrective activities that the school initiates. Most parents grant the school automatic respect and authority; many others are afraid to confront school personnel. In either case, the school often has an excellent chance to secure parental cooperation, or at least, passive acquiescence.

Special-education teachers must routinely consider the possibility of family alcoholism among their children. Hyperactivity, learning disabilities, bedwetting, and inability to get along with peers are all associated with family alcoholism in studies that are admittedly far from conclusive. But it is certain that the behavior reactions illustrated in Chapter 4 begin to manifest themselves at very early ages.

One of the most exciting aspects of CASPAR's program in Somerville, described in Chapter 9, is the work being done with children in grades 1 through 6. The key agents are the resource room or special-education teachers. With a CASPAR staff member, teachers conduct groups during school hours, composed mostly or entirely of children with family alcoholism, all attending with parental approval. In some cases, approval was obtained even when both parents were alcoholic, and the groups were responsible for several parents' joining or returning to treatment.

THE PROBATION OFFICER

Ronnie, 16, was just arrested for the second time. The charge: assault and battery on a police officer. The way he tells it, he and his friends were just standing around near the housing project where they live when the cops who always give them a hard time came and started pushing them off their corner. "The cops were looking for trouble,"

Ronnie says, "and since everybody had been drinking a little, they found it."

For his first offense, riding in a car stolen by a friend, Ronnie got a suspended sentence and a year's probation. He had been drinking on that occasion, too. He's been taken to the police station twice without being charged. Because this recent offense occurred while he is still on probation, Ronnie is a little worried that he may actually have to "go away," but he knows guys who did a lot worse and never spent a night in jail. Although he secretly envies the respect shown on the street for the ones who come back from stints in "the can," and the juvenile institution where he might be sent is supposed to be "a country club," he much prefers to keep his freedom.

Both of Ronnie's parents are alcoholic. He hasn't seen his father in about eight years, though his father is thought to live in a nearby town. Ronnie talks about finding his father, sometimes with the intention of telling him off, other times, to see how he is doing. His feelings about his mother are extremely mixed, too, but they are closely guarded. He is fiercely loyal to her, always ready to fight for her honor. He may complain about her to his friends on occasion, but if one of them were to malign her, Ronnie would go for his throat.

Ronnie plays the tough guy role without conviction; sometimes it feels to him like a reputation he has to live up to. But when he drinks, this role comes naturally, and even the friends he drinks with have commented on how nasty he can be. When they tell him he can't handle his liquor, he tries to take it as simply another putdown, part of the natural give-and-take of the street corner.

Ronnie is nominally enrolled in school. He is waiting to be admitted to a special vocational work-study program. In the meantime, he goes to school just often enough to keep after his counselor about transferring him.

Having been arraigned, Ronnie must now see his probation officer, Mr. Lavin, who, along with his colleagues, had been compelled to undergo alcoholism training. Mr. Lavin strongly and vocally disagreed with the views of the trainers. First of all, his own experience as a teenager and that of all the kids he sees have convinced him that almost all kids drink to get drunk. He believes that most kids get into some kind of trouble that doesn't indicate any long-term problem. Second, he feels that, whatever programs he can come up with, he can't do much for a kid who goes back every night to an awful family situation. However, part of his training involved observing a time-limited group for juveniles with alcohol-related problems. To his surprise, the kids seemed to like it, in their way, and to get something out of it. He was most moved by the number of youthful offenders who were able to talk, no doubt for the first time, about the drinking of their parents. He doesn't know much about Ronnie's background, but he thinks he would be an appropriate candidate for a group. He could more or less force Ronnie to attend such a group, but he would prefer it if Ronnie chose to participate.

Ronnie's relationship with Mr. Lavin, though adversarial on its surface, is fairly positive. They see each other sporadically, but Ronnie knows he can thank Mr. Lavin if he gets into the vocational program or finds a job. Mr. Lavin may call him on the carpet sometimes, but at least he listens, and he seems to be fair and straight with him. In fact, no other adult in his life is as consistent and helpful. And Mr. Lavin has a sense of humor.

The session begins with Ronnie's account of his arrest this weekend.

Mr. Lavin: So you think it was all the cops' fault?

Ronnie: Definitely. *(Pause, with a smile of complicity:)* Well, maybe not *all* their fault. I mean, I'll admit we were a little shitty. But we weren't bothering anybody until they came along.

Mr. Lavin: How many did you have?

Ronnie: I don't know, a few beers, a joint or two. *(Mr. Lavin looks skeptical; Ronnie smiles.)* Well, it was early, it was only nine o'clock.

Mr. Lavin: How come you were the only one charged with assault?

Ronnie: 'Cause the fat one came at me, started pushing me. What was I supposed to do? Then, if you touch them, it's assault and battery.

Mr. Lavin: But how come it was you? Did you mouth off? Listen, I'm not saying the cops are never wrong or anything, but you know what the story is; you know you can't win in that situation. So you just move, and when they leave you come back or you go somewhere else. If you bust them, all you get is a quick trip down here.

Ronnie: The thing I hate the most is when they take your beer and drink it. That's why they come after us. So, as soon as I see them I go apeshit.

Mr. Lavin: Because you're drunk.

Ronnie: I wasn't drunk. *(Mr. Lavin's expression says "Oh, come on!")* I was feeling good.

Mr. Lavin: Look, Ronnie, you're no dummy, right? You know that all you get when you shove a cop is trouble, and you can't afford any more trouble. That's all you get. It doesn't make you a tough guy. Joe is as tough as you are, and he's not down here on an A and B. I'm saying to you that you're in trouble because when you drink, you go too far and you do stupid things you'd never do if you were sober.

Ronnie: If I was sober, I wouldn't have been on the corner.

Mr. Lavin: Don't I know it. But see, some of your friends, they drink, but they don't get into beefs with the cops or slugging matches with friends. They don't go looking for trouble.

Ronnie: I don't go looking for trouble.

Mr. Lavin: No? Well, you manage to find it. You've told me yourself you have a temper when you're drinking. You come down here with your friends; I hear them telling you you can't handle it. Look, there's nothing wrong with drinking. I like to drink myself, but there's drinking and then there's getting drunk. You don't just catch a buzz, you get drunk, and then you get mean, am I right? And sooner or later you're back in trouble. You like getting hauled into court?

Ronnie: Sure, I love it. Don't be stupid, of course not.

Mr. Lavin: Do I look stupid? I'm getting paid to be here. What's your excuse?

Ronnie: (*Long pause*) So what happens now?

Mr. Lavin: What happens is that the judge sees two beefs in eight months and writes you a ticket to Billerica. Unless he sees you're doing something for yourself.

Ronnie: So get me into that work-study program.

Mr. Lavin: That's not enough. And that's for good boys. I'm not knocking myself out to get you in there if you're going to pull this kind of crap. I've got just one thing to offer you right now, and that's a group we run down here on alcohol and drinking. Once a week for six weeks, and it starts a week from Thursday.

Ronnie: So if I go to this group I get off?

Mr. Lavin: It's up to the judge. But you have a better chance. But I'm not suggesting this to get you off; I think it might do you some good.

Ronnie: (*With a grin*) Why, you think I'm an alcoholic?

Mr. Lavin: You said it, I didn't.

Ronnie: What's this group for? Do they make you take the pledge or something?

Mr. Lavin: No. It's all guys your age who got into trouble because of their drinking. Mostly all you do is talk or just listen. It's to get you to think about your drinking. Like, did you ever wonder why you drink the way you do?

Ronnie: I drink because it feels good, same as everybody else.

Mr. Lavin: Yeah, but you drink a lot, and you get ugly when you drink. What would you say if I told you that almost all the kids in these groups have alcoholic parents?

Ronnie: I believe it. A lot of my friends' fathers are drunks. I guess you could say my father's kind of a drunk, too, at least from what I hear. I remember he used to down practically a fifth of gin every night. And he'd get ugly, boy, did he get ugly. But that was eight years ago now. I don't know if he's still like that. He used to give me a taste now and then. That's probably why I like gin, when I can get it.

Mr. Lavin: See, Ronnie, I think kids learn how to drink from their parents, just by watching them, when they're very young. Or it could be something physical that you inherit in your blood, they don't know. But I think you have a better chance of controlling your own drinking if you understand your father's drinking. And like I said, we talk about this in the group because most of the kids are in that situation, or they were when they were growing up. What about your mother, does she drink?

Ronnie: She drinks, but she doesn't get nasty. When she overdoes it, once in a while, she just gets real sleepy and goes to bed. She really gets on my case when I come in drunk; she says I'm going to be just like my father. I could understand it, if she didn't drink herself.

Mr. Lavin: But does her drinking bother you sometimes?

Ronnie: Not really. She still gets supper on the table, even if it tastes like shit. So if I go to this group, do I have to talk?

Mr. Lavin: You don't have to. You may want to. But you have to come to every session, on time, and you can't be high or drunk or you'll get bounced. And the other rule is that nothing that anyone says can be repeated outside of the group. I'll be there too. I just come for the pretzels and chips. Why don't you come in and see me a half hour before the group starts, so that's three-thirty next Thursday. Okay? And Ronnie, try to stay out of trouble until then, will you?

Discussion

For reasons detailed in Chapter 5, it may prove impossible for Ronnie to learn a different way of drinking. Whether he can do so, or whether he must learn to abstain, the first goal of intervention is to enable him, as soon as possible, to acknowledge alcohol as the source of his persistent problems. For that to happen, Ronnie must be helped to reevaluate the drinking norms he accepted long before he chose friends who subscribed to the norms. Given the extremely high correlation between teenage alcohol abuse and parental alcoholism, the probation officer is obliged to presume that Ronnie's drinking may be a reflection of parental intemperance.

Ronnie has learned more from his parents than how to drink; he has also learned to deny the effects of drinking. The macho armor he wears, though abundantly supported by his peer subculture, was originally constructed to shield him from his feelings of anger and hurt. Moreover, it is easy for teenagers to explain away their problems because the standards for responsible teenage behavior are relatively weak and unclear. Even with this formidable protection, Ronnie is not invulnerable to his friends' comments about his drinking; and it should be noted that such comments are not unusual. Many teenagers, even those who drink heavily, recognize other teenagers who are developing serious problems with alcohol, and often use the word "alcoholic" to their faces, albeit with a teasing inflection.

Before he can think about doing without alcohol, Ronnie must be brought to state publicly his intention to cut down on his drinking.

When he cannot, he will employ the denial he has practiced for so long with regard to his parents' drinking. If he can face his parents' alcoholism with honesty, his chances of facing his own drinking problem should improve. Clearly, Ronnie's willingness to describe his father as an alcoholic is only a first step. If he continues to deny his mother's alcoholism (and remember that Ronnie knows no drinking except drunkenness, so when he says his mother drinks, he means she drinks to excess), he will probably continue to deny his own problem.

But being honest about his mother's drinking also means Ronnie must admit to feelings it has always produced in him. Untying that knot will be a slow and tender process indeed. What Mr. Lavin will have in his favor is that he is discrediting Ronnie's feelings of intrinsic evil. By stressing that Ronnie's drinking pattern is both learned and emotionally reactive, Mr. Lavin can introduce the notion that Ronnie is not bad or foolish, but miseducated. It is not desirable for Ronnie simply to blame his parents for his own problems with alcohol; he must certainly take responsibility for them. But if he can allow himself to feel hurt, deprived, and misguided, he may in time come to feel less worthless and recognize the possibility that things can be different. Much of his behavior can be understood as misdirected anger. He has to get that anger out.

Mr. Lavin honors Ronnie's veneer of toughness. It is all the boy has. In a sense, their relationship is based on the pretense that Ronnie can take it as well as dish it out. Within limits, Mr. Lavin can therefore be direct and even brusque, for Ronnie can best accept his sympathy and help in that manner. But when it comes to Ronnie's mother's drinking, Mr. Lavin must be all tact and gentleness—and all persistence. For Ronnie greatly prefers to be challenged about his own drinking, rather than about his mother's.

Drinking will be a recurring theme in Mr. Lavin's subsequent interviews with Ronnie. Ronnie may get angry at times with Mr. Lavin's endless fixation on drinking. At least for a time, he must be allowed to retreat when he gets overwhelmed with the emotions he is invested in suppressing. Ronnie has a world of damage to overcome, and it would be unrealistic to expect change as a result of a short-term experience. But it is a good place to start. Getting Ronnie a good job won't help for long if his drinking continues unchecked.

Ronnie and his peers in the group will have a hard time talking about their feelings and being serious with one another. The group leaders are sensible to tolerate a certain amount of wisecracking and other outlets for nervous energy. Within limits, they might even participate in it, for that is the way in which many teenagers establish whatever intimacy they can bear. And the group should not be essentially didactic. The participants need to learn more about themselves and their experiences, not about alcohol and its effect on the body.

Variations

Aspects of the scenario between Ronnie and Mr. Lavin may be applicable to any situation in which a youthful problem drinker's unacceptable behavior comes up for discussion. Alcoholism and drug-treatment programs, including intervention programs such as those for drinking drivers, should make serious efforts to help clients examine the drinking of their parents, in both individual and group settings.

Less obvious settings for an analogous approach are the school, youth employment office, and recreation agency. Guidance and disciplinary personnel at the junior high and high school levels must frequently confront students about drug-taking and drinking. Frequently, the school assumes that their parents are models of temperate behavior, when just the opposite assumption seems often justified. These obvious infractions are sometimes requests for help with a parent's drinking as well as with the student's.

Many municipalities receive funds from the U.S. Department of Labor for programs that train young people for work in government and nonprofit agencies; and some large corporations have their own youth employment programs. Even where employment counselors are vigilant for signs of interference due to excessive drinking, there are rarely education or intervention groups offered for youngsters with alcohol problems. Even more rarely is the connection made between parent's and offspring's drinking. Employment counselors may have more leverage with teenagers than probation officers or school headmasters; they have something the youngster wants. There should be no hesitation to use that leverage on the employee's behalf.

Recreation leaders also have something children want. They can give it away or they can trade for it. Why simply take teenagers on a bicycle trip, when it can be a reward for doing something they will grow from but might never otherwise come out for, like a minicourse on alcohol? It often happens that such a trip, a dance, or other event is ruined by a drinking or drug-taking incident, perhaps involving several teenagers. These incidents more than justify spending some time on alcohol education. And they are also occasions on which problem drinkers identify themselves.

The youngster in Ronnie's situation may become angry, offensive, sarcastic, or withdrawn, at the mention of parental drinking. But the helper has nothing to lose. If Ronnie doesn't connect his own drinking with his parents', his chances of arresting his own alcohol abuse seem significantly slimmer.

THE PERSONAL FRIEND

Systematic, school-based alcohol education including segments on family alcoholism fields a small army of young helpers who don't live with the disease but are close to those who do. Louise is a 14-year-old member of that army. The alcohol education units she has encountered in several grades have helped her clarify her own attitudes about drinking and evaluate the options she may face in drinking situations. They have also made her more aware of alcoholism and its effect on family members.

It may be that Louise will pick up signs of family alcoholism that others might miss. But more likely, she will have the same opportunity as others to see her friends' distress and embarrassment. The difference is that she knows what to call the family situation. She is less inclined to think she is witnessing isolated incidents, and more likely to try to be helpful, instead of assuming that her best course is pretending not to notice.

Louise has a friend, Marcia, who attends a nearby school. They usually get together once a week after school, and sometimes on weekends, but never at Marcia's house. Since it was more convenient for her, Louise didn't ever question why Marcia never invited her home. But during their last phone conversation, Louise heard Marcia's mother in the background, loud, vulgar, maybe drunk. Louise began to wonder. She recalled several times when Marcia told her how lucky Louise was to have a mother like hers. And sometimes, when she was in a bad mood, Marcia got jealous and spiteful. They always made up later, but as she thought about it now, Louise felt bad; she never really tried to find out what was bothering her friend. Today, she's decided, will be different.

Marcia's mother is alcoholic, and her father is completely out of the picture. Her mother alternates between viciousness and violence, on the one hand, and overbearing, sentimental affection and devotion, on the other. The change can occur in minutes, without warning. Marcia feels anger, revulsion, great guilt, and self-pity. She has never told anyone about her mother. Once, she almost told Louise, but she panicked at the thought that Louise wouldn't want to be friends with someone from her kind of family.

The two girls are sitting in Louise's basement, late one afternoon. They have been talking for about an hour about their usual subjects: other kids, school, and TV. Marcia describes a poster she's made with her favorite stars' pictures.

> *Louise:* Sounds great. I'd love to see it. Maybe I can come over after I go shopping on Saturday.
>
> *Marcia:* No, I'm not going to be home. I have to go to my sister's.
>
> *Louise:* Okay, then I'll come next week.
>
> *Marcia:* Maybe. Or I can bring it here. It's really not *that* excellent a poster.
>
> *Louise:* Yeah, but I'd kind of like to see your house, your room, where you hang out, you know. We've been friends a long time. Do you realize I've never been to your house?
>
> *Marcia:* My house is like a pig sty, it's so filthy. It grosses me out to bring friends there. I guess I should clean it more, but . . . *(She shrugs.)*
>
> *Louise:* So what? This place isn't so clean. My mother says I'd be better off in a barn. If that's all you're worried about, forget it.
>
> *Marcia:* Well, it's not just me, it's my mother. She gets a little bonkers when people come over. You know, this isn't good enough, that isn't good enough, she gets crazy. It's not worth it.
>
> *Louise:* I never met your mother.
>
> *Marcia:* You're lucky. She's a trip. She's real fat and real unpredictable. But she has her good points.
>
> *Louise:* Can I meet her sometime? *(Marcia nods.)* Is something wrong, is she sick or something?
>
> *Marcia:* Yeah, she's sick. She's real nervous and touchy. I just don't want—you know, she can blow up over the smallest thing, anything you might say. It's embarrassing, and it wouldn't be any fun for you, either, believe me.
>
> *Louise:* Marcia, don't get mad, but when I called you the other night I could hear her in the background, and she sounded like she might have been drinking. And I just wanted to say it right out because we're friends, and if something is bothering you, you can tell me about it. 'Cause what are friends for?
>
> *Marcia:* No, I know you're trying to help. But she's usually not that bad. That was a bad night. And anyway, it's her problem, not mine. If she wants to do that to herself it's her business.
>
> *Louise:* That's not what they said when we talked about it in school.
>
> *Marcia:* You talked about it in school?
>
> *Louise:* This year in health, last year in English; I've had it three times now. We talk about alcoholics, but we also learn about how the kid feels; like he caused it, or it was up to him to stop it. We saw this film, and one minute the father is smacking the kid, the next minute he's

hugging him and promising to cut down. And they kept saying, "If you know someone in that situation, help them talk about it and understand what's happening." So here I am.

Marcia: Well, I don't like to talk about it. It's easy for you; you don't have to live with it.

Louise: That's right. What do I know? But if you could talk with other kids who live with a parent who drinks too much, would you do it? Your mother wouldn't know. No one would know.

Marcia: I don't think I can talk about it.

Louise: You don't have to talk, just listen. Okay? Listen, I'll talk to some people at school. I won't mention any names, all right? I'll just try to find out where to go. 'Cause I know there are kids who do this, who talk to other kids about their parent's drinking. And then we'll go together if you want, 'cause I have an aunt I think might be alcoholic and I worry about her kids. And I swear I won't tell anyone.

Marcia: I still don't see what good it'll do. What good is my talking about it? She's the one who drinks too much.

Louise: 'Cause you'll feel better. Doesn't it always feel better to talk to someone with the same problem you have? Besides, maybe you can help her. You can't tell me it doesn't bother you. You want to just sit back and do nothing, or you want to do something that might help?

Marcia: Now you got me all bummed out, thanks a lot.

Louise: Wait a minute now. You got a problem, you want to pretend it doesn't bother you—that's fine with me. All I did was try to help. You're getting mad at me, instead of feeling like, hey, maybe there *is* something I can do.

Marcia: OK, OK, let's drop it, all right?

Louise: (Pause) Will you come talk to someone with me? *(Marcia nods.)* Are we still friends? *(Marcia slowly smiles.)*

Discussion

If this conversation seems unrealistic, it may be because adults habitually and vastly underestimate young people. While far from commonplace, such dialogues occur with surprising frequency in communities where drinking and alcoholism are discussed openly. A noticeable pyramid effect is produced by systematic alcohol education, and this effect is accelerated where there are accessible resources for children with family alcoholism.

In probably a more typical interchange, Louise would also come from an alcoholic family. She would be trying to persuade Marcia to attend Alateen or a special group with her, and her whole approach would be different. She would share her own problems first, and that alone would help enormously. There seems to be some kind of unspoken bonding between children of alcoholics; very often their friends are also from alcoholic homes, though they may never have discussed it together. The result is that when a professional refers one child, many times two reach help.

Another way that Louise might help is to offer Marcia a place to which she can escape. Many children desperately need such a haven, and could turn to a friend when they could never turn to a service agency. On the occasion of such a strategic retreat, Marcia would be ripe for tender probing about her problem. It is not enough to develop the survival skill of constructive avoidance; though the importance of such learning is underlined when contrasted with its dangerous alternatives: staying home and taking lumps, or running away. Louise can offer Marcia safety, but she can also gently insist that she confront her feelings.

Louise started out with a suspicion and an intention. As often, the scenario is completely unpremeditated. One friend happens to be present when another friend needs to let off steam, and it all just comes out naturally. And Louise is only human; she gets angry when she goes out on a limb and gets small thanks, indeed. A little anger from Louise may do Marcia some good. She had kept silent in order to keep a friend; mightn't she try to overcome her shame for the same reason?

Variations

Louise and Marcia might well have been 24 or 34 instead of 14. The child continues to be affected by a parent's drinking long after leaving the home. Medical emergencies and family visits are just two of the types of incidents that can occasion what may be the first candid discussion of a parent's alcoholism. Many professionals find it more difficult to broach the subject with a friend than with a client, perhaps because they feel there is more to lose, or because they paradoxically endow personal relationships with more severe boundaries on privacy. Or they may feel practiced and comfortable offering help to a youngster but not to a peer. But, as Louise says, "What are friends for?"

Some recreation workers, coaches, and clergy have relationships with teenagers that more closely resemble friendships than professional alliances. They have natural opportunities to see general distress or specific signs of a family problem, but they have no mandate to intervene and therefore rely entirely on whatever intimacy they have developed. Yet there is no equality of disclosure. Children typically know little about adults' lives, and even if professionals grew up with family alcoholism and are willing to talk about it, the child may be made more uncomfortable than anything else. Nevertheless, on the whole, such mutual disclosure is recommended where appropriate. It may seem strange to the child at first, but its overall effect is extremely productive.

Facing inconclusive data and lacking authority to delve into the cause of a problem, friends and professionals with informal contact have difficulty finding the line between helpful probing and encouragement, on the one hand, and intrusion on the other. It is important to inch toward that line, instead of recklessly charging over it or, much more commonly, staying miles away from it.

Chapter 9
COMMUNITY STRATEGIES FOR SYSTEMATIC INTERVENTION

It is estimated that no more than 5 percent of this country's children with parental alcoholism receive help in understanding and coping with their problem.[1] For that figure to increase substantially, national policy and community practice will have to address the two basic requirements for systematic intervention: the establishment of a network of trained youth professionals to identify and intervene with the children and the development of resources to which they can confidently refer them. This book is addressed primarily to the first of these goals.

The professional's intervention role is dependent upon the availability of resources capable of providing more intensive help. Most communities presently lack such resources. Any attempt to motivate and prepare youth professionals to address the family alcoholism problems of their children must also suggest ways in which appropriate services can be developed.

To say that treatment resources are sorely lacking is not to slight Alateen. Where Alateen is available as an ongoing resource, it is probably unexcelled. But it is not nearly as widespread as Al-Anon partly because it has been difficult to find enough adult Al-Anon sponsors willing to take on so great a responsibility and so formidable a challenge. And Alateen's virtues are also limitations. Alateen cannot initiate programs or associate itself with other identification, prevention, or treatment efforts. Anonymous and leaderless, it provides no account-

---

[1]Whitfield, "Children of Alcoholics: Treatment Issues," NIAAA Symposium.

ability and follow-up to those who make referrals. And, as observed earlier, many children need substantial help before they can go to Alateen. They don't sufficiently understand alcoholism; they lack the confidence to walk into a roomful of strangers, all of whom may know one another; and they may be unable to get to meetings without the cooperation of parents who often actively oppose their participation. As we will see in Chapter 10, Alateen and Al-Anon are the preferred long-term resources for children of alcoholics. But most children don't have Alateen in their communities and many of those who do need short-term help to try it.

Generic youth professionals can play a pivotal role in the creation of community resources for children of alcoholics, though they often don't know it. They are closest to the children and, therefore, most cognizant of the need and the opportunity. Following is a scenario that doesn't happen often, but might if youth professionals appreciated their own efficacy.

A teacher identifies several children from alcoholic homes. He thinks they could benefit from some kind of group, but there is no Alateen meeting nearby. The school social worker doesn't conduct groups, and she is honest enough to admit she knows little about family alcoholism. The teacher goes to the principal, who authorizes him to find out what the local alcoholism treatment program can offer. That program has begun to offer individual or group counseling for children, but only for the children of patients in treatment. Its staff, however, though already overworked, is encouraged by the teacher's interest and involvement; a bit chastened by its own inability to provide a needed and relevant service; and concerned enough to participate in further discussion about what is needed and how it might be provided. They are not ready to take on an additional service; but they are eager to see if any other agency can.

At this point, someone within the school or the alcoholism program might convene a larger group to assess the need for a service for children of alcoholics. Representatives of mental health, social welfare, recreation, and probation agencies could be invited. Individual members of AA, Al-Anon, and Alateen could also be contacted. The result could be the beginning of a collaborative effort to build a community resource.

Perhaps this scenario is too optimistic. But the one that many professionals envision is probably excessively pessimistic. People may not know just what to do for children of alcoholics; and in most areas no one is taking responsibility for figuring it out. But many human-service providers are aware that these children are out there in numbers, and with significant needs now being overlooked.

TREATMENT ISSUES

Practical Issues

Traditionally, alcoholism treatment has centered on the effort to help the alcoholic stop drinking. But alcoholism is a family illness. All members of the family suffer because of it. Far from automatically getting better when the alcoholic stops drinking, many families sabotage sobriety. Family members need help for themselves, centered on their own needs and choices rather than those of the alcoholic. With such help, the alcoholic's chances of recovery also improve.

Treatment centering on the family as a system is becoming more popular in alcoholism as in mental health programs. It may be desirable to get all family members working on the same problem at the same time and within the same framework. But joint family treatment requires the simultaneous willingness of all family members to say and hear painful things about one another. Families reaching that point are relatively healthy. In the majority of alcoholic families, family treatment is possible only after one or more members have received substantial prior help and pushed other members toward joint treatment.

Most often, it is the alcoholic or nonalcoholic parent who initiates family treatment after seeking help independently. When a parent provides the impetus for family treatment, there are two potent seeds for failure. First, if either parent has not sufficiently progressed in his or her own treatment, having the children reveal what they have been feeling is often too threatening. Many alcoholism programs report that parents withdraw from treatment not only the children but themselves as well when parents are pressured to involve them.[2]

Second, when we remember the complicated feelings of anger and detachment the children feel toward their parents, combined with the natural thrust toward independence and rebellion that grows to its peak in adolescence, we may well ask whether the parent isn't the *least* likely person to initiate or participate in the child's receiving help. The discrepancy between the number of children in Alateen and the number of adults in AA and Al-Anon is in part attributable to both of these tendencies.

Family treatment is a goal to strive for (although this does not necessarily mean getting the whole family together in the same room); but it

---

[2]Kenneth Williams, "Children of Alcoholic Parents: Intervention Issues," paper presented at National Institute on Alcohol Abuse and Alcoholism Symposium on Children of Alcoholics, Silver Spring, Md., 25 September 1979; see also program papers by Ellen Morehouse and Tarpley Richards presented at the Symposium.

may be most successful when we have learned to reach and treat the children independently. This book focuses on the above process, and the assumptions behind it, discussed elsewhere, need only be summarized.

Children can get better whether or not their parents are involved in treatment, and whether they are supportive, acquiescent, ignorant, or opposed to the child's receiving help. Adults grossly underestimate young people: their resiliency and their capacity to understand and change. Children learn what they can get from their parents and where they can look, in terms of peers and other adults, for what they cannot get at home. If they encounter sympathetic help in sorting out their experiences, emotions, and needs, they may be considerably more responsive than adults with more practice and investment in keeping things as they are.

Many children are also more willing to accept help for themselves when their parents have no active role in that help, and even (or especially) when they oppose it. Their need for independence and protection from a family whose disease does them harm calls for resources that are exclusively their own. Many are prepared to trust such resources.

Children are the most accessible members of the untreated family. All children attend school or come to the attention of school authorities. There is no adult institution with a comparably systematic reach and endowed with such generalized authority and respect.

Finally, some evidence shows that if the child were the first instead of the last involved in treatment, more family therapy for alcoholism might ensue.[3] How many alcoholics reached treatment only after they perceived what their drinking was doing to their children? Children may be powerless in society, but within many American families they occupy a privileged position. Instead of viewing them as helpless, we might consider how much power children sometimes wield in the home.

Legal and Ethical Issues

We need to distinguish between the legal grounds for treatment and the ones for intervention. The role that is urged on teachers and other youth professionals throughout this book has no real legal risk. Teachers recognize educational or emotional problems, whether full-blown or budding, and let children know where they can go to ameliorate them if they choose. Teachers do not need parental consent to suggest

---

[3] Hindman, "Children of Alcoholics," p. 5.

that children see a guidance counselor or to let them know about nearby counseling resources. It is when children reach treatment that the question of parental consent arises.

The laws governing children's right to treatment without parental consent are "intentionally vague to allow the local family judge to exercise broad discretion about what to do in individual family situations."[4] Much of the legislation and precedent concerns the rights of children and their families when an attempt is made to remove them from their homes. It is not readily applicable to treatment that is explicitly aimed at helping children live healthier lives within their families and communicate more honestly with their parents.

Another side of the same legal issue involves the right of minors to health care without parental knowledge or permission. This is usually defined as medical or psychiatric treatment, and cases have most often involved access to contraception, abortion, and treatment of youthful alcohol and drug abuse.

In these and other related areas, legal precedent and recent legislation have strengthened the child's right to services.[5] The trend is toward enabling children to get the help they need whether or not their parents know and approve.

In spite of this trend, the upshot for many professionals is that they have few firm legal guidelines for deciding when treatment without consent lies within their own, the child's, and the parents' rights. In practice, the ethical conceptions of professionals may influence their course of action more than their sense of the muddied legal boundaries. They are concerned with their own protection, but they also want to avoid embroiling the family in a battle destructive to all parties. Most professionals are probably inclined to extreme caution, steering clear of any situation that might bring children in conflict with their families.

In working with children of alcoholics, the nature of the illness, the age of the children, and the definition of "treatment" might be considered in an attempt to predict legal grounds for services without consent. It is on this "prediction" level that professionals are often forced to operate, since the law is so ambiguous.

Denial, shame, and secrecy are intrinsic to alcoholism. A great many alcoholic and nonalcoholic parents will not grant permission for their children to receive needed help, through which the children then

---

[4] Kenneth Keniston and the Carnegie Council on Children, *All Our Children: The American Family Under Pressure* (New York: Harcourt, Brace, Jovanovich, 1977), p. 186.

[5] John McCabe, "Children in Need: Consent in Treatment," *Alcohol Health and Research World* 2 (Fall 1977): 3, 5–6, 12.

could help other family members. Many children will not begin to use a service if it requires them to obtain consent or informs parents of their participation. This likelihood of opposition and recrimination in the face of need has, in other health areas, influenced the legal trend toward children's independent access to services. But on a practical level, as noted earlier, this same quality of alcoholism, the determination to avoid disclosure, makes it very unlikely that parents will come forward with legal or other public challenges.

Where preadolescents are concerned, parental permission for treatment is virtually both a legal and a practical necessity for many good reasons. Most alcoholism programs, therefore, restrict their work with this age group to children of their patients. But programs for children of untreated parents can be designed to increase the likelihood of consent and reduce the need for direct parental participation. We will see examples of these strategies in the description of the CASPAR model.

Adolescents join a variety of organizations and participate in all kinds of activities requiring parental consent only if transportation of children or risk of physical injury is involved. If the treatment for teenagers with alcoholic parents were psychotherapeutic, permission might be needed. But groups that are primarily educational, recreational, and supportive have so far not been placed in the same legal category. Many teenagers spend the hours between end of the school day and dinnertime at their discretion. Their parents don't know exactly where they are. Teenagers certainly don't get written permission every time they go to the library, the drama club, or a friend's house to gossip and confide.

Some children of alcoholics need treatment that is psychologically sophisticated and long-term. But most simply need to learn and get support for a new way of comprehending and responding to the family situation. When they learn a healthier and emotionally more satisfying perspective, many have the experience and strength to change their coping styles, and a new readiness to seek and accept future help. A time-limited educational experience and supportive process, such as that described later in this chapter, arms children with a new prism for their subsequent experiences and new skills to try. How effectively they internalize what they learn will be apparent only later.

To be sure, there are risks involved in the child's being the only family member who is learning a new perspective and new coping skills and refusing to maintain the alcoholic family's equilibrium. Young children in particular must be discouraged from confronting alcoholic parents or otherwise endangering their own safety. On the other hand, the physical and emotional risks to the child who must wait for a parent to seek treatment in order to get help are immeasurably greater.

In summary, the law fails to provide clear ground rules for when treatment without parental consent is justified and when it is an infringement of rights. Given recent legal trends, the nature of the illness, and a remediation process that is essentially educative and supportive, there seems to be legal basis for assuming that consent and adequate disclosure are not required for adolescents but must be obtained for younger children. The crucial safeguard for nonclinical helping institutions, such as schools, is community support rather than explicit legal dictums. In some locales intervention as well as treatment might be viewed as an encroachment on parental rights. In the absence of ironclad legal grounds, the active support of respected elements in the community becomes even more vital.

THE CASPAR MODEL

Some of the most innovative and effective work with children of alcoholics is being done by the CASPAR Alcohol Education Program in Somerville, Massachusetts. Somerville is one of the most densely populated cities in the country, with a population of 85,000 living in an area of 3.2 square miles. The inhabitants are overwhelmingly Catholic, mostly of Irish and Italian descent. Adjacent to Boston and to Cambridge, the home of Harvard and MIT, Somerville is almost homogeneously working class. It is covered with three-story, wood-frame houses. There is light industry in the city, and almost no grass or trees. Somerville somehow has the feel of a small town: people are friendly (by northern standards), everyone knows everyone else, and many people live a short distance from where they grew up.

Somerville had no alcoholism treatment services in 1970 when Hilma Unterberger was appointed associate area director of the Cambridge-Somerville Mental Health and Retardation Center. Unterberger had years of frustrating experience in the Massachusetts Department of Public Health's Division of Alcoholism. With her colleague Lena DiCicco, she had tried to interest communities across the Commonwealth in preventive education to combat alcohol abuse. Securing two positions within the mental health center for alcoholism treatment, Unterberger did two inspired things: She filled one position with DiCicco; and she freed her from responsibility for direct treatment so that DiCicco could devote all her energies to educating the community and organizing services.

DiCicco built a committee that chose as its first project the establishment of a halfway house for recovering alcoholic men. In the early seventies, alcoholism was widely regarded as a moral failing, public drunkenness was a crime, and halfway houses were novel and threatening. The density of Cambridge and Somerville meant that no location could be found that would be out of the way of neighbors and commerce. In the struggle to secure that first house, the committee incorporated as the Cambridge and Somerville Program of Alcoholism Rehabilitation (CASPAR), and built a partnership arrangement with the Mental Health Center.

CASPAR drew its membership from the prestigious and the humble, church and civic activists, and AA and Al-Anon members. By 1974, the organization operated two halfway houses for sober men; a freestanding detoxification facility; an in- and out-patient hospital-based program; and a training and consultation service. Since that time it has added two more halfway houses, including one for women; a women's alcoholism program featuring consultation and day treatment; a social club for recovering alcoholics; and an overnight shelter for public inebriates. The respect and admiration CASPAR services had won by 1974 made its alcohol education program possible in spite of its controversial approach.

The alcohol education program actually originated in 1972, when DiCicco and her associate, Dixie Mills, conducted an eight-hour training workshop at the request of several Somerville public health and school nurses. They were eager for additional training for themselves and for other school personnel, and introduced DiCicco and Mills to the school administration. Di Cicco asked Somerville's superintendent of schools to designate a representative to serve on the alcoholism committee. His wife was named. A first and then a second workshop was conducted for school personnel, and soon the superintendent, under pressure at home and at the office, agreed to collaborate on a proposal to the National Institute on Alcohol Abuse and Alcoholism (NIAAA), Division of Prevention. The proposal was funded in July 1974, and the CASPAR alcohol education program began in earnest.

In 1976, the NIAAA named CASPAR as one of two models in early alcohol education that it would replicate, with joint federal and local funding, in communities across the country. Since then, dozens of communities have adapted the CASPAR education model, and hundreds of educators have visited or requested information. Their first question is usually, "How did you get started?" It should be obvious that patience and persistence in the building of community support is the key. Hopefully, conditions are somewhat different now than they were in the early seventies. It may not be so difficult for communities to acknowledge their need for the prevention of teenage alcohol abuse. But the overall lesson learned in Somerville is that a solid foundation is necessary and takes time.

CASPAR's goal is the promotion of responsible decision making about drinking. CASPAR presents alcohol as a neutral substance; abstinence and responsible drinking are equally acceptable. It tries to impart attitudes toward alcohol found in the American ethnic groups with the lowest rates of alcoholism, and it seeks to help young people explore options in different drinking situations before they actually face them. It also teaches about alcoholism and its effects on family members.

The original prevention program had five main components:

1. A training program for teachers, featuring a 20-hour basic course and an advanced practicum on methods in alcohol education. Originally concentrating on secondary school teachers with health education responsibilities, training was eventually opened to all interested school personnel, and elementary teachers were especially solicited.

2. The development of an alcohol-specific curriculum entitled *Decisions About Drinking*. The curriculum, written by CASPAR staff and 10 trained teachers, was field-tested, evaluated, and refined between 1976 and 1978. It contains structured and sequential units of 7 to 10 alcohol-specific activities for grades 3 through 12, and a teacher's guide. The program has been sold in every state in the U.S., in every Canadian province, and in many foreign countries.

3. A peer leader program that trains 14- to 18-year-olds as alcohol educators. Three things must be pointed out about this component. First, like most adults, CASPAR staff grossly underestimated young people. At the outset, no one dreamed that teenagers could be effective in leading alcohol education workshops of 16 to 24 hours. Second, peer leaders are primarily educators, not counselors. They run educational groups using lesson plans with concrete objectives; most of the counseling they do occurs informally in the context of these groups. Third, in selecting its peer leaders CASPAR's principal criterion was group diversity. For broadest appeal, the group had to have honor students, average students, and potential dropouts; abstainers, moderate drinkers, and even problem drinkers; youth whose family drinking histories were similarly diverse; and children from different ethnic groups and geographic areas.

4. A community component, featuring a steering committee, public education projects, and training for youth-related agencies.

5. A full-time evaluator who, with program staff, designs and implements a thorough evaluation of all CASPAR education activities.

In the spring of 1976, the most advanced members of the original team of 10 peer leaders began to experiment, under staff supervision, with after-school and school-based alcohol education workshops. Participants were drawn from students in grades 7 through 12 who had indicated interest by filling out an optional tear-off page at the end of a CASPAR student survey. That same spring, the peer leaders recruited and helped staff to train a second group of 12 peer leaders. When summer came, the director of Somerville's youth employment program asked CASPAR to provide two-hour workshops for all 550 of the teenagers enrolled. After each workshop, peer leaders distributed cards with options for participants who wanted more information. One option was a group to talk about the drinking of someone close to them. Over 60 young people requested that kind of group. In the fall, as teachers began to field-test the curriculum, more children of alcoholics surfaced.

Meanwhile, mostly at the instigation of the lone peer leader who was involved in Alateen, almost half of the 22 trained peer leaders had begun to acknowledge their own family alcoholism. The CASPAR staff began to provide additional, intensive training for peer leaders from alcoholic homes who were interested in working with other children of alcoholics. The results of that training program were a number of structured activities concerning family alcoholism; a clearer idea of how a group might be composed and conducted; and several peer leaders who were deemed ready to work with other children.

The first two CASPAR groups were directed by one staff member and one peer leader. It soon became obvious that the presence of an adult, who was also the only person without an alcoholic parent, actually detracted from the group. With fingers crossed, and scrupulous supervision, CASPAR staff members tried a group led by two peer leaders, with a third sitting in, simultaneously learning how to lead a group and facilitating the creation of an open, trusting atmosphere. In the next two and a half years, more than 150 youngsters, ages 12 to 19, participated in peer-led groups on family alcoholism averaging about 22 hours in duration.

Somewhat later, CASPAR developed the other two parts of its program for children of alcoholics. One is located at a nearby court, where CASPAR staff and CASPAR-trained probation officers conduct 12-hour groups for youthful problem drinkers, more than 75 percent of whom are children of alcoholics. Probation staff have continued these groups on their own, which was the original intention. And in the 1978–79 school year, a staff member and a CASPAR-trained special education teacher began to offer workshops for children in grades 1 through 6, during school hours. These groups were continued and expanded the following year, funded entirely by the Somerville School Committee in a year of shrinking budgets. In the 1980–81 school year, school department funding was continued, but the source of the money was changed from federally reimbursable programming to the more stable regular budget based on city tax revenues. In October 1980, CASPAR began a new NIAAA grant, the first federally funded program in the country intended to explore, evaluate, and model innovative work with children of alcoholics.

CASPAR's intervention program was an inevitable and organic outgrowth of its primary prevention effort. Its lesson: Make alcohol education available, appealing, and nonmoralizing, and persons who live with alcohol abuse will identify themselves and ask for help. Of the more than 250 children of alcoholics who participated in CASPAR groups between 1976 and 1979, two-thirds had parents who were not receiving treatment. It should be noted that at no time did CASPAR have more than two and one-third staff on its program. More will be said about this at the end of the chapter, when CASPAR's applicability to other communities is discussed.

CASPAR STRATEGIES

Pre-identification

This stage involves measures making it more likely that sizable numbers of youngsters will identify themselves as children of alcoholics. These measures include the training of teachers, other youth professionals, and peer leaders, and their implementation of alcohol education activities in the classroom and the community. Much has already been said about the training of teachers and the way in which nonmoralizing, student-centered alcohol education helps even children of alcoholics who cannot ask for help. All young people need the opportunity to learn about alcohol and prepare for decisions regarding it. CASPAR findings after only four years indicated marked attitudinal change and increasing behavioral improvements.[6] Alcohol education helps children of alcoholics name the problem, gives them information and hope, and makes a legitimate classroom topic out of the object of their shame.

In the first five years CASPAR trained a total of 35 peer leaders in three cadres. Senior peer leaders have considerable responsibility for recruiting, training, and supervising novices, most of whom had previously participated in afterschool groups. Peer leaders undergo about 50 hours of intensive training, after which they must pass a rigorous

---

[6] Robert E. White and Ronald Biron, "A Study of the Psychological and Behavioral Effects of the *Decisions About Drinking* Curriculum," CASPAR Alcohol Education Program, Somerville, Mass., 1979 (mimeographed).

qualifying exam. Throughout their peer-leader careers, they get on-going training at weekly meetings and regular staff supervision. They must also satisfy academic and personal goals or they are not given work assignments.

Only peer leaders from alcoholic families are allowed to lead groups for children of alcoholics. The peer leaders get additional training requiring them to be as candid and thorough in their own learning process as they will ask their group members to be. They must not only know the right things to say, but must work at practicing what they preach. They also need special group skills. A new peer leader observes at least one group before being teamed with a veteran to lead another. As in all things, experience is the best teacher.

> The more we did the groups, the better they got. We got more comfort-able dealing with situations. Like, the first time someone cried, Nancy and I stood up and went to walk out of the room. I was closest to my chair so I sat down and Nancy took the person out of the room and we went on doing what we were doing. Later on, we could think about what all of our options were, and it meant more because it actually happened. After that, we had a routine worked out; it went much more smoothly.

Identification

The CASPAR model makes it easier for children to ask for help, and for helpers to recognize their requests. The majority of the children who reached CASPAR treatment identified themselves to a teacher or peer leader during an alcohol education workshop. We have seen in Chapter 8 and elsewhere how children reveal themselves in their reactions, and how a teacher can use the classroom exercise as a springboard to an individual conversation about drinking and alcoholism. Some of the clues to possible family alcoholism that arise during alcohol education sessions, and more general clues as well, are listed in Appendix A.

It is crucial to remember that the signs are often subtle and ambiguous. The children are ambivalent because of their fear and guilt; they think they are betraying their families. They often need to feel that the helper encouraged them, is trustworthy, and will share responsibility for the revelation. Indicative of this need are the disparate recollections of one identification incident, as told first by an eighth-grade student, then by the teacher.

> He made us do a Dear Abby letter. I did it, and after he read it he asked me if he could see me after school. I didn't sign it but I guess he

knew my handwriting, and you know, he said, "Melissa, can I talk to you after school?" and I said, "Sure." I wasn't sure what he wanted to talk about. I was having problems with my mother, you know, really bad, fighting and everything. But I never hit her back. One night she just threw a pan at me and I just had enough, so I decided to talk 'cause he asked me and I finally just let everything out.

She wrote a Dear Abby letter, and then she wrote, "I want to speak to you after." I had no idea whose letter it was, and when she came up the next day, I was kind of surprised whose it was.

Referral and Intake

The optimal referral resource is one that professionals know well and respect and rely on for accountability and follow-up; one that is attractive and easy to sell to children; and one that minimizes the role the professional must play in transporting the child, providing information, or filling out records and forms. From the children's perspective, before the treatment process can win them over, they must see enough in the program for themselves, and enough to protect them from parents and friends, to give it a try. In the three subdivisions of CASPAR's work with children of alcoholics, different procedures are used to make the treatment groups as appealing as possible to children and referring helpers.

The preadolescent group, held during school hours in elementary school resource rooms, requires parental permission. The parents of all special-needs children—as well as those of other children who have expressed an interest—receive a letter from the school. The letter outlines the topics to be covered in an optional alcohol education group; family alcoholism is one of them. The school typically receives permission to involve 10 times as many children as it can accommodate. It can select the children with the most need and greatest chance of benefit, and stigmatize no one.

The letter carries the authority of the school, which for many parents is compelling and absolute. It makes a strong case for every student's need for alcohol education. Some parents of 6- to 12-year-olds believe that alcohol education is detrimental or unnecessary to their children, but many parents hiding their own or their spouse's alcoholism think twice about raising a conspicuous objection. And many parents, of course, are openly grateful for help with their children even if they are resistant to help themselves. Nothing is required of the parent once permission has been granted. CASPAR has found that even children whose only parent or two parents are alcoholic have been allowed to participate.

The program has innate appeal to children, too. The opportunity to talk about the adult subject of drinking is a cause for envy that makes being chosen for the group a privilege. The rules about confidentiality also give the group the quality of a secret club, guaranteed to appeal at certain ages. And the children have nothing to hide from their parents: Everything is aboveboard. For children whose parents are willing to listen, the letter has already introduced the subject and made it easier for the dialogue to continue.

Years before these preadolescent groups began, CASPAR had been shocked when peer leaders asked for CASPAR T-shirts. Soon they were sought and worn by many participants in their groups, by teachers, and by parents. All these people proudly displaying the name of an organization heretofore known for alcoholism rehabilitation! One member in the first group for 6- to 9-year-olds had a sister with a T-shirt, and asked if he would get one, too. The T-shirts became a kind of certificate of achievement and membership. These T-shirts, and the number of children waiting to get into CASPAR groups, show most eloquently that participation is anything but stigmatizing.

The teachers and other youth professionals who refer junior and senior high school students to CASPAR's after-school, peer-led groups have all been trained by the program, and know at least two staff members quite well. They refer by phone or ask someone to come to the school to meet the child. As often, they make the referral directly to a peer leader who goes to that school.

> When any of the kids are ready to go for help, I just get them in touch with Arnie and let him take them. He drops in all the time. And Alice too, like, I'll say, "Do any of you know Alice?" Because everyone knows her, she's very proud of her affiliation with CASPAR, and they might be more willing to talk to her.

In addition, certain experienced peer leaders function as consultants to the guidance staff. They have regular hours at the secondary schools, and they work at gaining the respect of the counselors and inviting referrals. Often they see young people on a one-to-one basis in school in order to get them to come to a group.

Because CASPAR offers after-school groups open to anyone—in addition to the groups just for children of alcoholics—and because of the peer leaders' high visibility and respect among the student body, attending a CASPAR group is not indicative of a problem with alcohol.

> Whenever I taught the unit Peter would take over the class. He never associated any kind of a stigma with belonging to the CASPAR program, and he made the kids feel that there was no stigma attached to it,

so it was easier for me to say, "Hey, why don't you go down to CASPAR and learn more?" He really sold the program, I mean, we'd talk about how lots of people go to CASPAR, everyone doesn't have problems in the family or problems with their own drinking, and no one knows which ones do and which ones don't. But Peter would just make it sound like it was so much fun, that a number of kids would say, "Peter, how do you get to be a peer leader?" He had a lot of girls interested.

The after-school groups take place from 3 to 5 P.M. at CASPAR's homelike office, a short walk or bus ride from the secondary schools. The convenience makes it possible for many youngsters to attend without telling or lying to their parents. But the key that entices the students and truly protects them from parents and peers is the positive incentive CASPAR builds into its program. Sometimes the incentive is course credit; a teacher will allow a child to make up for poor grades by attending a CASPAR workshop.

However, the predominant incentive, excuse, and justification is money. Not only are peer leaders paid (and that should go without saying, since money is our preeminent reward and their work is invaluable); but the young people who spend six hours in school, and then come to learn about alcohol and alcoholism for two more hours, are also paid. They receive a check at the end of the workshop for the hours they attended; the typical check is about forty dollars. That's still a lot of money to a ninth grader or to an older child without a job. Here is what forty dollars per child buys in Somerville:

● The child's initial interest and willingness to try the group.

● The ideal explanation to give to parents and friends: "I go to CASPAR because they pay me; it's a job and I need the money."

● An assurance that the child participates seriously. In other words, it enables the peer leaders to keep group members focused, working, and disciplined in spite of the fact that they have been sitting in school for hours and in spite of the difficulty of the subject and its tendency to inspire flight and frivolity.

● The child's priceless collaboration in helping the other members of the group.

● Group diversity: school credit appeals to certain children, but money appeals to everyone.

For many people paying children to receive help is a distasteful idea if not downright anathema. Once they think about it, many people can see that their objections are irrational. How many adults take courses for their intrinsic worth and not for the tangible, usually financial, rewards attached to attendance? To reach large numbers of children of alcoholics, these children must be aggressively courted and protected through the use of something that has incontestable value to themselves and their parents. In our society at present, money best fills that bill. The practical problem of raising the money will be addressed at the end of this chapter.

The court-based groups for youthful problem drinkers use more stick than carrot. Probationers are mandated to attend, with the understanding that doing so may improve their chances of avoiding jail or reducing the probation period, and refusing to participate will be looked upon as unwillingness to straighten out. The groups are still designed to be as enjoyable as possible, but initial attendance is more the result of a firm push than a delicate seduction.

The Group Experience

The principal treatment mode is the small, closed, time-limited, structured group. To be sure, some children are not able to attend groups and need individual attention; and others need more intensive psychological help, academic tutoring, or vocational training, in addition to the alcohol groups. But the small group, sometimes composed entirely of children of alcoholics and always devoted to discussion of alcohol-related issues, is central and desirable for most children of alcoholics.

CASPAR groups vary in size from 6 to 8 members in the preadolescent groups to a maximum of 12 in the adolescent and court-based groups. Groups for 6- to 8- and 9- to 12-year-olds consist of 10 to 15 sessions, 30 to 45 minutes in length; adolescent workshops are 10 to 12 sessions of two hours; and there are six 90-minute sessions in the court-based groups. The age difference between the oldest and youngest members is rarely more than two years. All groups have two facilitators; in the young children's and court groups, both are adults, whereas in the after-school groups both are teenagers.

Group work breaks down the isolation of the children. They make friends who not only know the things they have been most afraid to reveal but share them. The secrets are out: Nothing blocks the development of friendship and so much promotes it. The children assiduously honor the group's confidentiality, because they rely upon it for themselves and because it is so emphatic a group standard.

Many of these children have never felt the sense of belonging and acceptance they experience at CASPAR. They find a warm, caring, safe, and trustful environment, with consistent and responsible models whom they are expected and ready to emulate. Too often, their home has not been such an environment. Some participants need time to adjust, time to discover that they can be truthful, emotional, helpful, serious and playful, angry and excited. The remarkable thing is that many children flower so quickly; in many CASPAR groups, the very first meeting has most of the participants letting their feelings out and supporting one another.

Aside from being a place where consistency reigns and expectations are clear, the treatment group must be fun. For many of these children, laughter is a rare commodity. They need and deserve a good time, and are obviously more likely to sustain contact if they enjoy themselves. The first 15 to 30 minutes of each workshop's early sessions are devoted to warm-up activities that get the youngsters laughing, trusting, and building relationships with one another. Peer leaders are encouraged to find the humor in participants' situations and stories and to allow children to use laughter to release tension. The final session is usually an all-day retreat that combines learning with recreation and social bonding. Often there is a reunion several months later.

Adult and peer leaders use detailed lesson plans with activities designed to promote maximum participation and tailored to specific cognitive and affective objectives. The peer-leader team presents its staff supervisor with a complete outline for the entire workshop. Before each session, the team and supervisor go over each activity in detail; and after each session, they evaluate the group, discuss potential problems, and assess the needs of individual participants. Peer leaders spend an average of five hours each week in planning, evaluation, and supervision. There is also a weekly two-hour meeting of all peer leaders in which group skills are reinforced and suggestions are exchanged.

In addition, peer leaders spend about two hours each week reading and answering members' journals. In the last 15 minutes of each meeting, participants write in journals that remain at CASPAR. These journals can be seen only by the group's peer leaders and by staff, and can be destroyed at the end of the group if desired. The children write whatever they wish; usually they need some questions or suggestions to respond to. Then one or both of the peer leaders respond in writing. The journals have been invaluable in cementing the relationships between leaders and participants. The children get crucial encouragement and praise for their work and their strengths; they get concrete advice; they give the leaders feedback and say what needs are not being met; and they get a private way of releasing their most guarded secrets.

The content of group activities addresses the following cognitive and affective *major objectives:*

Helping children learn a new way of understanding family alcoholism. First, they articulate the beliefs and feelings they have formed over the years about themselves and their parents. Next, they learn accurate information and an emotional perspective that counteracts feelings of shame, anger, rejection, helplessness, hopelessness, and confusion. Among the many effective exercises with this broad objective, Agree/Disagree sheets and brief descriptive paragraphs are particularly noteworthy. The former features statements such as those discussed in Chapter 2. An example of the latter is a short description of an alcoholic family, with questions like "Who would you least like to be in this family?" and "What kinds of effects outside of the family would this family situation have?"

Helping children evaluate constructive coping options.   This involves acknowledging the connection between the parent's drinking and their own patterns of behavior within and outside of the family: starting fights, manipulating, cutting school, sleeping excessively, drowning in work. More subtle emotional patterns are also examined: Denial, distrust, dishonesty, negativism, and self-abnegation are common examples. Emphasis is put on avoiding arguments and violence in the home, and finding positive outlets for anger and disappointment. Roleplay is especially useful in helping members compare and evaluate coping options.

One of the most delicate and important coping skills concerns how children tell their parents about their participation. As one peer leader recalled:

> We've had one or two kids get punished or barred from groups, coming home and getting bold and telling their parents, their alcoholic parents, they were an alcoholic. Dropping bombshells at the dinner table: "Excuse me, by the way, I learned in a group today that you're an alcoholic and this is what I think about it."

Children roleplay how to talk to their siblings, nonalcoholic parent, and alcoholic parent about what they are learning. They examine their own goals in such discussions and the feelings they provoke. Some children never tell either parent about the groups, but most manage gradually to win the support of the nonalcoholic parent, and more than a few engineer a caring and constructive exchange with the alcoholic.

Helping children feel better about themselves.   Improved self-concept is a treatment goal. In part, it is addressed by activities to reduce the negative feelings created by family alcoholism. But that is only half the job. Children of alcoholics are often painfully aware of their deficiencies, but have great difficulty naming their positive qualities. In addition to persistent praise, the group offers exercises inviting children to take honest pride in their considerable strengths. One such exercise is called The Coat of Arms in which participants create artistic insignia to represent several of their most desirable characteristics.

Preliminary CASPAR studies suggest that children's overall self-esteem is closely connected with their feelings about their families. Group participants are not blaming their parents; they are learning to understand and love them without harming themselves. CASPAR evaluators are beginning to find significant improvement in feelings about family among children who have participated in group activities.[7]

Helping members clarify attitudes about drinking. Effective treatment pays particular attention to the children's images and ideas with respect to drinking and drug-taking. They are introduced to responsible drinking as an alternative to the drinking they have always seen; they must learn the healthy and unhealthy reasons for drinking; and they explore the options open to them in situations involving alcohol. Some are already using alcohol and drugs to cope with their pain. They cannot evaluate and come to terms with their own drinking, now and in the future, unless they have a conception of what normal, responsible drinking looks like.

Increasing children's receptivity to help. A positive experience serves to increase the children's willingness to ask for and accept help, whether it be from agencies, relatives and other adults, Alateen, or friends. Some activities are designed to help members examine the feelings at the root of their resistance to help and to give them concrete information about resources. In most groups, children visit a detox center or a halfway house and attend an Alateen meeting. The message is repeated and underlined: You deserve help; needing help is normal, and recognizing the need is healthy; and it's up to you to get what you need. Again and again, the group plays the same tune in different keys and tempos: You come first, and you are responsible for taking care of yourself.

Reinforcement and Follow-up

The children's needs and capabilities are assessed during the time limited treatment groups. Children who want help in talking with their

---

[7]Robert E. White, "The Impact of 1977–78 Peer Leader Training in Selected Behavioral and Psychological Dimensions," CASPAR Alcohol Education Program, Somerville, Mass., 1979 (mimeographed).

parents receive it directly from CASPAR staff. Children who may need psychiatric care, alternative living situations, tutoring, or special education programs are referred to appropriate resources. The CASPAR staff has trained or consulted with most of the people to whom children need to be referred, making it relatively easy to secure ancillary services.

CASPAR considers itself most successful when group participants become regular members of Alateen and Al-Anon. Because the programs are anonymous, it is difficult to determine how often that happens. Nor can CASPAR methodically solicit information about children's progress from the schools. But the peer leaders, teachers, and guidance counselors who referred and worked with these children maintain contact with them, and the CASPAR alcoholism program glowingly reports when family members reach treatment as a result of children's exposure.

Most important, direct contact with CASPAR and its messages does not end with the group's last meeting. Ninth graders, for example, will have alcohol education again in the tenth grade, and may also be exposed to it by an employment program or recreational organization. They will probably know present or future peer leaders. Some children of alcoholics go on to participate in basic alcohol education workshops, and some become peer leaders themselves.

ADAPTING THE CASPAR MODEL IN OTHER COMMUNITIES

No one was more surprised than CASPAR staff at the apparent success of the federally sponsored effort to replicate its alcohol education activities in communities having little in common with Somerville. Two of the replication sites are in southern rural areas, and are more racially mixed and generally abstinence-oriented. The third site is near Hartford, Connecticut, a community comparable to Somerville. Nevertheless, all three CASPAR spinoffs have made considerable progress. Other replication sites have been added. Dozens of other communities have adapted the primary-prevention program on their own.

But CASPAR's work with children of alcoholics is still untested in other localities. The program takes great advantage of its urban setting; suburban and rural localities may find some CASPAR strategies inapplicable.

It is heartening to note that the entire CASPAR program—from training teachers, other youth professionals, and peer leaders to treating the children of alcoholics they identify—has been accomplished with a program staff of two full-time persons. That is to say, a school system or mental health or alcoholism program that can provide administrative support can mount a program like CASPAR's in a community of almost 100,000 people at a cost of less than $60,000. Such a program might include two positions, ample educational materials, and money to pay young people, and still leave something toward overhead and incidentals.

In current times, such funds are simply beyond the reach of most communities and are not forthcoming from state and federal sources. The issue becomes one of allocating scarce resources according to priorities. Could a guidance counselor from the school system and a mental health or recreation professional from a local community agency, for example, be relieved from some of their caseload to try a limited program? Could an alcoholism treatment program devote an existing staff position to reaching and treating children of alcoholics? New money will not fall from the skies. Our communities and institutions cannot easily afford to serve children of alcoholics. But they must ask themselves if they could afford *not* to serve them.

Incidentally, the money used to pay peer leaders and group participants is easiest to raise locally. Many civic leaders, community groups, and merchants who regularly deplore the irresponsibility of teenagers would probably contribute when confronted with youth who are trying to play a constructive role, saying subtly but unmistakably, "Put up or shut up."

The essential elements of the CASPAR model for replication purposes are:

● Solid community support;

● Systematic, repeated, student-centered alcohol education directed toward all children;

● A network of youth professionals, trained in identifying and intervening with children of alcoholics;

● A treatment resource accessible to children without requiring parental assistance;

● Incentives and protection for the children who participate; and

● A major intervention and treatment role for trained peer leaders.

Some of the other programs across the country that have been working with children of alcoholics are listed in the Resources section at the back of this book. The NIAAA, the National Clearinghouse for Alcohol Information, national and local councils on alcoholism, and the state alcoholism authorities are ready to provide information and assistance to communities.

Chapter 10
ENVIABLE RESOURCES:
AL-ANON/ALATEEN

How many people can be assured of finding help and support throughout their lives, wherever they may be, and at no cost? Many teenagers and adults who grew up in alcoholic families, as well as those who have spouses or close friends with alcoholism, are in just that enviable position. Unfortunately, many don't know about Alateen and Al-Anon; and some professionals share their ignorance or have prejudices that keep them from introducing these unique resources to those who need them.

No program is for everyone. But it is remarkable how quick some professionals are to conclude that "Alateen isn't for this kid." It is the height of presumption for any helper to downplay, or discount entirely, a resource on the grounds that a child probably won't find it appealing. Given the need and the desperation many children of alcoholics feel, any resource presented in a positive light by someone they trust and respect might be made attractive. On the other hand, the children are ashamed, hopeless, and prepared for defeat, predisposed to excuses and rationalizations for why Alateen wouldn't suit them. This is part of their family illness, and professionals play into it by indulging their own reservations and communicating them overtly or covertly to the children.

The best way to find out about Al-Anon is to attend several different meetings. With the exception of anniversary meetings, when the group celebrates another year of its existence, Alateen meetings are closed, and only young people affected by another person's alcoholism may attend. But many Al-Anon meetings are open to the general public. All groups have the option of declaring themselves closed to outsiders, so the groups that remain open do so precisely because they want professionals and other concerned people to learn about alcoholism and the Al-Anon program. Though outsiders usually feel trepidations about intruding, they are projecting feelings that the members don't have and are quickly made to feel comfortable and appreciated.

Just as many children of alcoholics need to learn certain things about alcoholism before they can acknowledge its impact on their families, many professionals need accurate information about Al-Anon in order to go to a meeting and see for themselves. Many professionals will never attend a meeting or even hear a speaker from Al-Anon or Alateen. But if they know something about how the programs work and can describe them accurately, and if they can resolve the personal and professional biases that diminish their receptivity to what are not only the best, but too often the *only* resources for family members of alcoholics, then they can be instrumental in helping children of alcoholics find lasting help.

BACKGROUND AND STRUCTURE

Al-Anon Family Groups is an international self-help fellowship of adults who are affected by someone else's drinking. That someone else may be a spouse, sibling, parent, child, other relative, or friend. Women with alcoholic husbands still comprise the largest single population within Al-Anon; many of them are also daughters of alcoholics and, later, mothers of youthful problem drinkers. In recent years, adult children of alcoholics and husbands with alcoholic wives have been joining Al-Anon in increasing numbers. In some areas there are even Al-Anon groups specifically intended for adults who have alcoholic parents.

Al-Anon was organized in 1951, adopting the Twelve Traditions of Alcoholics Anonymous (founded in 1935) as its structural foundation, and the Twelve Steps and the Slogans of AA as the basis of its program of recovery. By 1980, more than 16,000 Al-Anon groups were operating in more than 75 countries.

Alateen is part of Al-Anon Family Groups. It is a self-help organization for young people, most of them teenagers, who are close to an alcoholic. The alcoholic may be a sibling, other relative, or close friend, but is most often a parent. Alateen is *not* a program for young people who are having problems with their own drinking, except insofar as many children of alcoholics develop such problems.

The first Alateen groups started in 1957; by 1980 there were more than 2,200. Each group has an adult sponsor who is active in Al-Anon. The sponsor is usually *not* the parent of a group member; and the sponsor's role is one of guidance rather than direction. Sponsorship has somewhat different meanings in Al-Anon and Alateen, and more will be said about it in a later section.

In this chapter, what is said about Al-Anon applies to Alateen as well, except as otherwise specified.

Many programs have tried to replicate the organizational genius that the founders of Alcoholics Anonymous embodied in the Twelve Traditions. Al-Anon's progenitors were astute and humble enough to embrace them whole, instead of altering or complicating them. The traditions govern each autonomous group, as well as the overall network to which each group belongs.

THE TWELVE TRADITIONS

1. Our common welfare should come first; personal progress for the greatest number depends upon unity.
2. For our group purposes, there is but one authority—a loving God as He may express Himself in our group conscience. Our leaders are but trusted servants—they do not govern.
3. The relatives of alcoholics, when gathered together for mutual aid, may call themselves an Al-Anon Group provided that, as a group, they have no other affiliation. The only requirement for membership is that there be a problem of alcoholism in a relative or friend.
4. Each group should be autonomous, except in matters affecting other Al-Anon Family Groups or AA as a whole.
5. Each Al-Anon Family Group has but one purpose: to help families of alcoholics. We do this by practicing the Twelve Steps of AA *ourselves*, by encouraging and understanding our alcoholic relatives, and by welcoming and giving comfort to families of alcoholics.
6. Al-Anon Family Groups ought never to endorse, finance, or lend our name to any outside enterprise, lest problems of money, property, and prestige divert us from our primary spiritual aim. Although a separate entity, we should always cooperate with Alcoholics Anonymous.
7. Every group ought to be fully self-supporting, declining outside contributions.
8. Al-Anon Twelfth Step work (that is, sharing the program with others, as explained below) should remain forever nonprofessional, but our service centers may employ special workers.
9. Our groups, as such, ought never be organized; but we may create service boards or committees directly responsible to those they serve.

10. The Al-Anon Groups have no opinion on outside issues; hence, our name ought never be drawn into public controversy.
11. Our public relations policy is based on attraction rather than promotion; we need always maintain personal anonymity at the level of press, radio, TV, and films. We need guard with special care the anonymity of all AA members.
12. Anonymity is the spiritual foundation of all our Traditions, ever reminding us to place principles above personalities.

The traditions have been incorporated in a structure that is a marvel of grass-roots organization. Each group is financially self-sufficient through members' contributions rather than dues. Members donate only what they can afford; for many, this might amount to twenty-five cents per meeting. Somehow the money generated is adequate to pay for group expenses such as refreshments, literature, and space. The contributions also account for about 20 percent of the operating expenses of the Al-Anon World Service Office in New York. The mainstay and primary function of the office is writing and publishing Al-Anon literature. Every book and pamphlet bearing Al-Anon's name is written by Al-Anon staff and passes through a rigorous review process culminating in the annual World Service Conference.

Operational decisions are made through a network of elected representatives. Each group sends a group representative to monthly district meetings; and group representatives elect five statewide officers, including one delegate to the World Service Conference. All policy, procedural, fiscal, and publishing decisions—everything done or written in Al-Anon's name—must first be approved by the Conference. Throughout the structure, checks and balances are built in as safeguards. But the group representatives are the voice of the fellowship and keep it responsive.

In many metropolitan areas the groups band together to fund and operate information service centers. If someone wants to locate the nearest meeting, get help in starting a new group, find kindred spirits with whom to communicate by mail from isolated areas, or bring a speaker to a school or civic group, these offices are prepared to help.

At Al-Anon meetings, members who choose to do so, and who have the permission of family members in AA, can use their last names. Many members use first names only. But outside of meetings anonymity is sacred; and at the public level, when speaking to nonmembers, for example, individuals must remain anonymous and never claim to be speaking for Al-Anon.

Each Al-Anon group has a regular weekly meeting. Most are held in the evening, though there are more and more morning and afternoon meetings, some providing childcare. Often meetings are held at the same time and place as AA meetings. Meetings are always one and a half hours in duration, and they begin and end promptly. They vary in size and format: In urban areas, meetings as large as 50 to 150 people are not uncommon, though smaller groups are the norm, whereas in rural areas fewer than 10 people may convene. Some meetings are speakers' meetings where three or four speakers address the whole group. More often, Al-Anon meetings are exchanges of experiences and insights among members. Each meeting has a chairperson, selected at the previous meeting, who is responsible for suggesting a theme, perhaps inviting speakers, and lending the meeting some direction and order.

Al-Anon is built to survive through the years, at minimal or no cost to its members, and wherever persons affected by alcoholism seek to use it. It is effective because it embodies principles that are basic to healthy living.

THE PROGRAM OF RECOVERY

If they are aware of Al-Anon at all, many professionals think it simply involves going to meetings, listening to others, and sharing sympathy and support. If that were all there is to Al-Anon, it might still be quite praiseworthy. But Al-Anon is a complete program of recovery, with concrete, sequential steps identical to those of AA. It is a holistic approach to life, based on principles that might apply equally well to people untouched by alcoholism (though such people cannot join Al-Anon). Al-Anon members strive to "work the program" at all times. Attending meetings is only one way in which members begin to internalize Al-Anon and reinforce its wisdom.

When family members first come to Al-Anon or Alateen, they are usually seeking ways to help the alcoholic stop drinking. What they find, however, is very different. Individual members of AA sometimes feel mistrustful of and threatened by Al-Anon because they think of it as a place where their relatives band together to accuse and denounce their alcoholics and concoct plans for controlling them. Nothing could be further from the truth.

Just as AA teaches recovering alcoholics to accept responsibility for their behavior and its consequences, instead of continuing to blame "people, places, and things," so Al-Anon concentrates on the family member's responsibilities. The alcoholic's drinking is independent and beyond the control of a spouse or child. All that family members can do is to understand their own feelings and reactions and learn new ways of living with a person they can accept or reject but cannot control. The Al-Anon program has the single aim of helping family members lead sane, productive, and happy lives, with the understanding that their ability to do so may improve the chances of recovery for the alcoholic. Even after the alcoholic has recovered, died, or left the scene, family members continue to need and receive guidance and support from others who are learning through shared experience.

The help that members give one another invokes a variety of guidelines to recovery. First, the Twelve Steps provide the basic framework.

THE TWELVE STEPS

1. We admitted we were powerless over alcohol—that our lives had become unmanageable.
2. Came to believe that a Power greater than ourselves could restore us to sanity.
3. Made a decision to turn our will and our lives over to the care of God *as we understood Him.*
4. Made a searching and fearless moral inventory of ourselves.
5. Admitted to God, to ourselves, and to another human being the exact nature of our wrongs.
6. Were entirely ready to have God remove all of these defects of character.
7. Humbly asked Him to remove our shortcomings.
8. Made a list of all persons we had harmed and became willing to make amends to them all.
9. Made direct amends to such people wherever possible, except when to do so would injure them or others.
10. Continued to take personal inventory and when we were wrong promptly admitted it.
11. Sought through prayer and meditation to improve our conscious contact with God *as we understood Him,* praying only for knowledge of His will for us and the power to carry that out.
12. Having had a spiritual awakening as the result of these Steps, we tried to carry this message to others, and to practice these principles in all our affairs.

The Serenity Prayer, found on plaques in gift shops everywhere, is for Al-Anon a cornerstone of the program members try to live.

THE SERENITY PRAYER
God grant me the serenity to accept
the things I cannot change,
courage to change the things I can,
and wisdom to know the difference.

Here are some of the various slogans that groups and members use to bring the program into their everyday lives, particularly when they are about to fall into patterns they have come to regard as unhealthy and unsatisfying.

> Let go and let God.
> First things first.
> One day at a time.
> Live and let live.
> Easy does it.
> Keep it simple.
> Listen and learn.

It would be a mistake to try to interpret or amplify the Steps and Slogans in a few paragraphs or pages, since the whole Al-Anon experience is a constant effort on the part of each member to understand and apply them according to his or her experiences and beliefs. Al-Anon literature, culled from the reflections of a great many members, illustrates these Steps and how they help in daily living. (Appendix B provides information about how to get such literature.)

PROFESSIONAL BIASES

Probably most important in the context of this book is the unfortunate fact that a nodding acquaintance with the Steps and Slogans sometimes triggers a strong negative reaction on the part of professionals who have their own deeply held opinions and prejudices. In statements expressing these negative reactions, the program is often referred to in one or more of these terms:
- Too religious
- Too passive and accepting
- Too cruel and selfish
- Too unprofessional

Each of these deserves careful consideration.

"Al-Anon and Alateen are too religious."
God is explicitly mentioned in five of the Twelve Steps and in the Serenity Prayer. "Let go and let God" is a cardinal slogan. Some meetings end with the Lord's Prayer, recited with hands clasped in a circle. And the meetings often take place in church halls. Many professionals are turned off or offended by what they perceive as a strong religious

orientation. Even if they are not, they often conclude that the teenagers they might refer would be turned off. Afraid that they would lose their credibility if they extolled the virtues of Alateen to young people who would find it too religious and "straight," many professionals mention it only casually and without conviction.

AA, Al-Anon, and Alateen emphatically proclaim themselves to be spiritual rather than religious programs. They are affiliated with no formal religious group, and number among their members a great many atheists and agnostics. It is not necessary to believe in God; but participants who find help in the program generally come to believe in a "Power greater than ourselves."

Children of alcoholics, just as their alcoholic parents, experience a loss of values in the course of their illness. They find themselves repeatedly feeling, saying, and doing things that they are ashamed of, and promised themselves they would never do again. They may lie regularly, or publicly ridicule their parents, or privately plot their brutal murder. Above all, they don't know what to believe in anymore. The rules of conduct they learn in the family are organized around keeping the alcoholic happy and the family secret intact. The larger sense of right and wrong gets twisted, distorted, and subordinated to the family's need. The children learn that there is an immense gap between what people preach and what they practice. Life itself seems unjust, perverse, meaningless.

Al-Anon's intent is to instill and reinforce basic human values and to fulfill the need for a meaning to life that is larger than the daily struggles within families and individuals. The program calls for a code, if not to live by, then at least to strive for; and not for the sake of the individual or the family, but for a larger, greater good. Believers can accept the code as God's own. Nonbelievers might think of it as an honorable and just way in which to live with other human beings or, on the most basic level, a way to belong and contribute to the group.

The spiritual nature of Al-Anon is probably harder to describe than it is to feel. When a teenage boy, for example, comes to Alateen, he has been trying in vain for years to control his mother's drinking, mitigate his feelings of hatred and worthlessness, fool the world, and make sense out of chaos. The first thing he learns in the program is that his life has become unmanageable. All sorts of things are happening to him, and being done by him, which he has not been able to prevent or control. He comes to admit that "this thing is bigger than I am." With profound despair he sees through the illusion that if he learns just the right tricks, he can bring sobriety to the alcoholic and happiness to himself.

At the same time, however, he sees a group of people struggling with the same problem as his, but with considerably more success. Like a great many newcomers, he is astonished at the palpable serenity and actual happiness of many members. He can go away believing that the world is chaotic, hopeless, and basically not worth inhabiting, but no one *wants* to believe that, and the group is offering him another choice. He might reject the notion that a Higher Power mysteriously governs the apparent disorder of life; but he can see people finding comfort and strength, love and understanding, as well as cruelty and inconsistency, in life. He sees individuals who are getting from one another things he wants; he sees that they have hopes of getting more, even while they acknowledge that there is so much they cannot control. He envies them their equanimity, their ability to smile in the face of the limits of their power. They do all they can for themselves, but they also accept it that life often seems senseless, unjust, and different from what they wish it to be. He sees people who can embrace life as it is, and still find a meaning in it outside of themselves.

In short, when he stops believing he can win in single combat with the world, he is susceptible to other definitions of winning, a new conception of the rules of the game, and a larger sense of why it should be played. The self-pity he has turned into a self-fulfilling expectation of failure is difficult to sustain in the face of so many people in more dire straits who don't tolerate it in themselves or sympathize with it in him. He begins to see himself as someone who can contribute to and derive security and satisfaction from a fellowship, a larger community, or a family in God. He starts to feel connected to a larger purpose instead of immersed in an isolated family at odds with the world and each other.

That larger purpose, or Higher Power, is meant to be concrete, proximate, and accessible from moment to moment, Steps 5, 6, 7, and 11 speak to the importance of constant contact with the source of one's values and meaning, whether that source be God, nature, human dignity, society, or the Al-Anon group (in AA, "God" has sometimes been used as an acronym for "Group of Drunks").

A person may consider religion distasteful and dishonest, and spirituality a crutch. But one can hardly dispute the need for find a meaning in life and values that derive from that meaning. In the America of the 1980s, this sense of larger purpose and meaning is noticeably weaker than it has ever been. The fact that so many professionals quarrel with Al-Anon's spirituality is most of all indicative of our contemporary malaise, the loss of a sense of timeless values characteristic of what has been called the "culture of narcissism." Al-Anon members simply believe in the limits of their own wisdom and power. They learn to hope and trust that the things they can't understand and control will take care of themselves. It is doubtful that any other age has had serious problems with this tenet.

"The programs are too passive and accepting."

Outsiders sometimes criticize Al-Anon for emphasizing an individual's powerlessness and the need to accept whatever comes, instead of promoting a stronger sense of efficacy. They confuse pragmatism with passivity and underestimate the confusion with which children of alcoholics view their own power.

Children of alcoholics feel responsible for their parents' drinking. If they cause it, they should be able to stop it, but their every effort ends in failure. Their attitude toward this most pervasive fact of their lives contaminates their general sense of efficacy. Paradoxically, they continue to believe that they have great power, as demonstrated by the family chaos often attributed to them; and consciously or subconciously search for more subtle ways to forge if not a loving and happy home then at least a peaceful one. But their repeated inability to accomplish this principal goal undermines their belief in their capacity to accomplish any goal. They come to think of themselves as mysteriously, even involuntarily powerful, but impotent when it comes to getting what they want.

The key is that they don't distinguish between what they can and cannot influence. They expect to control everything or nothing. Al-Anon teaches members to find the middle ground. Most of us lose sight of it too, from time to time, but young people with family alcoholism never knew the middle ground existed. One child of an alcoholic might study hard for an exam and worry even harder afterward; another might not study at all and not give the test a thought, even after the F is in the books. Al-Anon advocates studying hard beforehand and "letting go and letting God" afterward.

Far from inducing passivity, the program is all about change; change based on an honest, far-reaching, and continuous personal assessment, the likes of which few people outside of Al-Anon ever attempt. Guidelines for the "fearless and searching moral inventory" undertaken in Steps 4 and 10 are available from Al-Anon headquarters. Anyone who considers the program too accepting would do well to examine these guidelines.

Central to the changes Al-Anon members desire is the capacity to see and accept the limits of their power and the responsibility for doing everything up to those limits. Everyone defines the limits for themselves. When has one done one's best, whether to provide a safe and nurturing family life or to combat world hunger or nuclear proliferation? When does the "Let go and let God" begin? In Al-Anon, as in the rest of the human community, members answer the question for themselves, repeatedly—provided they ask it in the first place.

Some visitors feel that the program is too passive because it doesn't sufficiently encourage people to leave abusive situations or otherwise rid themselves of the alcoholic. Other people voice just the opposite reaction.

"The program is too cruel and selfish."

Some people object to the first-things-first attitude, which they might paraphrase as "first I take care of me, then I worry about you." Most of all, they have difficulty with how Al-Anon teaches family members to deal with the alcoholic. It should be obvious that many people use the Steps and Slogans in many different ways. "Don't accept the unacceptable" is a catchphrase that tells one member not to tolerate life with the alcoholic any longer, while it keeps another member from letting the alcoholic cast him out of her life.

Another saying is sometimes heard around Al-Anon: "This is a selfish program." Indeed, members are encouraged to think first, of what is right or wrong; next, of what they themselves want or need; and only after, of what others ask. Children of alcoholics have learned to revolve around the alcoholic's needs, to live to please others; then they resent the persons whose welfare they put before their own. They have to learn to take care of and please themselves; only then do they stop "collecting resentment stamps."

Most of the natural impulses governing family members' responses to the alcoholic have unhealthy and destructive results for all concerned. It may seem cruel to let the alcoholic sleep in her own vomit; insensitive to refuse to sit up and talk with her far into the night; and insane to let her lose job after job, instead of telling the boss that she's sick. But to Al-Anon members such reactions are not only necessary, for themselves, but also helpful for the alcoholic in the long run. And AA members heartily agree. Al-Anon teaches family members to let the alcoholic take full responsibility for the drinking and feel the full measure of its consequences. What members try to do vis-à-vis the alcoholic is to "detach with love." They want to love the person without loving the alcoholism and without becoming entrapped in its cycles. Often the love has been burned out, and it takes some time before it returns. Or it never returns at all. Again, Al-Anon literature best amplifies on how family members can help or hinder the alcoholic's recovery and their own in the process.

A selfish program? When newcomers have attended enough meetings to decide to give Al-Anon a good try, they usually ask one or more people they respect to sponsor them. Asking members to sponsor you means asking them to be available to you any time of the day or night, to help you understand and work the program, overcome your fears, talk you out of crisis, correct your "stinking thinking." Sponsorship is one way to enact the Twelfth Step, and it is as important for sponsors in sustaining their recovery as it is for newcomers. (Studies show that tutors benefit from peer tutelage even more than those they teach.) But sponsorship is also an awesome responsibility and a great deal of work. Al-Anon is a selfish program, but it brings out qualities of friendship we sometimes think have vanished from the face of the earth.

"Al-Anon is too *unprofessional.*"

This contention implies that the program is simplistic, inconsistent, haphazard. Many professionals assume that children and other family members of alcoholics need sophisticated psychological help. Certainly some do, and the pity is that so few therapists know the first thing about family alcoholism. But for most children of alcoholics, the problem is a good deal simpler. They have developed defenses, personality traits, and self-images based on a fallacious view of family alcoholism and their own involvement in it. They need to learn a new perception of their experience and to try out new ways of responding, both emotionally and behaviorally. When new ways prove more satisfying (and it often requires sustained help and support before they begin to do so), many children of alcoholics can internalize what they have learned and achieve lasting, remarkable changes.

The program prepares newcomers for how gradually its precepts may be taken in. "Pay lip service" and "Bring the old body around—the mind will catch up later" are two slogans emphasizing that if one hears and repeats the Al-Anon program often enough, it will start to have meaning and real application.

The foundation of self-help is identification. Visitors sometimes remark on the similarity of the stories they hear at meetings and wonder how members can attend meeting after meeting without feeling bored. But the listeners are too busy identifying with the speakers, deriving hope, inspiration, caution, or perspective from their insights. Al-Anon members don't give advice or "take anyone else's inventory"; they simply say what has worked well for them and what has not.

Professionals are sometimes bothered by a perceived inconsistency within Al-Anon. They find great differences between groups as well as in the various interpretations that individual members give to the Steps and Slogans. This diversity is an essential part of Al-Anon's broad appeal. Some groups spend a great deal of time talking about God. In others, religious overtones are minimal. Regardless of class, educational background, race or ethnic origins, everyone can find some group with which they can be comfortable and some individuals with whom they can most closely identify. Helpers are therefore wise to suggest to newcomers that they try several Al-Anon groups before they draw any conclusions about the program's ability to help them.

As a self-help program, Al-Anon is radically different from individual or group therapies that rely upon a detached professional with a very private and mysterious bag of psychological tricks. Not all populations can help themselves; some require professional skills and the outsider's distance from the problem. But children and other family members of alcoholics can get their best help from one another. They can understand alcoholism and the alcoholic, their own reactions, and a new way to live, by sharing the experiences of their comrades.

Al-Anon may appear revivalist, evangelical, jingoistic, rhetoric-filled, superficial, or behaviorist. But it is based on fundamental and ancient ideas of helping. Behind its Steps and Slogans can be found, if a person needs them, psychological and behavioral concepts profound enough for most clinicians. For family members in Al-Anon, there is no single measure of recovery comparable to sobriety in AA. The best way to learn what Al-Anon does for its members is to attend a few meetings.

Alateen is more problematic. It helps most teenagers who join. That so few join is attributable to several obstacles. The children don't seek or accept help; and few youth professionals intervene to encourage them to do so. As a consequence, there are not enough teenagers ready to constitute more Alateen groups. But in some areas, there are enough ready adolescents, but no ready Al-Anon sponsors. Sponsoring an Alateen group is a huge undertaking, and though it can help the sponsor immensely, it is threatening and frightening. Al-Anon has long been concerned with its failure to elicit more Alateen sponsors from its ranks.

In communities where Alateen exists, the program needs help from youth professionals. They have to get young people to the point where they will try the program, and to do so they must be objective about what it offers. In most communities, there are no Alateen groups; and while professionals can make Al-Anon aware of the need, they cannot start Alateen groups themselves. But they can start groups that may substitute for or lead to Alateen or Al-Anon. They can find or help create other resources; they can put children in touch with one another or in touch with Al-Anon by mail. Above all, youth professionals themselves constitute a major helping resource for children of alcoholics.

Appendix A
SIGNS AND SYMPTOMS
OF ALCOHOLISM

I. SIGNS OF ALCOHOLISM IN AN INDIVIDUAL

There are a great many formulations and descriptions of the common signs and symptoms of alcoholism. Some authorities distinguish between problem drinking and early stage alcoholism; others do not. More information about the disease, its symptoms and progression, can be obtained from Alcoholics Anonymous and the National Council on Alcoholism (addresses are listed below), and from state and local councils on alcoholism and alcoholism agencies.

The definition of alcoholism presented in Chapter 2 is likewise one of many. It emphasizes functional consequences: problems—with school or work, family or friends, or physical or mental health—which, regardless of excuses, stem from drinking. Losing friends, losing a job, or sustaining an injury due to intoxication is a tangible warning sign of a problem with alcohol. Other signs of a burgeoning problem are less readily identifiable, except by problem drinkers themselves. They have to do with reasons, occasions, and patterns of drinking. Some examples are:

- Drinking to forget or escape from problems;
- Drinking to face certain situations;
- Having several drinks before a party;
- Drinking alone;
- Drinking in the morning;
- Reserving a regular time for drinking, and looking forward to it.

The National Council on Alcoholism developed the following checklist, "What Are the Signs of Alcoholism?" According to the Council, 'yes' answers to several of the questions may indicate different stages of alcoholism: early stage, 1–8; middle stage, 9–21; beginning of the final stage, 22–26.

1. Do you occasionally drink heavily after a disappointment, a quarrel, or when the boss gives you a hard time?
2. When you have trouble or feel under pressure, do you always drink more heavily than usual?
3. Have you noticed that you are able to handle more liquor than you did when you were first drinking?
4. Did you ever wake up on the "morning after" and discover that you could not remember part of the evening before, even though your friends tell you that you did not "pass out"?
5. When drinking with other people, do you try to have a few extra drinks when others will not know it?
6. Are there certain occasions when you feel uncomfortable if alcohol is not available?
7. Have you recently noticed that when you begin drinking you are in more of a hurry to get the first drink than you used to be?
8. Do you sometimes feel a little guilty about your drinking?
9. Are you secretly irritated when your family or friends discuss your drinking?
10. Have you recently noticed an increase in the frequency of your memory "blackouts" (as described in question #4)?
11. Do you often find that you wish to continue drinking after your friends say they have had enough?
12. Do you usually have a reason for the occasions when you drink heavily?
13. When you are sober, do you often regret things you have done or said while drinking?
14. Have you tried switching brands or following different plans for controlling your drinking?
15. Have you often failed to keep the promises you have made to yourself about controlling or cutting down on your drinking?
16. Have you ever tried to control your drinking by making a change in jobs or moving to a new location?
17. Do you try to avoid family or close friends while you are drinking?
18. Are you having an increasing number of financial and work problems?
19. Do more people seem to be treating you unfairly without good reason?
20. Do you eat very little or irregularly when you are drinking?
21. Do you sometimes have the "shakes" in the morning and find that it helps to have a little drink?

22. Have you recently noticed that you cannot drink as much as you once did?
23. Do you sometimes stay drunk for several days at a time?
24. Do you sometimes feel very depressed and wonder whether life is worth living?
25. Sometimes after periods of drinking, do you see or hear things that aren't there?
26. Do you get terribly frightened after you have been drinking heavily?

Some other, generally middle-stage signs worth mentioning are: seeking medical or psychiatric aid (as a way of blaming the problem on something other than the drinking); becoming increasingly self-conscious; being consistently or increasingly hostile or violent when drinking; and hiding bottles or otherwise assuring the supply of alcohol.

Possibly the most telltale sign, the sign that follows from the persistent exhibition of a number of the symptoms mentioned, is the concern of someone close. If a friend or family member is worried about a person's drinking, it is almost always with good cause.

II. INDICATIONS THAT A CHILD
MAY BE LIVING WITH FAMILY ALCOHOLISM

A. General Indications

Certainly all of the observable behaviors listed below can be the result of a variety of circumstances, either temporary or ongoing, which may or may not be problematic for the child. Nothing can be concluded from any one sign or a combination of signs. However, the helping professional is obliged to consider the possibility of parental alcoholism in children whose behavior coincides rather closely with the syndromes described in Chapter 4, and who also manifest some of the patterns that follow. A few of these patterns, such as numbers 1 and 2, might only appear in teenagers old enough to take care of younger siblings. Others, notably numbers 3 through 5, would be more characteristic of preadolescents.

1. Morning tardiness (especially Monday mornings).
2. Consistent concern with getting home promptly at the end of a day or activity period.
3. Malodorousness.
4. Improper clothing for the weather.
5. Regression: thumbsucking, enuresis, infantile behavior with peers.

6. Scrupulous avoidance of arguments and conflict.
7. Friendlessness and isolation.
8. Poor attendance.
9. Frequent illness and need to visit nurse, especially for stomach complaints.
10. Fatigue and listlessness.
11. Hyperactivity and inability to concentrate.
12. Sudden temper and other emotional outbursts.
13. Exaggerated concern with achievement and satisfying authority in children who are already at the head of their class.
14. Extreme fear about situations involving contact with parents.

B. Indications During Alcohol Education Activities

Again, these indications may conceivably have other causes and should simply alert the professional to the possibility, a good deal stronger now, that the child is worried about the drinking of a parent. Symptoms occur during group or individual discussions about alcohol, drinking, and alcoholism.

1. Extreme negativism about alcohol and all drinking: "Why do they make alcohol? Why are they allowed to sell it?"
2. Inability to think of healthy, integrative reasons and styles of drinking.
3. Equation of drinking with getting drunk.
4. Greater familiarity with different kinds of drinks than peers.
5. Inordinate attention to alcohol in situations in which it is marginal, for example, in a play or movie not about drinking.
6. Normally active child becomes passive during alcohol education activities.
7. Normally passive child or distracting child becomes active or focused during alcohol discussion.
8. Changes in attendance patterns during alcohol education activities.
9. Frequent requests to leave the room.
10. Lingering after activity to ask innocent question or simply to gather belongings.
11. Mention of parent's drinking to excess on occasion.
12. Mention of drinking problem of friend's parent, uncle, or aunt.
13. Strong negative feelings about alcoholics.
14. Evident concern with whether alcoholism can be inherited.

REFERENCES AND RESOURCES

I. RESOURCES FOR USE WITH YOUNG PEOPLE

A. Curricula

Alcohol education is important for all children, but is particularly crucial for children of alcoholics, some of whom will ask for further help as a result of these group activities. The curricula listed in this section are alcohol education curricula, which include some activities about family alcoholism. They are *not* curricula for use with groups of children of alcoholics; in some cases the latter are available from model programs listed in the following section.

There are many alcohol education curricula. Your state's alcoholism agency may have its own updated list of recommended materials, including some developed locally. Other sources of information about alcohol education materials are:

> Milgram, Gail G., *Alcohol Education Materials: An Annotated Bibliography.* New Brunswick, N.J.: Rutgers Center of Alcohol Studies, 1978–79 (218 annotations).
> National Institute on Alcohol Abuse and Alcoholism. *Alcohol-Specific Curricula: A Selected List.* Rockville, Maryland: 1980 (11 annotations).

Of the curricula being used nationally, the two I recommend most are:

> Mills, Dixie, Deutsch, Charles, and DiCicco, Lena, *Decisions About Drinking* (Grades 3–12), 1978. Available from CASPAR Alcohol Education Program, 226 Highland Ave., Somerville, MA 02143.

Roberts, Clay, *Here's Looking at You*. (Grades K–12). Seattle: Educational Service District No. 110, 1976. Available from Comprehensive Health Education Foundation, 20814 Pacific Highway South, Seattle, WA 98188.

B. Pamphlets and Books for Children

1. Ages 5 to 10

Nonfiction

Black, Claudia. *My Dad Loves Me, My Dad Has a Disease*. 1979, 76 pp. ACT, Newport Beach, Cal.

Seixas, Judith. *Alcohol: What It Is, What It Does*. 1977, 56 pp. National Council on Alcoholism, 733 Third Avenue, NY 10017.

Fiction

Melquist, Elaine. *Pepper*. 1974, 14 pp. National Council on Alcoholism.

2. Ages 8 to 12

Nonfiction

Al-Anon Family Groups. *What's Drunk, Mama?* 1977, 30 pp. Al-Anon Family Group Headquarters, Inc., P.O. Box 182, Madison Square Station, New York, NY 10010.

Seixas, Judith. *Living With a Parent Who Drinks Too Much*. New York: Greenwillow (William Morrow), 1979.

Fiction

Sherburne, Zoa. *Jennifer*. New York: William Morrow, 1959.

Snyder, Anne. *First Step*. New York: Holt, Rinehart and Winston, 1975.

3. Ages 12 to 15

Nonfiction

Al-Anon Family Groups. *Alateen, Hope for Children of Alcoholics*. 1973, 114 pp. Al-Anon Family Groups.

————. *If Your Parents Drink Too Much*. 1974, 24 pp.

————. *It's A Teenage Affair*. 1964, 3 pp.

Hornik, Edith. *You and Your Alcoholic Parents*. 1974, 28 pp. Public Affairs Pamphlets, 381 Park Ave. S., New York, NY 10016.

What Everyone Should Know About Alcoholism. 1974, 16 pp. Channing L. Bete Co., Greenfield, Mass. 01301.

Fiction

Hammer, Earl Jr. *You Can't Get There From Here*. New York: Bantam Books, 1974.

Oppenheimer, Joan. *Francesca, Baby*. Oct. 7, 1976. Scholastic Scope Magazine, Scholastic Book Services, New York.

Stolz, Mary. *Edge of Next Year*. New York: Harper and Row, 1974.

Summers, James L. *The Long Ride Home*. Philadelphia: Westminister Press, 1966.

Woody, Regina. *One Day At a Time*. Philadelphia: Westminister Press, 1968.

4. Ages 15 to 18

Nonfiction

Alcoholic in the Family? 1977, 16 pp. Channing L. Bete Co.

Hornik, Edith. *You and Your Alcoholic Parent*. 1974, National Council on Alcoholism.

Silverstein, Dr. Alvin and Virginia Silverstein. *Alcoholism*. New York: Lippincott, 1975.

Someone Close Drinks Too Much. 1976, 15 pp. U.S. Government Printing Office, Washington D.C. 20402.

Wegscheider, Sharon. *A Second Chance*. Palo Alto, Ca.: Science and Behavior Books, 1980.

Fiction

Jackson, Charles. *The Lost Weekend*. New York: Farrar, Straus, 1944.

Mahoney, Barbara. *A Sensitive, Passionate Man*. New York: McKay, 1974.

Rebeta-Burditt, Joyce. *The Cracker Factory*. New York: Macmillan, 1977.

Smith, Betty. *A Tree Grows in Brooklyn*. New York: Harper and Row, 1947.

C. Films

1. Ages 5 to 12 (also useful for ages 16 to 18)

All Bottled Up. 11 minutes, color, animated. AIMS Instructional Media Services, Inc., 626 Justin Ave., Glendale, CA 91201

2. Ages 12 to 15

Like Father, Like Son? 15 minutes, color. Part of Jackson Junior High series, National Audiovisual Center, GSA, Washington, DC 20409

3. Ages 14 to 18

The Secret Love of Sandra Blain. 27 minutes, color. Norm Southerby and Associates, P.O. Box 15403, Long Beach, CA 90815
Soft Is the Heart of a Child. 28 minutes, color. Gerald T. Rogers Productions, Inc., 5225 Old Orchard Road, #6, Skokie, IL 60077

II. INFORMATION, SERVICES, AND MODEL PROGRAMS

A. Local Resources (consult telephone directory)

Al-Anon Family Groups
Alcoholics Anonymous (AA)
Alcoholism Information and Treatment Centers
Regional and Statewide Councils on Alcoholism
State Government listings

B. National Networks for Information and Literature

1. Al-Anon Family Group Headquarters, P.O. Box 182, Madison Square Station, New York, NY 10010
2. Alcoholics Anonymous (AA), P.O. Box 459, Grand Central Station, New York, NY 10017
3. National Clearinghouse for Alcohol Information (NCALI), Box 2345, Rockville, MD 20852
4. National Council on Alcoholism (NCA), 733 Third Avenue, New York, NY 10017
5. National Institute on Alcohol Abuse and Alcoholism (NIAAA), 5600 Fishers Lane, Parklawn Building, Rockville, MD 20852

C. Model Programs for Children of Alcoholics

1. CASPAR Alcohol Education Program, 226 Highland Avenue, Somerville, MA 02143
2. The Door—Multi-Service Center for Youth, 618 Avenue of the Americas, New York, NY 10011
3. Kolmac Clinic, 1003 Spring Street, Silver Spring, MD 20910

4. Nassau County (N.Y.) Department of Drug and Alcohol Addiction, 175 Fulton Street, Room 600, Hempstead, NY 11501
5. New Directions: The Family Center Youth Program, 5210 Hollister Avenue, Santa Barbara, CA 93111
6. Rainbow Retreat, 4332 North Twelfth Street, Phoenix, AZ 85104
7. Westchester County (N.Y.) Department of Community Mental Health, 148 Martine Avenue, Room 234, White Plains, NY 10601

BIBLIOGRAPHY

Ablon, J. "Al-Anon Family Groups: Impetus for Learning and Change Through the Presentation of Alternatives." *American Journal of Psychotherapy* 28 (1974): 30–45.

Aldoory, Shirley. "Research into Family Factors in Alcoholism." *Alcohol Health and Research World* 3 (Summer 1979): 2–6.

American Medical Association. *Manual on Alcoholism.* Chicago: 1977.

Aronson, H., and A. Gilbert. "Preadolescent Sons of Male Alcoholics." *Archives of General Psychiatry* 8 (1963): 235–41.

Baker, J. M. "Alcoholism and the American Indian." In *Alcoholism: Development, Consequences and Interventions,* pp. 194–203. Edited by Nada J. Estes and M. Edith Heinemann. St. Louis: V. Mosby, 1977.

Bales, Robert F. "Cultural Differences in Rates of Alcoholism." In *Drinking and Intoxication,* pp. 264–77. Edited by Raymond G. McCarthy. New Haven: College and University Press, 1959.

Barnes, Grace M. "The Development of Adolescent Drinking Behavior: An Evaluative Review of the Impact of the Socialization Process within the Family." *Adolescence* 12 (Winter, 1977): 571–91.

Behling, D. "Alcohol Abuse as Encountered in 51 Instances of Reported Child Abuse." *Clinical Pediatrics* 18 (1979): 87–91.

Biron, Ronald, James A. Carifio, Robert White, Dixie Mills, Charles Deutsch, and Gail Levine-Reid. "The Critical Incident Approach to Assessing Effects of an Alcohol Education Curriculum." *Journal of Alcohol and Drug Education* 25 (1980): 20–27.

Black, Claudia. "Children of Alcoholics." *Alcohol Health and Research World* 4 (1979): 23–27.

Booz-Allen and Hamilton, Inc. *An Assessment of the Needs of and Resources for Children of Alcoholic Parents.* Rockville, Md.: National Institute on Alcohol Abuse and Alcoholism, 1974

Bosma, Willem. "Alcoholism and Teenagers." *Maryland State Medical Journal* 24 (1975): 62–68.

Boston Globe, 19 January 1980. "Helping Kids with Alcoholic Parents"

Browning, D., and B. Boatman. "Incest: Children at Risk." *American Journal of Psychiatry* 134 (1977): 69–72.

Cahalan, Don, and Ira Cisin. "American Drinking Practices: Summary of Findings from a National Probability Sample. I. Extent of Drinking by Population Subgroups." *Quarterly Journal of Studies on Alcohol* 29 (1968): 130.

Cahalan, Don, Ira Cisin, and Helen M. Crossley. *American Drinking Practices.* New Haven: College and University Press, 1969.

Califano, Joseph A., Jr. Foreword to *Third Special Report to U.S. Congress on Alcohol and Health.* Rockville, Md.: National Institute on Alcohol Abuse and Alcoholism, 1978.

Cantwell, D. "Psychiatric Illness in the Families of Hyperactive Children." *Archives of General Psychiatry* 27 (1972): 414–17.

Chafetz, Morris E., Howard T. Blane, and Marjorie J. Hill. "Children of Alcoholics: Observations in a Child Guidance Clinic." *Quarterly Journal of Studies on Alcohol* 32 (1971): 687–98.

Clarren, S., and D. Smith. "The Fetal Alcohol Syndrome: A Review of the World Literature." *New England Journal of Medicine* 298 (1978): 1063–67.

Clifford, Bernard J. "A Study of the Wives of Rehabilitated and Unrehabilitated Alcoholics." *Social Casework* 41 (1960): 457–60.

Cork, Margaret. *The Forgotten Children: A Study of Children with Alcoholic Parents.* Toronto: Alcohol and Drug Addiction Research Foundation, 1969.

Cotton, Nancy S. "The Familial Incidence of Alcoholism." *Journal of Studies on Alcohol* 40 (1979): 89–116.

deLint, J. "The Prevention of Alcoholism." *Preventive Medicine* 3 (1974): 24–35.

Deutsch, Charles. "The Surprise in Pandora's Box: Teachers Help Children with Family Alcoholism." Paper presented at the annual meeting of the National Council on Alcoholism, Washington, D.C., April 1979.

Deutsch, Charles, Lena DiCicco, and Dixie Mills. "Services for Children of Alcoholic Parents." In *Alcohol and Health Monograph No. 3: Prevention, Intervention and Treatment: Concerns and Models.* Rockville, Md.: National Institute on Alcohol Abuse and Alcoholism, 1981.

———. "The Somerville Story: Evolution of an Alcohol Education Program." Paper presented at the 27th annual meeting of Alcohol and Drug Problems Association of North America, New Orleans, La., September 1976.

———. "Reaching Children from Families with Alcoholism: Some Innovative Techniques." *Proceedings of the 29th Annual Meeting of the Alcohol and Drug Problems Association of North America.* Washington D.C.: 1978, 54–58.

DiCicco, Lena. "Children of Alcoholic Parents: Issues in Identification." Paper presented at the NIAAA Symposium on Services to Children of Alcoholics, Silver Spring, Md., 24 September 1979.

DiCicco, Lena, Hilma Unterberger, and John E. Mack. "Confronting Denial: An Alcoholism Intervention Strategy." *Psychiatric Annals* 8 (November 1978): 54–65.

El Guebaly, Nady, and David R Offord. "The Offspring of Alcoholics: A Critical Review." *American Journal of Psychiatry* 134 (1977): 357–65.

Fine, E., L. Yuden, H. Holmes, and S. Heineman. "Behavior Disorders in Children with Parental Alcoholism." Paper presented at the annual meeting of the National Council on Alcoholism, Milwaukee, Wisc., April 1975.

Fogarty, Thomas F. "System Concepts and the Dimensions of Self." In *Family Theory*, pp. 144–53. Edited by Philip S. Guerin. New York: Gardner Press, 1976.

Fox, Ruth. "The Effect of Alcoholism on Children." *Proceedings of the 5th International Congress on Psychotherapy Program on Child Psychology.* New York, 1963.

Fraser, J. "The Female Alcoholic." *Addictions* 20 (1973): 64–80.

Globetti, Gerald. "Alcohol: A Family Affair." Paper presented at North American Congress of Parents and Teachers, St. Louis, Mo., 1973.

Gomberg, Edith. Paper presented at New England School of Alcohol Studies, Bristol, R.I., 21 June 1979.

———. "Women with Alcohol Problems." In *Alcoholism: Development, Consequences and Interventions*, pp. 174–85. Edited by Nada J. Estes and M. Edith Heinemann. St. Louis: V. Mosby, 1977.

Goodwin, Donald. *Is Alcoholism Hereditary?* New York: Oxford University Press, 1976.

Goodwin, D. W., F. Schulsinger, and L. Hermansen. "Alcoholism and the Hyperactive Child Syndrome." *Journal of Nervous Mental Disorders* 160 (1975): 349–53.

Goodwin, D. W., F. Schulsinger, L. Hermansen, S. B. Guze, and G. Winokur. "Alcohol Problems in Adoptees Raised Apart from Alcoholic Biological Parents." *Archives of General Psychiatry* 28 (1973): 238–43.

Gunther, M. "Female Alcoholism: The Drinker in the Pantry." *Today's Health* 53 (1975): 15–18.

Haberman, Paul. "Childhood Symptoms in Children of Alcoholics and Comparison Group Parents." *Journal of Marriage and the Family* 28 (1966): 152–54.

Hecht, Murray. "Children of Alcoholics Are Children at Risk." *American Journal of Nursing* 73 (1973): 1764–67.

Hindman, Margaret. "Children of Alcoholic Parents." *Alcohol Health and Research World* (Winter 1975/76): 2–5.

Homonoff, Emeline, and Arville Stephen. "Alcohol Education for Children of Alcoholics in a Boston Neighborhood." *Journal of Studies on Alcohol* 40 (1979): 923–26.

Jackson, Joan K. "Alcoholism and the Family." In *Society, Culture, and Drinking Patterns*. Edited by David J. Pittman and Charles R. Snyder. New York: John Wiley, 1962.

Kammeier, M. "Adolescents from Families With and Without Alcohol Problems." *Quarterly Journal of Studies on Alcohol* 32 (1971): 364–72.

Kearney, T., and C. Taylor. "Emotionally Disturbed Adolescents with Alcoholic Parents." *Acta Paedopsychiatr* (Basel) 36 (1969): 215–21

Keniston, Kenneth, and the Carnegie Council on Children. *All Our Children: The American Family Under Pressure.* New York: Harcourt, Brace, Jovanovich, 1977.

Kern, Joseph C., Joan Tippman, Jeffrey Fortgang, and Stewart R. Paul. "A Treatment Approach for Children of Alcoholics." *Journal of Drug Education* 7 (1977–78): 207–18.

Korcok, Milan. "Alcoholism is a Family Affair." *Focus on Alcohol and Drug Issues* 2 (May–June 1979): 4.

Lindbeck, V. "The Adjustment of Adolescents to Paternal Alcoholism." Paper presented at Massachusetts General Hospital, Boston, 27 April 1971.

McCabe, John. "Children in Need: Consent Issues in Treatment." *Alcohol Health and Research World* 2 (1977): 2–12.

McCarthy, Raymond G., ed. *Drinking and Intoxication.* New Haven: College and University Press, 1959.

McCord, William, and Joan McCord. *Origins of Alcoholism.* Stanford, Calif.: Stanford University Press, 1969.

McKay, James R. "Clinical Observations on Adolescent Problem Drinkers." *Quarterly Journal of Studies on Alcohol* 22 (1961): 124–34.

———. "Juvenile Delinquency and Drinking Behavior." *Journal of Health and Social Behavior* 4 (Winter 1963): 276–82.

McLachlan, J., R. Walderman and S. Thomas. *A Study of Teenagers with Alcoholic Parents.* Toronto: The Donwood Institute, 1973.

Maddox, George L. "Teenage Drinking in the United States." In *Society, Culture and Drinking Patterns,* pp. 230–45. Edited by David J. Pittman and Charles R. Snyder. New York: John Wiley, 1962.

Mainard, R., P. DeBerranger, and J. Cadudal. "Une Conséquence fréquente et grave de l'alcoolisme parental—les services commis sur les enfants." *Revue de l'Alcoolisme* 21 (1971): 31.

Mayer, J., and R. Black. "The Relationship between Alcoholism and Child Abuse and Neglect." In *Currents in Alcoholism,* pp. 429–44. Edited by Frank Seixas. New York: Grune and Stratton, 1977.

Morehouse, Ellen, Tarpley Richards, and Judith Seixas. "A Child's World of Fighting and Noise." *Focus on Alcohol and Drug Issues* 2 (1979): 16.

Morrison, J., and M. Stewart. "A Family Study of the Hyperactive Child Syndrome." *Biological Psychiatry* 3 (1971): 189–95.

National Council on Alcoholism. "Facts on Alcoholism." New York, 1976.

National Institute of Mental Health/National Institute on Alcohol Abuse and Alcoholism. *Alcohol and Alcoholism: Problems, Programs and Progress.* Washington, D.C., 1972.

National Institute on Alcohol Abuse and Alcoholism. *Third Special Report to the U.S. Congress on Alcohol and Health.* Rockville, Md., 1978.

———. *Fourth Special Report to the U.S. Congress on Alcohol and Health* Rockville, Md., 1981.

Newsweek, 28 May 1977, p. 80.

New York Times, 17 February 1974.

New York Times, 13 November 1980.

Nylander, I. "Children of Alcoholic Fathers." *Acta Paediatrika Scandinavia* 49 (1960). 1–134.

——— "Children of Alcoholic Fathers." *Quarterly Journal of Studies on Alcohol* 24 (1963): 170–72.

O'Gorman, Patricia. "A Conceptual Framework for the Primary Prevention of Alcohol-Use Related Problems, and a Framework for Individual Action." (In press), 1979.

———. "Children of Alcoholic Parents: Prevention Issues." Paper presented at the NIAAA Symposium on Services to Children of Alcoholics, Silver Spring, Md., 26 September 1979.

———. "Self Concept, Locus of Control, Perception of Father in Adolescents in Severe Problem Drinking, Recovering Alcoholic and Non-Alcoholic Homes." Ph.D. Dissertation, Fordham University, 1975.

Plaut, Thomas. *Alcohol Problems: A Report to the Nation.* London: Oxford University Press, 1967.

Rachal, J. V., J. R. Williams, M. L. Brehm, B. Cavanaugh, R. P. Moore, and W. C. Eckerman. *A National Study of Adolescent Drinking Behavior, Attitudes, and Correlates.* Research Triangle Park, N.C.: Research Triangle Park Center for the Study of Social Behavior, 1975.

Rada, R., D. Kellner, and W. Winslow. "Drinking, Alcoholism, and the Mentally Disordered Sex Offender." *Bulletin of the American Academy of Psychiatry and Law* 6 (1978): 296–300.

Richards, Tarpley. "Working with Children of an Alcoholic Mother." *Alcohol Health and Research World* 3 (Spring 1979): 22–25.

Robins, Lee N., William M. Bates, and Patricia O'Neal. "Adult Drinking Patterns of Former Problem Children." In *Society, Culture, and Drinking Patterns*, pp. 395–412. Edited by David Pittman and Charles Snyder. New York: John Wiley, 1962.

Room, Robin. "Governing Images and the Prevention of Alcohol Problems." *Preventive Medicine* 3 (1974): 11–23.

Rosett, Henry. "Effects of Maternal Drinking on Child Development: An Introductory Review." *Annals of New York Academy of Science* 273 (1976): 115–17.

Rouse, B., P. Waller, and J. Ewing. "Adolescent's Stress Levels, Coping Activities, and Father's Drinking Behavior." *Proceedings of the Eighty-First Annual Convention of the American Psychological Association* 7 (1973): 681–82.

Schuckit, Marc A., Donald Goodwin, and George Winokur. "A Study of Alcoholism in Half-Siblings." *American Journal of Psychiatry* 128 (1972): 1132–36.

Shade, Ruth H., and Willard J. Hendrickson. "Pill Culture Parents and Their Drug-Using Teenagers." *American Journal of Orthopsychiatry* 41 (1971): 289–98.

Sloboda, Sharon B. "Children of Alcoholics: A Neglected Problem." *Hospital and Community Psychiatry* 25 (1974): 605–06.

Smith, S., R. Hanson and S. Noble. "Parents of Battered Babies, A Controlled Study." *British Medical Journal* 4 (1973): 388–91.

Steinglass, Peter. "A Life History Model of the Alcoholic Family." *Family Process* 19 (September 1980): 211–26.

Straus, Robert. "Conceptualizing Alcoholism and Alcohol Problems." In *Defining Adolescent Alcohol Use: Implications Toward a Definition of Adolescent Alcoholism*, pp. 106–07. Edited by P. O'Gorman, I. Smith, and S. Stringfield. New York: National Council on Alcoholism, 1976.

United Nations, World Health Organization, Expert Committee on Mental Health. WHO Technical Report Series, no. 42, 1951.

Vaillant, George. "Paths Out of Alcoholism—A Forty Year Prospective Study." Paper presented at the Third Annual Alcoholism Symposium, Cambridge Hospital Department of Psychiatry, Cambridge, Mass., 8 March 1980 (mimeo).

Virkkunen, M. "Incest Offenses and Alcoholism." *Medicine, Science, and Law* 14 (1974): 224–28.

Washington Post, 10 June 1974.

Wegscheider, Sharon. *No One Escapes From a Chemically Dependent Family.* Crystal, Minn.: Nurturing Networks, 1976.

———. "Children of Alcoholics Caught in Family Trap." *Focus on Alcohol and Drug Issues* 2 (May–June, 1979): 8.

Weir, W.K. "Counseling Youth Whose Parents Are Alcoholic: A Means to an End as Well as an End in Itself." *Journal of Alcohol Education* 16 (1970): 13–19.

White, Robert E. "The Impact of 1977–78 Peer Leader Training in Selected Behavioral and Psychological Dimensions." Somerville, Mass., 1979 (mimeographed).

White, Robert E., and Ronald Biron. "A Study of the Psychological and Behavioral Effects of the *Decisions About Drinking* Curriculum." Somerville, Mass., July 1979 (mimeographed).

Whitfield, Charles. "Children of Alcoholics: Treatment Issues." Paper presented at National Institute on Alcohol Abuse and Alcoholism Symposium on Services to Children of Alcoholics, Silver Spring, Md., 25 September 1979.

Williams, Kenneth. "Children of Alcoholic Parents: Intervention Issues." Paper presented at the NIAAA Symposium on Services to Children of Alcoholics, Silver Spring, Md., 25 September 1979.

Woititz, Janet. Paper presented at the NIAAA Symposium on Children of Alcoholics, Silver Spring, Md., 25 September 1979.

———. *Marriage on the Rocks. Learning to Live with Yourself and an Alcoholic.* New York: Delacorte Press, 1979.

Wolin, Steven J., Linda A. Bennett, and D. L. Noonan. "Family Rituals and the Recurrence of Alcoholism Over Generations." *American Journal of Psychiatry* 136 (1979): 589–93.

INDEX

(cont. on next page)

(cont. on next page)